Jack Keller

Christmas AD 2015

"OH! IT'S YERSEL,
YA BUGGER!"

"OH! IT'S YERSEL, YA BUGGER!"

A Scottish Minister Looks Back On A Life Of Surprises

Rev. Jack Kellet

Matador
9 Priory Business Park,
Wistow Road, Kibworth Beauchamp,
Leicestershire. LE8 0RX
Tel: 0116 279 2299
Email: books@troubador.co.uk
Web: www.troubador.co.uk/matador
Twitter: @matadorbooks

ISBN 978 1784625 467

British Library Cataloguing in Publication Data.
A catalogue record for this book is available from the British Library.

Printed and bound by CPI Group (UK) Ltd, Croydon, CR0 4YY
Typeset in 11pt Aldine401 BT by Troubador Publishing Ltd, Leicester, UK

Matador is an imprint of Troubador Publishing Ltd

For Ena, Malcolm, Lorna and William – four Godsends

APPRECIATION

Without the encouragement and patience of my wife Ena, also the skills and time of my friends Rev. Marion Dodd, Joan Rowley, Norman Lockhart, my brother-in-law Alex MacKay and especially of my daughter Lorna Martin, these stories sculpted out of eighty-five years' experience could never have been prepared for publication. Thank you.

FOREWORD

What kind of person becomes a parish minister? And what kind of church is it where a frail old woman can greet a rare visit from the parish minister with, "Oh! it's yersel, ya bugger!" and then gets a kiss in response?

The parish minister has been a pillar for preserving Scotland as a linkage of caring communities for four and a half centuries now.

There are fewer of us about today, but a parish minister is still available to serve every person in Scotland, whatever their religion or non-religion, free of charge – of course! – and absolutely without any expectation that "Now I've scratched your back, you'll scratch mine."

We Scottish ministers have come from all kinds of backgrounds, including the working-class[1], undertaken a wide range of academic study with fellow university students of all faiths and none, then moved to divinity subjects and also trained to engage with all sorts and conditions of people.

This volume of 'autobiography' spells out the social background of a mainstream parish minister, finding himself surprised to be empowered by gifts of faith, hope and love, and charged to join with others – predominantly lay people – in the challenge to help folk in Scotland find "the life more abundant" that Jesus of Nazareth wills for them.

I share here with readers hard facts about the joys, the shame, the privileges and exceptional personalities of elders and others in the Kirk who joined with me in the job.

AD 2014 Jack Kellet

INTRODUCTION

"WHAT'S THE TIME, MR WOLF?"

(Born in the Edinburgh working-class)

In Edinburgh in the 1930s and 1940s, working-class children spent more time playing with other kids in the street than with their families. One of our favourite games – morning, afternoon and evening – was, "What's the time, Mr Wolf?"

Traffic danger did not exist, as no one in Waverley Park Terrace (Abbeyhill) had a car, and the coal lorry came just once a week. "One and six a bag" was the shout.

So, one bairn would be the wolf facing and leaning against the wall on one side of the street, with arms up over the eyes, while the rest of us lined up along the wall opposite, joined hands, and began to chant, " What's the time, Mr Wolf?" all the time dancing gingerly forward with eyes warily and excitedly on the wolf. The wolf would howl back 9 o'clock, 10 o'clock (or whatever) to the great relief of the other kids. And then, when the line drew close to him the wolf would shout "Dinner time!" and try to catch one of the screaming children before they got over to safety on the opposite pavement.

When a child was not quick enough and got caught, he or she would be 'het', Wolf for the next game.

I recall this memory because having kept the wolf away from my door for 84 years now, I realise that I will not be evading for much longer the inevitable Angel of Death – or what might come like a big bad wolf indeed: *bereavement*. Meanwhile, there may be time to set down stories of the past that a working-class boy of my time could never have imagined possible: it has been a life of surprises.

AND NOW, 3 heart attacks behind me, getting ready for the last adventure!

AD 2014   *Jack Kellet*

Inspiration

Old Hippy Prayer – "Dear God, prod me with the odd."

Anne Muir on "Just Stories" – *"Now, says St Paul, we see the world and the human condition reflected in metaphors – in stories."* (Not a Safe Place, Iona Community)

CONTENTS

A BOLSHIE AT BALMORAL – SURPRISES THAT AID UNDERSTANDING

MEETING THE QUEEN
AND THE CORGIS

"A-A-D-A-A-M!" the Queen shouted into the great east doorway of Balmoral Castle. "A...dam!"

Yes, it was the Queen, believe it or not, her hands cupped round her mouth to make sure that her shout would go right through the reception hall and up the stairs if necessary. This really was our Queen Elizabeth the Second – so relaxed, natural and responsive – the same Queen who for a period in later years was to be accused of being too controlled and unfeeling for the modern age. And that was an opinion which told me a lot about the misleading effects of the ignorance on the part of so called royal watchers and reporters in the media.

The year was 1981. Prince Charles and his bride had arrived home from honeymoon a few days earlier. I had been invited to preach at Crathie on the Sunday morning and had arrived to be a guest of Her Majesty for the weekend. The plan was for me to enter by the main gate of the estate by 6.30pm. I rolled up at the right time of course and a policeman emerged from the trees, took my word for it, spoke into his walkie-talkie, and told me to drive on up to the near gable end of the castle where the Queen's equerry, Squadron Leader Adam, would be waiting for me.

A letter ten days previously from the Queen's chaplain at Crathie had told me I would not meet the Queen until just before dinner at 8pm – when I should remember to say "Your Majesty," while giving a gracious little nod of my head, and then be careful to say "Ma'am" whenever the Queen chose to speak to me thereafter. But when I drew up at the castle no one was there. I suddenly recalled that a previous chaplain-for-the-weekend had his bag removed from the boot by a valet, and that the next morning the valet reported to him before breakfast with the old raincoat the minister also kept in the boot for crawling under his banger of a car to find out what was wrong, all beautifully cleaned, pressed and folded in white tissue paper! So I got out of my old car and had just started to lift out my bag, when I was startled by the sound of small dogs scurrying out of the castle and hurrying to the area behind me where there were some trees. And then I saw her in her headscarf striding out on the heels of the six corgis. She gave me a smile and a wave. I felt myself quite nonplussed, which was a sudden and strange feeling, as I had not been nervous at all of meeting the Queen. (Years later, I happened to read that in his autobiography, the celebrated and well connected Ludovic Kennedy, who had actually in his boyhood played with the royal children, had been too nervous decades later to accept an invitation to stay at Balmoral. But I was controlled by the concern to find some opportunity to tell her Majesty the distressing effects her government's policies were having on the people of Leith at that time.)

Now, this kind of chance meeting had not been prepared for! And I immediately found myself confessing embarrassment and tongue-tiedness when the Queen, having passed me, suddenly turned on her heels and strode towards me with her right hand outstretched and a most lovely smile taking over her face:

"I'm sorry," the Queen said, beaming in welcome. "I thought I recognised you as one of my staff, and then realised you must be our minister for the weekend… Is no one here to see to you?"

4

I told her what the policeman had said. Up went the Queen's right index finger as if to say "Got it in one" and the next moment she was running up to the porch – I mean 'running':

"A-A-D-A-A-M!"; A-DAM!"

These corgis...

On the Sunday of the weekend when we had finished lunch out in the garden and the Queen rose to go, I – at her right hand – stood up too, and then stepped back from the table with the intention of making room for the Queen to return to the castle.

"E-e-k!" I realised with horror I'd stood on the foot of one of the said corgis who had rushed into the garden when the meal had finished in order that they might be fed! The Queen just gave me that smile again.

Later that evening, I had the chance to ask Prince Charles how he had got round to asking the Queen for permission to marry Diana, and he replied that he'd caught her in a corridor when she stopped by a radiator to feed her corgis...

PRINCE ANDREW

When my valet had shown me to my room on the first floor, he unpacked my weekend bag and put things into the magnificent yew chest of drawers along the wall opposite my bed and then said he would go and run my bath, apologising that the bathroom was a few yards down the corridor facing my door. Not being used to two baths in the one day, I was swithering about how to tell the young lad not to bother when the next intimations led me to conform: "Dinner is at 8 o'clock, Sir, and I will be back to take you down to the drawing room at 7 o'clock."

Then turning in the doorway, "It may be, Sir, that the Queen will ask you to say grace. Would you be prepared to do this, please?"

When I had replied that this would be a great privilege for me, the valet paused for a moment and then, gazing at my face more intensely, added:

"I hope you won't mind, Sir, but I've been told to ask you if the grace is likely to be long or short."

On hearing that the grace would be short, the relief on the valet's face was very obvious and, much more relaxed, he confided, "Oh, Prince Andrew will be so pleased. He said that when we had the Moderator last week the grace was so long they thought it was the sermon!"

(When, some years later, I shared this experience with an older minister who had been at Balmoral long before me he told me that he had anticipated being invited to say grace before dinner and had actually spent more time working out words which would be appropriate for the royal family in such circumstances than he did for the Sunday sermon. And no sooner had he opened with "Oh gracious God, we thank you for this food," than the Duke of Edinburgh said "Amen" and that was that!)

Scrubbed up particularly well and now wearing a black dinner jacket (as required in advance and hired for the occasion) I was duly escorted down to the drawing room and the door opened so that I could slip in.

A very lively conversation was going on from two settees beside a roaring fire, with – to my initial surprise, because at that time I shared what was generally conveyed by the media that she had let the Queen down and therefore could surely not be in royal favour – the Princess Margaret dominating the scene, "holding court" as it were. But Prince Andrew also stood out as he was wearing a white jacket, and being asked where he got it: "I found it in the wardrobe in my room," he said. "Fits me perfectly. Must have been Uncle David's."

It was a further surprise to me to hear the banished King Edward VIII being referred to in what seemed to be a familiar way.

In the breakfast room next morning, Prince Andrew left his table companions to come over and speak to me. "Minister, I want to apologise to you. We must have disturbed you when we were horsing about along the corridors during the night and somehow managed to bump into your door. I'm sorry."

Now, the Princes Andrew and Edward had quite a number of teenage friends, male and female, staying with them for the weekend and it had been no surprise for me, of course, that there had been some running about and squealing during the night! I assured Prince Andrew that I was not put out at all and thanked him for his concern. Sitting himself down across the table from me, he proceeded to ask me if I'd enjoyed the journey up from Leith on such a beautiful day, referring to the landmarks that let me know he knew the road well.

More politeness

One of the guests Prince Andrew introduced to me was the brother of the Duke of Roxburghe. To start our wee conversation, I mentioned that my wife and I had registered a Note of Interest with a Kelso estate agent for a cottage on the Roxburghe ancestral lands but the sale was completed without alerting us, as was our due. The next day, when he was about to leave for London, the Roxburghe brother made a point of seeking me out and offering if he could help in any way.

A wee bit "cheek" too?

And then on the Sunday evening, the moment I walked into the drawing room for dinner, Andrew called out to me from the company around the fire place:
    "*Congratulations*, minister!"
    "What's that for?" I asked.
    "15 minutes 32 seconds! The length of your sermon!"
    "Mm, how do you know that?"
    "I put my stop watch on you all!"
    ("Cheeky bugger" was the reaction of Tom Gordon, a parish minister-friend, when back in Edinburgh he asked me how I got on!)

SURPRISED BY THE RAF SQUADRON LEADER EQUERRY

*– and surprises also from the Parish Minister, a young
lad fellow guest, and the Queen herself.*

Adam had come running down the stairs, apologising loudly that he had been caught up by a phone call, took my weekend bag from me and showed me into the office he was using just off the hallway. He was very friendly and man to man, as if we had known each other for years.

In a minute or two, my valet would settle me into my room and look after me. Here was a card for me with his name on it – possibly misspelt, as can be seen below.

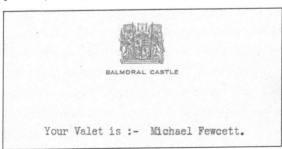

BALMORAL CASTLE

Your Valet is :- Michael Fewcett.

A list of my fellow guests had been typed and stuck onto the post at the bottom of the stairway up to the first floor. (Taking a quick glance when passing later I recognised some aristocratic family names, and I remember the Marquess of Milford Haven and especially the brother of the Duke of Roxburghe because, before leaving, he came over and asked if he could help me get a retirement cottage in the Borders.)

9

Adam also told me that at dinner I would find myself placed next to the Queen on her right.

Now, I had heard from someone beforehand that one did not speak to the Queen unless she addressed you first and now here was Adam alerting me not to worry if the Queen did not engage with me right away as she usually talked to the person on the one side for the first half of the meal and then turned to her other neighbour for the second half.

All this proved absolutely not to be the behaviour of the most warm, gracious and friendly personality who came right up to me in the reception room before dinner and then resumed the conversation at table the moment after I had said grace.

There was just one "little thing more" from the equerry on my first briefing and, totally unprepared for such a thing, I was shaken, nonplussed. The question was: how was I with dirty jokes?

I am sure the Queen herself would have been horrified. But I later realised that no doubt this check was required by others in the castle!

My next real engagement with the equerry was just after Sunday lunch when Adam approached me and said that the parish minister's wife had invited me down to the Manse and he would escort me across the estate. There would be a couple of daughters to meet and one of them had baked two cakes. I was keen to go because while I had been disrobing in the Crathie vestry after the service the minister (now deceased) had confided in me that he found great difficulty in preparing sermons and dreaded having to visit hospitals. I thought my presence with him and the family might be supportive.

It turned out that the parish minister was in his element as a gracious host. And I discovered that he had been given two duties for me. I should leave a tip of three guineas for the valet, and here was a draft of the letter of thanks I should copy out myself for the Queen. (Believe it or not the grammar was in need of correction!)

Walking cross country back to the castle we met the Queen "out for a walk", all by herself and supremely relaxed.

There were some things she wanted to discuss with her equerry, but standing in the lovely sunshine we had quite a long chat together.

I said that as a boy I had been brought up close to Holyrood Palace and it used to be rumoured that the two little princesses often walked in the King's Park. "Yes, we did," the Queen responded. "I still do."

"Surely you are recognised now?" I ventured.

"Oh no, I like to walk whenever I get the opportunity. One summer sailing up here through the islands I went out a walk and as I was making my way back I came upon a man stretched over a rock gazing through binoculars at the Royal Yacht."

I asked him: "Have you seen much?"

"Not a thing," he replied. "I've been staring for more than half an hour and I've not seen the Queen once."

"Maybe she's out for a walk," I said, before carrying on down.

Balmoral, just like home

Back in my room, I suddenly began to hear the loud voice of an excited young boy – perhaps a fellow pupil of Prince Edward – speaking on the telephone in the passage outside my door.

"Mummy, I'm having a great time here, it's just like home."

MORE ABOUT PRINCESS MARGARET

– Including a gaffe from me and a concern for Diana

When I had slipped into the drawing room at 7 o'clock that evening (22nd August 1981), I was about to be involved in relationships with the royal family that a few years later would make me surprised and even angry at the ignorance and misunderstanding of the media's so called royal correspondents, who revealed more about their own shallowness and nastiness than what was true about their subjects' lives.

Princess Margaret was now quizzing the company round the fire about when they had first been informed of the date of the wedding because she felt she herself ought to have been one of the first to know and was not. (Later in the evening I was to see Margaret press her nephew on the accuracy of this perceived injustice and watched Prince Charles avoid a direct answer, and even squirm a little in embarrassment.)

Embarrassment for me, too

But, for now, Princess Margaret noticed that the minister for the weekend had come into the room, rose to her feet immediately and walked across to me. I had sat down on the nearest seat to the door, an old (nursing) chair, upholstered in Royal Stewart tartan and positioned alongside a long curtain over the windows. The next evening the princess explained to me that she had come over to me instantly as no one used this chair; it was the one Queen Victoria sat on, next to the window as she suffered from (did she really say?) "hot flushes", and liked to be near the draught coming in.

There was no way I could have been discomfited by this disclosure since I had not been alerted in advance to the family rule. But I did find myself embarrassed by the presence of the Princess in front of me. She stood too close. Because she turned out to be a small woman, I had, of course, to look down to her face as we spoke. Her white dress was cut extremely low, at least for these days in the society I moved in. Her breasts, brown from the Mustique sun, were very prominent indeed. There was no room for me to step away. It crossed my mind that this lady's governess and exceptionally occasion-conscious mother must have told her how to behave in such circumstances!

Even as I listened to her talking I couldn't stop myself pondering my little predicament and remembering a warning from one of my elders that senior people in society could have "fun" with ministers. James Hunter, superintendent of the Scottish Lighthouse Board had told me that High Court Judges were ex-officio Directors and one of their duties (perks) was to sail round the islands on a summer "inspection." Captain Hunter used to arrange for them all to attend an evening service and the parish minister would be invited to dinner on the ship afterwards. (Some?) Judges would take great delight in trying to get the minister drunk.

Charles and Diana

And then I noticed in the background the Prince of Wales and Princess Diana slipping quietly from another door through the drawing room and into an annexe from where I thought I could hear some young voices and a television set. Diana appeared much taller than I had imagined from TV appearances and – I thought disturbingly – she seemed to be stooping slightly as if over-conscious of her height.

I took the chance to tell Princess Margaret that my wife and I had greatly enjoyed watching the televised marriage service. But Margaret's instant response was a complaint: "The cameramen focussed on me when I was looking very sad, as if I disapproved of it all, when the truth is that this was during the hymn *I vow to thee, my country*, which always moves me deeply." When I replied that Diana herself had chosen this hymn, Margaret said she hadn't known this, and added, "*That girl* has had a terrible upbringing and the Queen is very much hoping that she will make us her family."

When tragedy came to Diana, and so much uninformed guess work with unfair comment appeared in the mass media, I was glad that I remembered this concern and had noted the actual words in my room the same night.

Incidentally, though I could never have guessed then at some of the reasons later revealed to help explain Diana's distress, I did hear that past experiences with the mother who had let her down over the years and was now herself resident in the Scottish Highlands had made Diana feel extremely uncomfortable about life up here. She certainly didn't indicate any interest in speaking to the Scottish minister, as all the others in the family did. Charles, however, when greeting me warmly that evening, told me that he looked on this place as home.

Though I chose not to mention it to Princess Margaret, I actually had had a disappointment myself about the televised marriage service. Good man though the Archbishop of Canterbury was, he had exposed his lack of parish experience when caught out by Charles' mistake with the fundamental marriage vow and had not got him to repeat it correctly.

Arrival of the Queen: "Snap!"

Suddenly, as I talked with the Princess Margaret before dinner, the Queen was with us, so delightfully relaxed, full of the *joie-de-vivre*. Immediately, she slapped a ring hand onto her sister's: "Snap!" She turned to me. "I'm wearing the same ring as Margaret. My sister got hers as a present from the King" (or was it President?) "of Benin when she paid a royal visit. When I was due to go there, I was asked discreetly what I might like as a present and I said the same kind of ring!"

Just before dinner was announced, I found myself – in more ways than one – alone with Princess Margaret in the friendly atmosphere the Queen had engendered. I asked if any other foreign visits were now arranged. On hearing that she had been invited to Basutoland I chatted back that it was very nice of them to invite her, whereupon the Princess looked me straight in the eyes to say, "It's very nice of me to go!"

Ah well, the Bible does tell us there is a time to keep silent. And no doubt even bolshies unfazed by royalty should be politeness itself and be able to hold their tongue when they have chosen to accept an invitation to be a guest with someone else's family!

THE FIRST DINNER WITH
THE QUEEN

'God save our gracious Queen' – Amen to that! Here and now I am delighted to be able to produce physical evidence of graciousness shown to an unknown and obviously 'working-class' subject; ever ready with his Christian socialism and Presbyterian egalitarianism, in no sense a sycophant career-driven for preferment.

There we were seated round a long oval polished wood dining table. For the first time I could see all my fellow guests, quite a number of them clearly young friends of the princes, boys and girls. I found myself at the right hand of the Queen, with her Lady-in-waiting (Mary Morrison of Islay) on my right. Prince Philip I had reason to look for right away but he was not present.

When we had started on our main course, I asked the Queen if this was venison we were eating; my wife was a home economist and would want to hear about the food! "It's roe deer," she replied. "Better." And then she passed me the menu – which only she had – and asked if I'd like to take it home for my wife. Seeing my delight, she asked if I'd like to have some more, turned momentarily to the butler standing behind her, and within a minute or so passed me an envelope containing seven menus and also the card listing her Pipe Major's music for the evening!

Conversation being so easy and spontaneous, I mentioned that my wife would love to retire to Deeside. We had come up two or three times to Mrs Schofield's Hotel, which she offered to ministers in January at half price, partly to help keep her staff in work over the winter. The Queen's face leant even more closely to mine and she asked, "Have you got your wife tucked up close by this weekend?" (I'm sure the Queen was going to ask me to invite my wife to join me.)

Thus, once again, I was also reminded of the platform of ready acceptance that generations of parish ministers had built up so that the work of their successors might be eased.

Security

As our meat plates were being taken away and our pudding course being served, I took advantage of this *tête-à-tête* to say that it had been distressing to see on TV the recent frightening incident during the Horse Guards Parade, when a man in the crowd produced a pistol, an event so serious that Prince Philip had immediately broken ranks and ridden to the Queen's side. And today I hadn't noticed any signs of 'security' at all up here. The reply of the Queen showed that her real security worry was for her daughter Anne and the occasion when a man managed actually to get into her car and seriously wounded her driver.

"Of course, my security people are wanting changes. What do you think?"

Prime Minister Ted Heath

When I saw the pudding before me, I asked what this was. The Queen explained that tonight we were having a Swedish recipe for redcurrants. And then she asked if, when walking round Loch Muick, my wife and I had ever ventured upstream to the Dubh Loch. "One day I was walking on the high path along the hillside, talking with Prime Minister Mr Heath, and no one else there except my man some way behind, when a little yellow plane suddenly appeared overhead. That was a fright. Mr Heath's face turned as red as that," (pointing to my pudding).

"It turned out to have been American tourists wanting a look!"

After dinner mangoes

Our meal completed, the Queen said there was now a little surprise from Prince Charles and Princess Diana. A member of staff appeared bearing a large basket of mangoes. Charles explained that as he and Diana were waiting in Cairo Airport to board their plane for the flight home, President Anwar Sadat began looking at his watch anxiously, and then they saw a small military vehicle being driven at speed on to the tarmac. The soldiers on guard responded instantly to this unexpected danger, but the President beamed in pleasure and relief: here was a crate of mangoes as a parting present.

Now, mangoes were really an unknown fruit in Scotland at that time. I remembered how we national servicemen were introduced to this most delicious and juicy of fruits when off duty in Port Said thirty odd years before. But we just bit into them between our hands – and had to take care that the running juice fell on the pavement and not on our khaki drill uniform. I couldn't see myself coping at such a table, so waved the footman past. I then watched out of the corner of my eyes what the Queen did and hoped I'd get another chance on the Sunday, which we all did.

On the way back to the drawing room I heard Margaret ask her sister if there could still be space for her this year in the very limited royal area for the State Opening of Parliament.

Raiders of the Lost Ark

My valet had told me that we were to see a film after dinner. Prince Andrew had been pressing for the newly-produced 'Raiders of the Lost Ark', not yet publicly available in the UK, and the censor's age limit for viewers meant that Edward was not old enough. The Queen's decision was awaited!

I think it was the Queen's Lady-in-waiting who told me that Prince Philip suffered from very sore knees when having to stand for a long period but he did love the pictures and the Queen had therefore transformed the ballroom so that it could be used as a cinema.

The Queen herself had chosen to be elsewhere after dinner so I found myself being led upstairs by Princess Margaret and seated at her right side.

Back in the drawing room, with just the 'oldies' settling down now and whisky (or whatever) having been dispensed, Margaret was 'holding court' again from her seat beside the fireplace. The chat proceeded easily, but after a wee while Margaret stood up, rather abruptly I thought, looked across at me, and said to my surprise, "You must be needing to prepare for the service tomorrow." As I moved to my room, I wondered if this was when the dirty jokes would be due to begin; but maybe the Princess had noticed that, despite the excitement of the film, I'd actually nodded off in the dark and warmth of the cinema!

6. menus

MERLAN EN COLERE
SAUCE VERTE

———

FILET DE BOEUF BRITANNIA
SALADE

———

CREPES ISLANDAISE

JEUDI LE 13 AOUT 1981

HOMMARD CANADIENNE

———

ALOYAU DE BOEUF ROTI FROID
SALADES VARIEES

———

MILLE-FEUILLE DE FRAMBOISES

DIMANCHE LE 16 AOUT 1981

FILET DE MERLUCHE ST.GERMAIN

———

SELLE DE CHEVREUIL ROTI BADEN BADEN
SALADE

———

ROTE GRUTZE

SAMEDI LE 22 AOUT 1981

CREPES D'OEUFS AUX TOMATES

———

ALOYAU DE BOEUF ROTI A L'ANGLAISE
CHOUX DE PRINTEMPS
HARRICOTS VERTS
POMMES RISSOLEES
SALADE

———

FRAMBOISES RISSOLEES

DIMANCHE LE 23 AOUT 1981

CARRE D'AGNEAU BOULANGERE
SALADE

———

ROCHER DE GLACE DALMATION

DIMANCHE LE 9 AOUT 1981

DARNE DE SAUMON GRILLEE
SALADE

———

ROCHER DE GLACE DE BANANES

MARDI LE 11 AOUT 1981

PIPE PROGRAMME

MARCH   THE 71ST HIGHLANDERS

STRATHSPEY   DORA MACLEOD

REEL   THE SMITH OF CHILLIECHASSIE

MARCH   KIRKWALL BAY

PÌOBAIR AN BHANRIGH

MORE SURPRISES ON THE SUNDAY

I got quite a few more surprises about the royal family's life on the Sunday.

The valeting service

When my valet came to my room on the Sunday morning at the time I had suggested, he was carrying the black clerical shirt I had travelled up in, now cleaned, pressed and carefully folded in white tissue paper. When I said that I was greatly impressed by the speed and efficiency of this, he responded, "Oh, yes, sir, we have a very good service. One day, a gentleman arrived with only one pair of shooting trousers. They were covered in mud when he came in for lunch and we had them cleaned, dried and pressed ready for him to go out in the afternoon."

As I now reached for the clothes he was putting out for me, he flyped my socks!

Princes kissing

When the princes arrived in the breakfast room, the first thing they did was to kiss one another. I'd never before seen kissing between boys/men, and wondered if this was a tradition originally brought over by Prince Albert. Even my mother and father never kissed me in the years I remember. But things are very different in our family now, of course. Our adult grandchildren wrap their arms round us when we meet.

It is some years since my younger grandson Iain told me that handshakes are for friends and acquaintances, not family.

Margaret and the media

When we were all later assembled outside in the sun, ready to be driven to church, Princess Margaret took me aside and told me she would not be attending service. Press photographers and reporters would be swarming all over. She would have her own quiet time in the garden. Pastoral concern led me to recite, in supporting, the well known "Nearer to God in a garden, than anywhere else on earth," and Margaret nodded. (But to see Jesus crucified between two thieves in a rubbish dump outside the city wall is not to believe this personally.)

And then Margaret said that the Queen did not want the girls to attend church because the press would be descending on their families and printing "exclusives" about Andrew and the next royal wedding.

South Leith connection

Engaging with my (Daimler) chauffeur on the way through the huge roadside crowds to Crathie Kirk, I discovered that his mother came from a Reid family in Duke Street, Leith.

Curtseying to the Princes

Sometime after Sunday lunch, family and guests gathered again in the sun outside the castle as the young guests prepared to leave for home. I learned a bit more about myself when the girls curtseyed to their friends the princes, and I found myself surprised when I ought to have expected it, shouldn't I?

A family dinner on the Sunday

My valet had alerted me earlier that dress for Sunday night dinner might be informal, because 'all' the guests would be away, but now the Queen had confirmed otherwise. Dress jacket or no, the table's size had been reduced, and there was much more across-table family chat and banter over the meal.

Almost the first thing the Queen said to me was to ask if I'd enjoyed my walk through the castle grounds early that morning. I was starting to reply that the colour of the heather on the mountains was spell-binding, and the rose-beds in the gardens much more perfect than I'd ever seen before, when I suddenly realised I'd maybe made a *faux-pas*, and asked if I'd really been free to wander. "Oh yes," said the Queen, "It's just that I saw you from my bedroom window."

I asked if the Queen still, after so many years, found the surroundings here exceptionally beautiful. She responded, "I find them – what's that word you used in the sermon this morning? – Idyllic." I ventured that on my walk I'd been surprised to see the carved record on the castle walls that King George VI had purchased Balmoral. "Yes, my father had to do that himself," came out somewhat feelingly.

Prince Andrew piped up across the table to his mother, "Have you heard from Papa today?" And then, after an answer in the affirmative, "How did he get on?" The Queen replied that Papa had come in tenth.

"Tenth!" responded Andrew, as if disgusted. And immediately the conversation was not between a Queen and a Prince, but between a mother defending her husband against an upstart son!

Prince Charles, as is his wont, came in to explain the situation to the only guest (obviously out of the loop). "Papa has been carriage-driving in Switzerland. And we have to remember that the other competitors have specially-bred ponies, while Papa uses just what we have in the palace stables."

(Later in the year, I happened to notice a press release that the Queen had given her husband a gift of carriage-racing Welsh ponies for his birthday.)

Prince Philip

The particular reason I had expected Prince Philip to be at Balmoral that weekend was because I had invited him to open South Leith Parish Church's new halls in Henderson Street the next summer and presumed he might have got his staff to arrange my visit so that he could check me out.

In the 1970s South Leith Kirk Session had decided we really needed modern halls nearer the old Kirk, and I had written to the Duke of Edinburgh, "I am writing to ask for your help and I am not asking for money!" I knew he had sailed out of Leith during the war and I told him of the Kirk's royal connections – with James V, Queen Regent Mary of Guise, Mary Queen of Scots, James VI, Charles I – and asked if he would send a note of encouragement that we could publish in order to help raise funds for our building plans and their good purposes.

The next day, I was stunned to notice in the papers that the Queen and Prince Philip were leaving right away for a royal tour of Australia. But back, by return of post, came the ideal message: "Buckingham Palace. The Kirkgate Buildings project deserves to succeed and I am sure it will." Signed *Philip*.

Early in 1981, with the new premises now rising from the ground, and before my invitation to Crathie and Balmoral arrived, I had written about the planned opening ceremony and was awaiting a reply.

But quite obviously now, with the Duke not present, this was not the reason for my presence in Balmoral after all and some other kind source had brought the wonderful experience about for me.

The Queen Mother

Sunday dinner over, I found myself returning to the drawing room, absolutely at ease in the company and conversation of the Queen, Princess Margaret and Prince Charles. After a few minutes, however, the Queen broke away and made for the door just to the right of the fireplace and the long table which bore the Sunday papers. But in just a very few minutes, back the Queen bustled to our little group and exclaimed, "What do you think of that? She's too busy to take a call from me!" After a moment's exchange between them, I ventured to seek confirmation of this surprise, "Am I right in understanding that the Queen and Head of the Commonwealth has been prevented from contacting her mother?"

"That's it," the Queen replied. "I'm worried about the Queen Mother because she's got a very sore leg, and when I phone up to the Castle of Mey, I'm told that she is holding a cocktail party and has said that she is not to be disturbed. *Sore leg and holding a cocktail party*!" Smiles all round. Prince Charles, again characteristically considerate to a guest not in the loop, turned to me to explain that he himself often doesn't get through to Granny. "I'm told I'm being put through and then she presses the wrong button and cuts me off!"

Here and now there's another wee insight into the Queen Mother that I can share.

The Queen Mother and the new minister at Crathie

Some years later, Ena and I were having a few days' January break in Ballater. Keith Angus at Crathie had now been succeeded by a different kind of minister, Robert Sloan. The parish minister at Ballater told me that the Queen Mother, who joined public worship in Crathie every Sunday during the weeks she lived in her estate bordering Balmoral, was furious when she discovered that the new minister had replaced the King James' Bibles with a modern translation, and she let the Kirk Session know. The next Sunday, when the chauffeur had driven the Queen Mother up to the back door of Crathie church as usual, she instructed him to go in and find out what Bible was to be used that day. When he returned to the car, she told him to drive her straight home.

With the Princess Margaret after dinner

Standing together in the drawing room apart from the group seated and standing round the fire, it turned out that Princess Margaret wanted/needed someone to listen to her experiences during a long and painful time in her life – and I was there, Providentially.

At the right time, I excused myself as I wanted to go upstairs and write to my wife.

BALMORAL CASTLE

Sunday, 23 August 1981.

Dearest Ena,

I thought you might like this little
bit of evidence that your husband really is
up at Balmoral! You won't get this
note till I'm home, but the one thing
I have not handy and that I don't want
to ask for is a stamp. At least you can be
certain I was wanting to communicate with you.

Prince Philip was on the Continent horse-
carriage driving and doesn't arrive till I leave,
so it seems the invitation was not to give me
the once-over — or a third degree — about
his possible opening of the New Halls.

The Queen had me sit at her right hand

28

for dinner last night and again for lunch — out
in the garden! — today. She has been very kind to
me, as have the Prince of Wales, his brother and
Princess Margaret.

So has been a small house party, with
myself the only 'outsider' guest and the only other
guest young friend of the Princes and the Princess
of Wales.

I have liked the thought that my Mother
and your Mother started life in very humble
domestic service, but now I have a valet of
my very own!

You don't know what the future has in
store for you!
＝ All my love,

Jackie
—

ADIEU TO BALMORAL

After breakfast on the Monday, somebody led me into a neighbouring room where a large model of the estates was laid out, and there was some discussion about where good shooting would be sought that day.

And then – after a very fruitful meeting with Prince Charles about the needs of Leith – I was escorted by the Queen's kindly Lady-in-waiting down to the car park. My valet had told me that the Queen had 'put a brace of grouse' in the boot of my car. On the way, Lady Morrison invited me to call if we were ever back on holiday in Islay, and then, seeing my car, showed surprise. "Why did you buy a Japanese car?" I replied that it was because of the second atom bomb we'd dropped on them. But this wasn't the whole reason, of course, and it was not a reply I expected her to understand instantly, if ever.

PERMISSION FROM THE PRINCE
FIT TO BE KING

Prince Charles gave me a big grin as we sat down tete-a-tete in a side-room of Balmoral Castle. "Well when you get back to Leith will you be telling people about all this?" Charles's arms spread out in one of his typical gestures and his grin became a big friendly smile all over his face.

When I replied that the weekend had been fascinating, a different world for me, and I had been hoping to be allowed to tell people all about it, the permission and approval came instantly with a warm, "of course!"

The date was Monday 24th August 1981. Charles was just back from honeymoon with Diana, but was obviously keen to start work again. I couldn't miss seeing the red "Ich Dien" on his shoulders.

"I asked for us to meet together this morning," he said, "because I wanted to ask you about your sermon yesterday. Do you mind?"

"I am delighted," I responded. "I wish people would discuss the service properly with me every week. And, as it happens, a previous chaplain–for–the–weekend alerted me that Prince Philip would want to quiz me."

"Well, my father's away, so here I am. Tell me more about Leith."

Now this was the kind of opening I'd been longing for since the invitations to Crathie and Balmoral came in the post. Lots of people have asked if I wasn't nervous about going. Such feelings never emerged. What did come to the fore after the initial surprise and delight, was a childhood memory: Miss Goodfellow at Abbeyhill primary school in the 1930s telling our class of fifty working-class bairns how Queen Margaret of Scotland travelled the country, inviting local people to come with their concerns about the way the country was being run, so that she could try and put things right. (Oh the importance of a good primary teacher!)

It just never occurred to me that I might have pastoral responsibilities over the weekend – although to my surprise some did arise – because for months past the Queen and the whole royal family had been seen at their happiest and most popular ever. But as a parish minister from an area of very visible physical and social depression and multi-deprivation I was confronted every day with undeniable evidence that government policies were not working to help relieve the unfair lot of the poor. The post-war socialist dream of the abolition of poverty had vanished from the leading politicians' agendas. The wealthy businessmen who made their money in Leith no longer lived in Leith and no longer had to walk to their offices through the streets that confronted them with the lot of the poor, so that they saw others' suffering. In their separated comfort, they could be unaware, and an easy prey for pride and prejudice.

So I had decided to preach on the need for all of us – like that good upright churchman of old – Nicodemus – to be born again. Here we were at Balmoral and Royal Deeside –warm, well fed and provided for – as if in the womb. The first time we'd emerged from the womb, we were the cause for concern, the centre of attraction. But to emerge from the cosy womb of an idyllic holiday as mature people with eyes open this time was no longer to be terrified for our own safety, as at the first birth, but to see all the poor souls around who needed help that we could give.

Nicodemus had been charged by Jesus to realise that his admirable behaviour in private piety and generous giving and leadership responsibilities within the institution of the church was not the complete model, not the be-all-and-end-all of the good life, but actually the preparatory discipline that would enable the spirit to blow him where God willed. Our calling is not to seek our own peace, but to allow all fears to be cast out and to engage in "perfect love" for the world as Christ himself did.

Now Prince Charles was to pick up on a number of issues I had raised, like the amount of our taxation that was gobbled up for nuclear weapons as a first priority – a policy determined by fear. Our society's (then largely unrecognised) "institutional racism" was something I knew about through the experience of two of my children, and Charles sought to explain the real difficulties the police force had in attracting black recruits. But Charles' main concern was to enquire about the lack of jobs for young people leaving school and the visibly distressing results in the Leith I knew.

It was obvious that Prince Charles wanted to do something to try and help. In the spring following he invited a wide range of businessmen and women to a conference on youth unemployment in Leith, and then to set up a ginger group.

Prince Charles has quietly persevered in such good works over the decades. It is disgraceful that media people whose own lives can be messy from time to time like those of the rest of us, should have magnified Charles' mistakes without mercy, and that so many "academic" commentators should be so unthinkingly condescending in the face of rare proven worth.

Here are two further instances from my own limited experience.

In 1982, a generous grant was awarded by the Prince's Trust to enable young lads in the 10th Leith (South Leith church) company of the Boys' Brigade to make all the cupboards the church and the community needed for their new suite of halls in Henderson Street.

At the turn of the century, now retired to Walkerburn – a wee village in the Scottish Borders that had fallen on hard times following the closure of its mills – I learned to my surprise that four youth club leaders had been invited "out of the blue" to dinner at Holyrood Palace with the Prince and his wife Camilla, some sixty representatives of Charles' "Business in the Community" being present. The regeneration of Walkerburn was the main concern of the evening, and the four were astonished at the Prince's knowledge of their village and its plight. Charles challenged each of the businesses represented to do one thing for Walkerburn. Computers for jobs, training, building work, and offers of days out for the youth club were among the promises made and delivered.

Our country is very fortunate indeed to have a Prince well fit to be King!

BORN AND BELONGING
IN THE WORKING-CLASS

"BORN IN THE WORKING – CLASS"

As important for us as Springsteen's "Born in the USA"
is for Americans.

Whooping cough

My earliest family memory is waking during the night to realise that a doctor was in the house. I climbed out of my cot in time to hear him say to my mother that he would be back in the morning to sign the death certificate for my baby sister. (To his surprise she actually survived the whooping cough crisis.)

"Spanish blue eyes"

A great thrill for me was playing with my whip and peerie out on the Causewayside pavement. 'Girls' (as women were referred to) going to and from work in Banks the Printers down the street would stop to admire my prowess. (Years later my mother told me they stopped to gaze into my deep blue eyes, with such long eyelashes!)

What it meant to be working-class

My father was eventually able to 'buy' – get a mortgage for – a house of his own when I was 6 years old. Working as a grate-builder for James Gray and Son in George Street, he was always very proud that he was paid a halfpenny-an-hour more than the other tradesmen and, although he was always subject to the same two and a half hours' notice, he was the only workshop employee never to be paid off during the Depression. You can see one of his fireplaces in the Open Arms at Dirleton. But many of the jobs were for the really big houses "in the country," and he had to find digs away from home.

It seems astonishing to me now that at such an early age, while still in Causewayside, I was crossing a main road that carried buses all on my own, and walking down to the shops for messages. But then, there was my father's working away, and my mother's younger children (and pregnancies) keeping her in the house.

Crossing a busy road at 5-years-old

One vivid memory of these formative times was my having to carry the accumulator for the wireless quite a distance to the shop that would recharge it. "Be very careful. It's full and you mustn't let it spill. It's acid." And then going back the next day to collect and carry, again so riskily, the recharged accumulator.

The first time (and only time) I deceived my mother

Another unforgettable memory must have been at a time when my father was working locally. "Go down to the shops and get four slices of corned mutton for your daddy's piece. I've wrapped the money in this paper. Hold on tight." As I returned home, I stretched both arms out, as if I was an aeroplane, to 'fly' across the road. No sooner had I reached the other side than the slices of corned mutton slid out of the greaseproof paper and fell flat onto the pavement. And it had been raining! What a moral dilemma for a wee boy! I kept schtoom.

Working away from Edinburgh

The owner of James Gray and Son for most of my father's days was Mr R.E. Douglas, a prominent, local politician and churchman, so you might assume he would be "responsible" with his workers. But when my father finished his first day's work at a "country" job, far from Edinburgh, he often had to go out in the dark door-to-door to find digs for himself and his apprentice. (A double bed was the normal thing.) It was not until long after the end of the Second World War that the firm made advance arrangements for their tradesman's accommodation.

My mother would sometimes pass on stories of my father's experience.

On one occasion, at a table in his country digs, the woman of the house said to him, "Make yersel at hame Willie. Just saucer yer tea." This story was retold with glee because my parents were both fastidious about proper table manners. But what my father did with his tea there I don't know.

On another occasion, a lady of the big house for whom my dad had been working for a couple of days, came out as he was leaving and thanked him most profusely for his good work and his concern to minimise disruption. This happened during the time of food rationing and scarcity, so when she asked if my dad would like a few tomatoes from her greenhouse, he was delighted. Back she came with a wee bag and said, "that will be one and eleven pence!"

In the city too

Working in City private houses had its problems too. One lady told my father – who worked a ten hour day – not to use her bathroom.

Of course, tradesmen from different shops often worked in the one house at the same time. (Lord Hoy of Leith was one of the painters doing their rounds with my father in the 1930s when he was "Jimmy Hoy from St Leonards and didnae hae a bool in his mooth.") When they were "drumming up" their tea together – leaf tea into boiling water in an old syrup or treacle can – they would pass on the tips of their trade so fellow workers could make the best job of improving their own homes. But one common view still rankles with me: manses were not usually welcoming houses to work in.

"The times they are a changing" in Parliament, too

In 1945, with all the war had taught the general public, the times they were a–changing fast. Jimmy Hoy was the Labour Party Candidate for Leith and as such was discharged early from war service in the army to fight the General Election. The people of Leith wanted change and rallied in their hundreds to Leith Links to hear and support the socialist programmes for a changed Great Britain, with a National Health Service and Public Ownership to transform the lot of miners, railway men, power workers and the rest.

When I was invited to conduct his funeral, I wondered if ever again an Edinburgh working-class boy who left school at fourteen to be a house painter could possibly be elected as an MP, and appointed as a member of the House of Lords.

A Lord High Commissioner for the poor

When a Labour government came back into power, I wrote to Harold Wilson suggesting that it would be good for multi-deprived Leith if (Labour) Lord Hoy could become the next

Lord High Commissioner to the General Assembly, but the powers-that-be decided otherwise.

Some years later, however, a retired and more senior Labour government minister (and church woman), genuinely concerned for the poor, was appointed in Harold Wilson's time. Margaret Herbison, when Minister of National Insurance, had written to all parish ministers – and no doubt to all priests – pointing out that many older people seriously needing Social Security benefits were refusing to apply for what they wrongly thought was charity, and would we do our best to help such get their rights. "Plus-ca-change, Plus-ce n'est pas la meme chose!!"

CHILDREN'S STREET GAMES IN EDINBURGH'S WORKING-CLASS CULTURE

"The Street" really was as important a milieu for our character formation as the family, effecting indeed the moulding job that boarding schools do for upper and middle-class kids – although with very different results, of course. When young girls and boys played "What's the time, Mr Wolf?" they joined hands together unselfconscious of different gender. Both also played Peevers – the pavement game adopted down south as Hopscotch. Girls, on their own, would play the Diabolo and skipping games.

For the boys, football was the great game. We would form two sides from whoever was available, of any age. The lampposts and the wall alongside would form goal areas. Local residents never objected to the noise of our shouting – mind, there was no swearing in those days – despite the risk to their window panes. The street was car free, safe and an accepted milieu for us by the older generations.

With more adult boys, after their work and without proper footballs for playing on the parade ground up the King's Park, there was still no age barrier, and we would join the game in the holly; that is, the hollow at the entrance to the park at the front of the stairs down from Waverley Park Terrace. Sometimes we would take time out to climb the Elsie Inglis Hospital wall in order to pinch the mint in the resident engineer's garden. This was not so much for the fresh taste into our mouth as for the excitement of getting back over before the outraged man could catch us. One time, he was too quick for me and grabbed my hands on the top of the wall as I tried to dreep down to safety – and I wet my trousers.

A bully at the bools ("Holey and Guttery")

I don't remember any bully at all apart from one very good knuckler at the bools. He was a little older than the rest of us around and he always demanded more than his prowess actually achieved. But one day, in the holly – maybe because we were waiting for some boy to arrive with a ball, older lads took turns in giving us wee ones a thrill by holding us by the ankles and swinging us round, with our bodies mid-air. On my turn, I heard someone shout "Let him go!" Whether by intention or just losing the grip, I duly landed on my nose across the cinder football pitch!

"The Boni" and "the Milkies"

A great event for all in Abbeyhill was the Boni – the bonfire, twice a year, Halloween (not Guy Fawkes Day) and in May (Victoria Day). For weeks beforehand we would be round the houses and the shops, asking for old wood, boxes, linoleum, anything that would burn. We were allowed to store the boni in the yard behind a house in Waverley Park Terrace, and we would sit astride the high wall to protect our pile from "the Milkies."

The Milkies were the boys from neighbouring Milton Street, and we would sometimes try to retaliate for any theft by crossing the back greens which divided us. But invariably we failed to "win" anything.

Another confrontation I remember with the Milkies was when a "regiment" of about twenty boys marched into our street, and stopped in ranks of four, swinging their weapons, balls of tightly packed newspaper held by a long string. This was my introduction to St Patrick's Day, though actually there were no Catholics living locally and there was nothing religious about the fight they wanted! ("The Wavies" used to say the "Milkies" were dirty fighters who wrapped a stone in their paper ball weapon!)

Hitting Sir Walter on the nose

The last boys' street game I want to record was how we each tried to hit Sir Walter Scott on the nose. We didn't know it was the great Walter Scott, and weren't old enough to know about the Waverley Novels, where Waverley Park got its name. But a stone bust of the great Scot was built into the high corner of the tenement between Waverley Park and Waverley Park Terrace. Someone would have an old tennis ball and we would take it in turn to aim for the nose and hurl the ball high. Again no objections from the neighbours! (Sir Walter Scott's nose was not damaged like mine!)

"ONLY CHILDHOOD AILMENTS"

This was the answer usually inserted on applications for life assurance by people of reasonably good health and appearance. But when I now look back on my own (unworried) childhood, I'm astonished that I survived at all. Could my experience have been normal for working-class kids?

Firstly, I was definitely, though unaware of it, "delicate" in my early years. My mother's physical and nervous weakness meant that as a baby I had had to be farmed out some distance away. Then, as I recall, my mother used to take me for sun-ray treatment to a clinic beside the Methodist church in Nicholson Square. (Such was the disciplined obedience expected of working-class mothers in those years that once, when she arrived, with my two younger sisters in a pram that I was holding on to, the nurse on duty on the door wouldn't let us in for my treatment because we were five minutes late!)

Along with all children around, I think, I had bouts of whooping cough and measles at home. Tonsillectomy demanded a short (frightening) stay in hospital. When scarlet fever came, I had to be taken to the 'Fever Hospital' (City Hospital); no visitors allowed, but I learned later that mothers could come and see how their child was from a secret window. I had to have eight teeth removed, with gas, at the Dental Hospital. Earache came and was extremely painful; there was my mother having to cope at home and taking me, accompanied by three young sisters now, up to the Royal Infirmary on more than one occasion ("threatened mastoid," we were informed).

During the war, in 1940, two sisters and I were evacuated to the new Middleton Camp School. I have always remembered a very active and outdoor life during my fifteen months' stay (away from the risk of a blitzkrieg), but three afflictions interfered.

At lunchtimes, I could not get up from table (rheumatics?), and two teachers used to put their arms under my oxters and wrench me up.

Then I developed swelling of my gums and was put in the little Camp Hospital where no doubt with pill treatment I've forgotten, the nurse fed me every day a tin of mandarin oranges – otherwise absolutely unobtainable for the duration of the war.

Back into the Camp Hospital I went in 1941 with a sore throat: a swab was taken and diphtheria diagnosed. Off to the City Hospital again for some weeks.

What a learning experience this was for an eleven year old and for his family, of course! My dad was away to do his bit in the war (RAF) by this time. My mother was given a number for me and had to buy and consult the Edinburgh Evening News every day, where all patients' numbers were listed in groups according to their condition and progress.

The Fever Hospital ward contained about twenty male patients, and I don't remember another boy. The first shock was the almost instant enema! My bed had no pillows and the nurses told me I had to lie absolutely flat at all times. My food would be fed to me. After a fortnight or so I would get one pillow, and then – all being well – a second pillow a week or two later, when I'd be allowed up on one elbow to feed myself. The food was very good –despite war time rationing, of course – and we got tea, bread and margarine mid-morning and mid-afternoon – all with a little smell of disinfectant. The M & B pills had a horrible taste.

Suddenly, I had "swollen glands" – a recurrence, I think – and hot poultices of smelly linseed oil were wrapped round my neck.

46

The nurses were kept very busy and didn't have time for chat, but Matron came in at six o'clock every day, stopped to speak to me and asked if I had any questions she could help with, so I asked how it could be that I got diphtheria when my mother had had me vaccinated as an infant. Matron pointed over to the beds opposite, letting me lift myself up a bit. "Have you seen the charts facing outwards on the end of each bed? The big numbers in red are 100, 000 and 500, 000. This is the degree of seriousness. The number on the end of your bed is just 3000."

Another thing I was intensely aware of is how hard the maids worked, needing a lot of strength and energy to clean and then polish – another all-pervading smell! – the mahogany floor.

Came a day I was allowed up to make 'aeroplanes' – I was going to be a Spitfire pilot after all, when I was eighteen! – and zoom them all over the ward. Running out of paper from letters, etc, I was even encouraged by a fellow patient to tear a page from one of the books available and use this.

Shock horror!

And then, just before I was well enough to be discharged there occurred an event that actually troubles me still, at 83 years old, even with all my experience since in the army and as a parish minister in two cities. It was a lovely sunny day. The ward sister told me that two of the men in the ward were going out for a wee walk in the grounds and would I like to join them?

What a delightful surprise, and out I went. They were – it seemed to me – old men and, of course, were absolutely unknown to me. Perhaps a modern eleven year old, with today's awareness of well publicised risks, might have been on their guard. But in the climate of those times I was a total innocent, and obviously the ward sister and nurse foresaw no danger.

From the moment we were out of the building, and for the hour or so it took to go round where they led, the two men began to talk to me about a particular young nurse. Had I noticed how pretty she was and how she kept "staring at you, doting on you? When we get back in, you should walk up behind her and put your hand up her skirt. She would love it."

GOING THE MESSAGES

"Going the messages" was an important part of my daily life in the 1940s. With my father away to the Forces and my mother keeping the house, with three girls younger than me and, of course, no washing machine, dishwasher, fridge or vacuum cleaner, this was a necessary duty.

"The store"

So, once a week I cut across the park for "the store" as everyone called St Cuthbert's Co-operative Society – to collect the rations. The queue was always long and slow. The things people needed were not piled high in front of the customers. I had to hand my note to the sales assistant, when my turn came, and wait patiently while the essentials were brought, using the steps up the wall or from down we knew not where. Prices were written onto the line for me to take home. The ration books were marked up for the items that were on the rations. The note and the money were tucked into a flying cylinder that whizzed along a high wire across the shop to the cashier's office.

My mother chose not to use the store butcher but I would often be in the baker's shop for bread, Paris buns, and sometimes for a treat, cream cookies. (A lady in the baker's reported me once to my mother for saying "Gee us some buns"!)

The butcher butchering and the mutton broth

The chosen butcher was in Easter Road and I would go there for a flank of mutton boned and rolled and for steak mince. The mutton – you didn't get 'lamb' in those days – was prepared on the counter in front of me and the steak, my mother instructed me, had to be sliced and put through the mincer before my eyes too. (The butcher meat ration, I remember was 1/ and 2p for every adult and 7p per child; the 2p and 1p were for corned beef only.)

The mutton was boiled, and removed when tender to cool and to be sliced for eating later. The liquid was boiled up again with vegetables and (dried) peas. The peas were the treat, and as children we spooned them out with delight, counted them and arranged them round the rim to eat last.

I would also be sent to Lang the pork butcher across the road to get ham bones for lentil soup, and if he had any – haggis. Sometimes these non-rationed goods would be supplemented from another shop by salt cod so hard and salted that it had to be steeped in water for two or three days before cooking. Then I went to Rankine, the favoured fruiterer in Easter Road. My mother never bought from Berger's, much nearer at the top of Rose Lane (now Abbey Lane). (Berger's was the shop wee boys from the street ran past, pinching carrots from their boxes outside on the pavement as we ran home from watching lantern shows about the evil of sin in the Band of Hope!)

The chemist (with nothing but medication)

Looking back, I'm surprised how often I had to go to the chemist in Cadzow Place. Common ailments in those pre-NHS days could not demand the expense of a doctor, and the little chemist, with its drawers and bottles of medicines labelled very prominently, provided an essential service for everybody's normal life. No shelves of ladies' makeup, perfumes and toiletries in those days!

So, regularly, syrup of figs, or cascara; we did not like the recommended Gregory's Mixture. When 'the cold' was caught I was sent up for "squill mixture": syrup of squills and ipecacauanha wine and glycerine. When one or other of us was pealy-wally, peaky, hingy, faughie or run-down or needing a tonic, it would be a jar of (yummy) malt extract, failing which, a bottle of white emulsion – with its peculiar taste – or a bottle of yellow sulphur powder (to mix with black treacle and take by the spoonful). For my mother, I would sometimes be getting a box of Dr Beecham's Pills. For rubbing on my father's hands, hacked all over from working with builders' lime and cement, the medication was a block of smelly SnowFire (liniment – methothalate).

The greengrocer

When, post-1945, I was in the greengrocer round the corner in Spring Gardens to buy Scotch tomatoes from Lanark – in season of course – the owner, Mr Allan, could not stop himself haranguing the queue of customers about our terrible Labour government and nationalisation!

The corner shop and TB.

'Jimmy Taylor's' on the corner between Waverley Park and Waverley Park Terrace, was always a very busy shop indeed; bread, rolls, potatoes, tobacco, Spam, all sorts of tinned foods – including many "essentials" on the point rationing system. He and his family lived in 16 Waverley Park and he himself was always a very obliging neighbour. As a young lad, I could always get a pie, wee tin of peas and a penny packet of custard when I was going off on my bike for the weekend.

The memory that horrifies me now is a practice that we all just accepted in those days as necessary and sensible. Opening a large tin of Spam or corned mutton prior to slicing on the bacon-cutting machine the amount he'd been asked for, Mr Taylor would remove one end of the long tin with a tin-opener, pierce a hole in the other end, raise the tin to his mouth, and blow hard through the hole so that the meat would slide out. "Hygiene" was not thought about! And a day came when Mr Taylor was diagnosed with tuberculosis…

Boys smoking

Even young lads today thinking it is "cool" to be seen smoking would find it hard to comprehend the lengths we went to in the early 1940s to get a cigarette. Our health was not a consideration in more ways than one.

We used to walk along the pavements looking for fag-ends to pick up. In those days, the man who did not smoke was a rarity. My mother's sorting out of my father's wage-packet on a Friday night provided as an essential priority for the twenty Players cigarettes my father would collect with his paper on the way to work every morning. (Incidentally, women did not normally smoke in that age and those who did were regarded as "fast.")

The habit for smokers was to drop their fag-end on the pavement and stamp on it to make sure there was no risk of fire. So for young lads wanting to be like men and with no money this was like manna from heaven. No matter whose mouth the fag-end had been in, not even the sight of lipstick on the odd one, and without any thought as to what might have befallen since the fag-end had been dropped, we picked up all we could with great glee.

We had tried smoking cinnamon but here was the real thing. Shops would not sell us cigarettes anyway because of the law, but, if someone had a little pocket-money, we could buy cigarette papers and make our own. Even the word "hygiene" was unknown to us. And the word "cool" did not have its modern meaning, but we experienced the feeling, all right!

WORKING-CLASS SCHOOLDAYS IN THE 1930S AND 1940S

So many illnesses and hospitalisations before I was twelve! How did I have any chance at all of proper primary school education? Also, the war broke out when I was ten, bringing with it chopping and changing!

Sciennes

Things started very well. The local Corporation primary school for Causewayside was Sciennes. My first teacher (in 1934) was a Miss Thompson. It was obvious she liked her pupils – I think I took this for granted then. I remember we were introduced to reading, writing, spelling, arithmetic and craftwork – all without a raised voice or harsh word. What was even more important – might this have been a norm in those days? – was Miss Thompson took us to her home four or six at a time to have tea. I can't remember whether it was for afternoon tea or high tea, but there we were sitting around the dining table with Miss Thompson on one end and her mother on the other end, a teapot being poured from on high to make us laugh and relax.

Abbeyhill

It was when I was six that my parents bought the house (ground floor tenement flat) at 4 Waverley Park Terrace, so my transfer to Abbeyhill School was the first change, and there the mood was quite different. We assembled on a landing and marched to our classrooms to martial music on a loud gramophone.

I didn't have Miss Bruce for long enough to know her as a person, but she was a disciplinarian alright and a good teacher. The scary word in the playground, however, was that if you got (Puggy) Bruce you would find yourself at the next age change in the class of "slave driver" Miss Goodfellow!

Miss Goodfellow – "slave driver" – and a secret angel

Now, Miss Goodfellow really was a bully, obviously set on terrifying everyone, with no sign at all of having affection for any of us, far less a teacher's pet. But I realised much later that she did more for my good than any other teacher over the years. It would seem an impossible responsibility that she had – 50 pupils from good homes and bad absolutely unselected, all to discipline and help to reach the highest standard possible for sitting the Qualifying – that is, the exam critical for future education. (Once, years later, when Chaplain of Leith Academy, I was on the platform with Edinburgh's Deputy Director of Education and asked him how 50 pupils per teacher could have been tolerated by the authority. He reacted by telling me the number could never have reached 50: statistics showed the average size in 1930s was in the mid-30s. I looked out an old class photograph which showed 49 present that day).

Normal practice for Miss Goodfellow was to walk round the class and check our sums on the slate and writing in the jotter, with her leather belt (Lochgelly) – instant retribution – coiled up in her pinnie pocket. Spotting a mistake, she would haul the culprit's hand out towards her and wield the belt as quickly as her scorn inflamed her tongue.

When Miss Goodfellow was teaching from the front and some talking occurred in class as she was writing on the blackboard she would on occasion turn in all too obvious anger, and hurl the heavy wood-based duster up the raked floor to hit the wood panelling behind us, with a huge clatter.

Looking back, she no doubt missed us deliberately, but we felt that the chatterers were the actual target.

Sarcasm and personal insult

Sarcasm and personal insult were constant weapons too. Years later, a former classmate serving at a Post Office counter in Leith Walk, reminded me of a time she arrived late for class, nursing a sore knee, and embarrassed by the huge hole in her black stockings. Miss Goodfellow asked why she was late, the wee girl answered, "I went and fell," and thereafter for months this answer was mimicked in scorn.

Second World War and second change of school

The Second World War began on 3rd September 1939. A couple of days beforehand, we – my mother and her four children – gathered at Abbeyhill rail station with other families all with our gas masks over our shoulders, to be taken for our safety "to the country" – evacuees!

Before getting on the train we were all given a paper carrier bag containing corn beef, evaporated milk, a packet of plain biscuits, a round of Kraft spreading cheese, an orange and a bar of Duncan's fruit and hazelnut chocolate.

We had no idea where we were going or for how long. One mother in our carriage asked out loud how long we were away for, and another replied that the list of contents in the bag said rations for 48 hours so we'd be back home on Monday!

Nine months in Fife

The train crossed the Forth Bridge, after which children and families were being disembarked at different stations. When our turn came and our carriage emptied onto the platform, we discovered we were in a village called Strathmiglo. The man taking charge of us was the "Billeting Officer" – and we were soon to learn Mr Wannan was the school headmaster. The evacuees were taken to various houses where the villagers had been instructed that their spare rooms had been commandeered. When the Kellets got their billet my mother was so upset by the frosty reception (perhaps understandable!) "from two severe old ladies dressed in black" that she began to weep, sought out Mr Wannan, and he agreed that we, along with my Auntie Nan and cousin Charlie, could have the "sole" use of Rowanlea, a grand unoccupied but fully furnished house owned by Mr Scott the Mill Owner, situated on the corner of Cash Feus and facing the village green.

Mr Wannan, whose class I was in with children of different ages, turned out to be a very pleasant teacher. At his desk, he stretched himself out, with his feet on another chair, and smiled while he talked. Whenever a pupil misbehaved in some way, he would say "Bring out your ruler. Now hold out your arm and clench your hand, knuckle up". One, two, three strokes resulted.

Punishment for me!

There was no pain for me in the classroom – mainly because Miss Goodfellow had already drummed into me all that Mr

Wannan had to teach – but very shortly I was to receive the only parental beating in my life.

My father, as a grate-builder, was in a Reserved Occupation (excused call up) at this stage. He lived at home in Edinburgh and came up to join us in Strathmiglo after he finished work at noon on the Saturdays.

There came a Saturday when I had been hearing from older boys brought up in "Strath" about the technique and joy of guddling trout. So, as darkness approached, I ventured across the green to the banks of the River Eden, lay down and began to move my hands slowly along under the bank, feeling for lurking fish. Then some boys appeared along the opposite bank and, seeing me and what I was doing, started to throw stones into the water for fun. They paid no attention to my whispered appeals for them to stop, and when the splash of a large stone certainly spoiled any chance I had I was enraged, got up and ran to the stepping stones in order to cross the river and chase them off. It was getting darker of course and they had a big start on me when I began to chase and shout. When I realised that they were going to get away, I stopped, and it was swear words that came out from me. Then, when I turned for home and reached the stepping stones, I became aware in the pitch black of the burning red light of a cigarette being smoked on the home bank. This was my father who had obviously come out to check that I was alright and bring me home. But now the quiet man was furious with me and yelled, "Get home right now and get up into your bedroom!" My father followed me up the stairs, now with a cane walking stick in his hands, told me to lie on the bed, and whacked my backside. (What a shock he'd got!)

STRATHMIGLO NO MORE:
MIDDLETON CAMP SCHOOL

Although a bomb had landed in Holyrood Palace Gardens, the Blitzkrieg we'd heard about in Warsaw had not been repeated in Edinburgh. Rumour had it that Hitler was sparing Edinburgh as he hoped to make our palace his Scottish home. So back we came home in the March (1940). By now, the government was completing the new school camps they had planned in the 1930s to get children out of Auld Reekie and into the country air for their health. So Middleton Camp School, just south of Dalkeith, became like a working-class Public School for the next fifteen months. Two or three wooden dormitory blocks, a classroom block, and then ablution blocks for boys on one side and for girls opposite. A hall for games and dances – with the football pitch beyond it – occupied the space at the top while the middle space at the bottom provided the dining room and homes for the headmaster and the camp manager. There was a small hospital (complete with a nurse) sited on its own further back. The teaching staff were residential, having come out from Edinburgh schools. The maids – who gave us their country accents – came in daily from Middleton and Birkenside. The football coach came in weekly for the boys from Newtongrange, where he trained the Star. Mothers – and fathers, of course, if they were not in the Forces – came in by service bus on a Saturday, and sometimes with wee ones too young for the camp school education. (It is just astonishing the level of provision the government made for us. In those days they must have had values in mind, more important than the financial cost!)

Children, of course, were much the same as they are today. An extremely nourishing cereal had been brought across the dangerous Atlantic from Canada for our breakfast, but we didn't like it!

We were free to wander and play on the large Middleton House Estate, and some of us ran away!

"ANGELS UNAWARES" (HEBREWS 13v2)

Now, at Abbeyhill School, Miss Goodfellow the slave driver's regime demanded constant concentration and competition for success. In arithmetic, we would be urged to fill both sides of our slates with sums, bring them to the front to get a white chalk tick in the bottom corner, then clean the sums off the slate again, to get the highest number of chalk ticks by the end of the day! We were told famous children's stories from Scottish history: Bell the Cat, Bruce rising tall on his palfrey – this one complete with actions – to bring his battle-axe down on De Bohun's head; the lady putting her arm across the door of Falkland Palace to save King David; "It cam with a lass and It'll gang with a lass." History included also the Seven Wonders of the Ancient World, while Nature took in the parts of a daffodil and also the beauties of Lake Como. In the Bible, the Old Testament had stories of brave men and women while Psalms 23 and 100 we had to learn by heart. Grammar: now that was an important one, the clauses being named and distinguished time and time again.

There were always questions being thrown at us to keep us alert, and very often Miss Goodfellow's forefinger pointed at the top boy or girl and then travelled along the back row of desks until she got the correct answer. "Up top," she would say, and the pupils who'd been unable to answer would all move one place down.

The scorn that withered was always a constant. Years later, my youngest sister told me that Miss Goodfellow kept telling her, "You can't be a sister of John Kellet." And only recently I learned from her that our ("highly strung") mother had gone up to challenge Miss Goodfellow after she had made the same hurtful remark to my middle sister, Margaret. (Margaret and Millie both got the marks required for a senior secondary school). 100% may have appeared against so many subjects on my report card – amazing my parents and uncles – but I did not escape the withering scorn. When I had returned to Abbeyhill after my first evacuation, Miss Goodfellow greeted me dismissively with the news to me that my nose was bigger than it had been when I went away!

But then, when I was in the City Hospital with diphtheria in 1941, a large and very neat parcel arrived. It contained two games – Monopoly and Sorry – a present that astonished me, from Miss Goodfellow, more than a year after I left her class.

Now my next change of school, aged twelve, was to George Heriot's. Some months before, I'd been taken from Middleton to sit two competitive bursaries; for Heriot's and the Royal High. My parents' life experience meant that they knew nothing at all about such schools and the existence of bursary competitions. Just who could it have been that contacted them and got the necessary applications and so on?

"Angels Unawares". Could it have been the staff at Middleton whose names I am unaware of, and who, to the pupils' knowledge, never singled anyone out as a Dux, as being worthy of commendation or special attention? Or might Miss Goodfellow have proven herself the unexpected angel once again?

SEMI-DETACHED AT
GEORGE HERIOT'S SCHOOL

Realising I was working-class

It was at George Heriot's School, when I was approaching twelve years old, that I first became conscious of the class structure of Edinburgh society. What a strange new world I was in, from the first moment I turned off Lauriston Place, and walked through the gateway, made all the more imposing by forming a Janitor's house from its two sides.

At this first visit, for the Open Bursary Entrance Examination, I was still an evacuee at Middleton Camp School, and the nurse accompanied me because I had only recently been discharged from the diphtheria ward at the City Hospital. From the ancient, absolutely wondrous quadrangle, I was directed downstairs across the playground to the Examination Hall with its hammer-beam roof, already almost filled by what seemed hundreds of boys of my age.

The Royal High School Open Bursary Competition was another I had been entered for, and both schools notified the results very quickly. It was disappointing that I had failed to win a place at Heriot's, having come thirteenth, but I did not have to accept the invitation to the Royal High, where I had come sixth, because a couple of successful candidates for Heriot's preferred the Royal High, and so Heriot's now offered the award after all.

Class Distinction

Summoned to a meeting of the new Bursars to hear arrangements for admission to the first year, I felt very much odd-boy-out! The others all seemed to know each other, certainly to have come from fee-paying schools, and most, indeed, from Heriot's own Junior School. The 'accent' I did not realise I had was commented on.

When classes started, the fact that I did not naturally belong became all the more evident. It was established, for instance, that I lived in a tenement. Then it became clear that the normal thing was to play rugby (and to have parents who could afford the kit, of course), while I was football-mad. Going on around me also was a lot of talk about 'the tennis' over the summer.

Having for long organised the cricket in the Kings Park for our street, using an old fashioned bat from my grandfather's coal cellar, I enquired about playing cricket as the new season approached. My mother – my father being away at the war – insisted that she could afford the whites. I noticed that the boys in-the-know all turned up their shirt collars at the back, and would tie their cable-stitch jerseys nonchalantly round their neck and shoulders. After the first summer, I had out-grown the new whites and realised I could not expect my mother to find the money for another outfit.

One working-class boy in my first year English-class – a Foundationer – that is, a "fatherless boy" having his fees and books paid for, with a small income too, provided by the Governors operating the George Heriot Charitable Trust – was ridiculed by the English teacher at the roll call on many mornings. This man taught us hardly anything, never moving from his seat and desk up on his little platform, because he was working on the teams and the fixtures for the rugby and cricket. But he did make time to correct and re-correct Robert Porteous for the way he pronounced his name. "What did you say?…No! 'Pawrrti-us', not 'Poaches'. 'Pawrrti-us'."

Where I really belonged

Further evidence of the class distinction that kept me from a feeling of really belonging among the Herioter families is that for my first three years I went to school in the company of the boys and girls from Waverley Park who walked from the Terrace across the Kings Park to James Clark's Junior Secondary. Arriving at the Dumbiedykes, I would leave them to walk up St Leonard's Hill while I cut off to climb Arthur Street *en route* for Heriot's.

By the time my pals left 'Jimmy's', at age fifteen and started work as apprentices, my milk-boy pocket-money had helped buy me a second-hand bike, and I started cycling to school. But even after three years among understandably proud 'middle-class' Herioters, the company I knew I belonged to was elsewhere – with the Boys' Brigade at Holyrood Abbey church and the Christian Workers' League in the Canongate.

Latterly very likeable classmates

Mind you, there were very able and latterly very likeable boys in my class. Among them, the classmate in whom the Heriot/Goldenacre consciousness was most evident was Drew Wightman, and I found myself surprised when his in-group confidence led him not only to reveal that he was in the Boys' Brigade but actually to produce his BB Week card and invite our Register Teacher, Mr Norman Abercrombie, to make a donation! At the end of our fifth year, again astonishingly to me, Drew organised a secret whip-round and donated a book to 'Abers'.

Decades later, by which time Drew had become Head Postmaster, I had two significant contacts which confirmed the content of Drew's character as a man. First, he responded very graciously when I wrote to appeal against the sacking – actually the justified sacking – of a Leith postman I'd recently married; secondly, when I conducted Edinburgh Presbytery's Quinquennial Inspection at Juniper Green parish church, I found Drew to be an elder.

Donald Berwick was another well-ensconced fellow pupil who had been at the Junior School and who came to play an important part in my adult life. When in 1969 I was called to be minister of South Leith, there was Donald in the congregation – and his sister Margaret was very soon to become the 500-year-old Kirk's first woman elder. Donald himself now had his own civil engineering business, and contributed his energy and skills to help rescue our new halls building from structural mistakes made by the builder and the architectural team we were employing.

Bill Peat – very good at playground football! – appeared in Leith too, after he had resigned his appointment as a Reader in Physics at Heriot Watt University, gone on to train as a parish minister, and then been called to the charge of Leith St Serf's. *Quelle surprise!* It never occurred to either of us at school that we might end up as parish ministers!

Outstandingly good teachers, dedicated to their pupils

One of the very best of teachers I have ever benefited from was Mr ('Chinkie') Westwood. His eccentricity was relished by the boys but eventually his audacity led to sacking by the Governors, after parents created a scandal in the media because he had taken senior boys to see what adult life was like in the nearby Greyfriars Bobby Bar. This particular experiment was no doubt beyond the pale, given the puritanical 'protectiveness' of the then climate of respectability. But here was a dedicated teacher who also took senior boys into the General Assembly and the High Court to learn about public speaking and the nature of debate; who, in my own experience, brought modern poets into the classroom and was able once to keep control and persist unambiguously teaching his lesson while he sat bathing his sore feet in a basin.

After his highly publicised sacking, Mr Westwood enrolled at New College for a Bachelor of Divinity Degree and then submitted his first year essay on Tertullian, the early church father, in Greek poetic couplets. About this time, I happened to see him one Saturday in crowded Princes Street, waving his cane to me in greeting and still – like Hercule Poirot – wearing spats!

Mr ('Pat') Campbell, a very good Maths teacher for my Highers Year, had a personality and a unique gimmick that delighted the class. He would open the lesson by standing facing the centre of the (green) 'blackboard' with chalk in his left hand, start to write the theorem for the day, and complete each line after transferring the chalk to his right hand.

Years later, I was suddenly to see Mr Campbell on a Sunday in Craiglockhart church, when I stood in as holiday supply, and there he was, one of four office bearers bringing forward the offering (and obviously well qualified to count it).

Mr Norman Abercrombie ('Abers'), Head of Foreign Languages, was my Class (Register) Teacher for five of my six years. I looked up to him from the very beginning because my Nana had been a waitress in the dining room and she told me what a kind man he was. But his strictness was very clear from our first day and it took a little while before we picked up the accompanying humour and also warm humanity of the man; I still smile at his story of the fellow-soldier in France who came back from a farm absolutely delighted because when he bought twa eggs, he got three!

Now, Abers had lost a leg on the Western Front in the Great War, and the word went round among us to be wary on Monday mornings, because he removed his 'wooden' limb at the weekend for a long rest and then found the stump very sore on Monday mornings.

First thing on Mondays the drill was that we had to open our ink exercise notebook which the French master inspected as he walked along the two aisles between our desks. In my first year, I somehow imagined that I could be safe concentrating under the desk on a largish picture book about the Spitfire: there was outrage! And still I did not learn. One Monday morning not long afterwards, my attention was once again elsewhere and when I guessed that Abers had now passed a couple of rows behind me, I turned to whisper something to the boy immediately behind me. The be-suited disciplinarian needed just one stride to get within striking distance and his right hand clattered my ear with colossal force. The shock and the pain could never be forgotten. (Nor has the surprise and delight of being recognised as first equal for the Dr Lowe Prize in Modern Languages!)

Now, with their background, my parents never experienced the angst that takes over middle-class parents as they press their offspring into hours of study (and also worry) at home. I never saw the advantage of becoming a swat at the expense of things more important to me. And my feeling of apartness from the spirit of the school, even five years on, is further evidenced by the fact that I sought school permission to end the summer term early, though this meant that I would miss the prize-giving, in order to take a job as a butcher's boy and thereby earn enough money to afford the week's camp in Iona with the Christian Workers' League, where I really belonged.

But Mr. Abercrombie was an admirable teacher, giving time after school – for those who could be free to gain the benefit – to teach Russian and also the game of Chess, as well as coaching cricket at Goldenacre in the summer. He was the one teacher I visited at home in his retirement after I became Minister at South Leith.

Founder's Day

Every first Monday in June, the whole school (and guests), in my time, could be assembled in the quadrangle. We would sing the oft rehearsed school songs – 'We hail the day with grateful mirth, that brings to mind George Heriot's birth' – and close by marching out in twos, saluting the statue of George Heriot as we passed.

On two occasions after I became a minister, I felt honoured to be invited by the school to which I and many others owed so much in order to lead a prayer and then to conduct a service in the school chapel for Foundationers and their families. On the second occasion, I was Minister at South Leith and so was able to stay for the black tie celebratory dinner in the evening. The Chief Guest was Lord Mackay of Clashfern – the 'non-political' Lord Chancellor (of All England) appointed by Margaret Thatcher.

The high point of the annual dinner was the production by the Chairman of the Governors of the long silver loving cup, with its two handles, which was made by George Heriot himself.

The chairman at that time was Mr James Ross, the proprietor of the then Edinburgh Rock Manufacturing company. He invited the Chief Guest and then myself to sup wine from the loving cup.

James Peter Hymers Mackay, two years older than me, was another non-rugby playing, working-class boy with Leith connections and a Christian faith he practised even to his cost, who had won a bursary to Heriot's Secondary School.

I do wonder just how many 'fatherless boys' and bursary winners, educated and supported by the Heriot Trust over nearly four hundred years now, have not only done well for themselves but also used their early working-class background and Heriot education so that the poor of the world might be blessed. (Perhaps a young Bursar of the modern age might research this for a PhD?)

Nulle surprise, sadly

Jimmy Ross was an extremely friendly host, even asking me things about my sermon. I took the opportunity to say how glad I was that Heriot's had recently decided to begin admitting girls. He replied that they had to: they needed the money!

Thus, over the years, we all do keep coming across evidence that supports Karl Marx's thesis for economic pressure being the determinant factor for bringing change in society. Also, that applying the gospel to revolutionise our cherished traditions really is difficult.

LIFE IN THE STAIR

Number 4 Waverley Park Terrace was regarded as a "good" stair. There were eight houses, four floors, two houses to each floor. The fixed regime in the stair was imposed and enforced by one resident, Mrs Duncan, the widow who lived opposite us on the ground floor. Her family had owned the dairy next door. The dairy was now closed and used as a store- room for the "general store" on the corner of Waverley Park and Waverley Park Terrace. Our stair was a good stair because the outside door was always locked; you needed a stair latchkey to get in. The brass bells outside the stair were all polished every day. And it was kept very clean inside. Children were not allowed to play in the stair and not allowed to play or even go into the back-green. Each household had to wash their stair and landing once a week. Then there was a back passage from the ground floor through to the back-green and every house had a turn for washing it. A notice was hung on your door to say it was your turn to clean the back passage. There were turns for hanging out your washing. Each house had a morning or afternoon or evening when they had priority for hanging out their clothes to dry in the back-green.

An occasional event was the arrival of a singer in the back-green. Now these were men who had been badly affected by the Great War. In the Depression, there was no work for such men, so periodically a man would come, somehow get into the back-green, (probably by climbing up from the King's Park), remove his cap, put it on the ground in front of him and begin to sing up to people's windows. Usually the singer cupped one hand against his ear to make sure he was producing the best sound. We would be entertained by or we would ignore, "It's a long way to Tipperary" and "Nellie Dean". After he'd finished, the singer would look up at the windows and hold his cap out. Pennies would be thrown down to him.

Our particular stair was not one where people were in and out of each other's houses. Everyone was respectful of everyone else's privacy. What I do remember about the family immediately above us, is that Mr Davie was a railwayman, and we used to see him leaving from time to time with a bell and a folding platform, because he spoke in public about the Union and the Labour Party.

Another resident was the brother of homeowner, Mrs Towart. He had spent part of the First World War as a prisoner of war, working in the salt mines somewhere in Eastern Europe, and he had been very badly damaged mentally and physically.

Before we ourselves left Waverley Park Terrace, another family moved into the top flat. I remember Mr Aitchison losing his job and my mother would get me to take up a jug of soup. She would make broth with peas and barley, or else lentil soup flavoured with ham bones and I would be asked to say that my mother had made too much and we hoped Mrs Aitchison could use it up.

FOOTBALL, FOOTBALL, FOOTBALL –
AND SCORING A GOAL AT DENS PARK!

Throughout my childhood and youth, any two lads would be welcomed into any football game, even by boys we did not know, just so long as there was not already eleven on each side and that there was indeed a "cock and a hen".

Football, football, football. It got me places, helped make me an organiser, kept me from becoming an airy-fairy out-of-touch political or theological theorist, and even gave me a moment of glory!

I was attracted into my first game of football when I was five, sitting on top of the gate of the former St Anthony's School in Causewayside, watching older boys relishing a match in the playground. Joined by another boy I did not know, we shouted to ask if we could get a "cock or a hen": that is, one of us on to each side.

The Hearts and the Hibs

My father and his two Edinburgh brothers were committed Hearts supporters and I started to join them (when they weren't away at the war) and also my cousins, at the same stance on the terraces of Tynecastle one week and Easter Road the next.

In those days, unlike today sadly, Jambos and Hibees did not hate and abuse one another. There wasn't the money to watch your team both home and away. Our family used to joke that we only went to Easter Road to see the half-time Hearts result raised up on the scoreboard; no pocket radios or mobile phones then. The Saturday spectators could number 40,000 and woe betide anyone who was under the influence of alcohol and started swearing. A shout would go out from a local authority–figure close by, "Boys present!" or occasionally "Ladies present!" And this would be enough to stop the bad language. (This really is the way the mainly working – class crowds on the terraces at Tynecastle and Easter Road behaved then!)

Thanks to the 35th (Holyrood Abbey church) Boys' Brigade

In my early teens, I was the boy in the street who made sure we had a ball to play football up the King's Park. Because of the war, footballs could not be bought – even had we had the money. But I discovered that the ex-guardsman railwayman and BB Captain in the next stair had not thrown out the old burst footballs. They were made of leather panels in those days and the stitching would tear or wear out before the leather. So I would go up to Captain Spence's house and ask for one of the burst balls, take it home, use a sister's kirbygrip to thread a thin string through the holes, and go back to get the captain to blow it up.

I obviously impressed Captain Spence, because when the Boys' Brigade League resumed after the war, he made me joint captain of the team. (Organiser I was, but sadly this appointment as joint captain of the team did not last for long!)

Very serious competition

I realised how very competitive and important even boys' football could be for small proud communities round the capital when, one Saturday, the league programme took us to one of the mining villages, possibly Wallyford or Gilmerton. The 35th travelled by rail on the "suburban line". The moment we arrived at their station, old men came right up to the carriage doors, shouting to us that the rain had made the pitch unplayable and the referee had cancelled the match. "If you stay on the train, it will take you to Gorgie in time for the Hearts cup-tie." But our officers were not taken in and we pushed out to confirm the deceit and play the game. (Sadly, our opponents were too good for us anyway!)

For some small communities in amateur football the only three possible results for a match were win, draw or protest.

To this day football is an important and essential part of life in the (mainly working-class) Boys' Brigade.

Football, football!

Until my late teens, I played football (or organised cricket) morning, afternoon and night during the school holidays. On Saturdays I'd play football in the morning, watch football in the afternoon and go to the dancing at night in order to talk about football. And this was the normal life for working-class boys.

In the Scottish working-class world the Sunday Post was bought every Sunday not just for Oor Wullie and The Broons but for Jack Harkness's extensive and intensive coverage of Scottish football.

Later, in the very serious minded CWL – founded in the 1940s by the Iona Community in the Edinburgh Canongate – we formed a football team instinctively. I remember a match against the Younger's "Brewery Boys", who played in the clogs provided for their work. Our CWL team entered the newly revived Churches' League and won the (wooden) cup.

When I was sent abroad on National Service, my father wrote to me just once – my mother wrote every week, of course – and this was to tell me how much I could look forward to thrilling to the skills of Conn, Bauld and Wardhaugh after my release.

Football in Egypt (1948–49)

We didn't have much opportunity to play football when on National Service in Egypt, but one time the Adjutant asked me to stand in for the referee who'd called off at the last minute. It happened that the Argyll and Sutherland Highlanders captain's team lost and lo and behold, he promptly arranged a repeat match because they hadn't had a proper referee!

One other game I remember vividly was an occasion when we – exceptionally – played in the Fouad (Port Said) Stadium against a local team. We Brits just took it for granted that we would slaughter the Maltese, Egyptian, French and Greek employees of the Suez Canal company. But our traditional dribbling, kick and rush tactics were totally outclassed by the passing – perfect passing! – game then completely unknown to us.

Passing backwards? Passing across the goal? Not trying to dribble one man after another? Such tactics were absolutely against the rules we'd learned as essential for winning from a very early age!

Politics

Back home, when the deservedly celebrated John P Mackintosh, MP – whom I'd got to know at Edinburgh University during his lecturing days – had published in the

New Statesman one of the very first academic arguments to the British public in favour of devolution for Scotland – emphasising the distinctive nature of our educational system, legal structures and National Church – I thought I had to draw attention to the main thing that made Scottish working–class boys feel very Scottish – football!

(John's middle-class education in an English-type Public School must be held responsible).

Every time Scotland played England – the "Auld Enemy" – at football, whether at Hampden or Wembley, we could only know what was happening by listening to BBC wireless. And the BBC always employed as its commentator a man with a very English voice, which made all the worse his very English bias that was never sensitive to our Scottish perspective. (Such was the widespread resentment that it's a wonder the SNP took so long to come to the fore.)

Football – the call to the ministry

It was while holidaying with my wife, Ena on the Isle of Iona in 1955, that I realised I was meant to be a minister – in a new housing area parish. Six years of Edinburgh University later, I found myself being interviewed by the General Assembly's National Church Extension committee. Three men sat behind a table in the 121 George Street Offices, while some twelve or so other ministers and elders stood or sat around me. The chairman happened to be the Reverend TD Stewart Brown, the minister of South Leith I would succeed some eight years later. He just touched the papers before him, lifted his head to look at me and said, "Well, Mr Kellet, we've read your church experience and academic record but tell us what you know about life out in the world?" My reply brought instant warm laughter all round: "Well, my first religion was the Heart of Midlothian Football Club!"

There were no more questions about my eligibility, just when could I start?!

Football and scoring a goal at Dens Park

This was one of the highlights of my life. Bobby Ancell, the manager of Dundee Football club – the first team to succeed in European football – had trained our players for a number of weeks. On the big day, there was a huge crowd. A moment came when I saw the right winger race ahead of the opponents' defence to gather a long pass lofted towards the corner flag. From near the half way line, I sprinted from my left wing past the burly centre-half, anticipated the cross that must come, and masterfully volleyed with my left (normally unused) foot high into the net to the goalie's right.

The acclaim from the thousands attending was thunderous.

The Dundee Courier next morning reported my goal as a lucky fluke!!

Now, all of the above is absolutely the truth. But honesty also requires me to say that there was no chance of our team playing in Europe. This game was actually a revival of the traditional challenge match between Dundee butchers and ministers/priests! We discovered beforehand – can you believe it? – that the Roman Catholics couldn't find a left winger! So, the right winger was playing on the left wing. And I did sprint very fast indeed because the centre-half was producing a butcher's cleaver from under his jersey...

"MILLIE MACKAY'S GOT A HOLE IN HER EYE, THE DOCTOR SAYS, SHE'S GOING TO DIE"

Also The Two Blacksheep, Bah! Bah!

(Playground girls' skipping song, London Street Primary School, circa 1914)

My mother had a hard life, one that sadly may have been typical for many working-class women of the time, with what would be seen nowadays as near-impossible stumbling-blocks to get over. It is a remarkable thing about Millie Mackay that somehow she faced all that came to confront her, coped with the consequences, got on with her responsibilities, and daily sang her way through the years as if all such were normal.

When she was just ten years old her mother ran away from her father, taking just the younger child with her, leaving Millie crying after them in the street to be taken too, and now left to cope with the father who had been making life a misery. A daily duty was to haul the tin bath into the middle of the floor, and have water boiling on the fire, all ready for her miner father getting home from the pit.

In a society then of Calvinist judgementalism, my mother had to cope with the public knowledge that she was illegitimate; the hand-written copy birth certificate procured from the Musselburgh Registrar in 1923 reproduces the declaration made by her mother that her "husband" is not the father of the child, and further she has had no personal communication with him since they ceased to reside together 18 months ago. What effect this record on the original birth certificate may have had on the attitudes of the school staff in London Street, one way or another, I don't know. But my mother's memory of the children singing the personally directed playground skipping song was a happy one.

Millie's secondary schooling was in James Clark's, St Leonard's Hill. Thereafter, she could count, read, write, spell, and manage a household well for the rest of her days.(At the age of 91, she was in the middle of a letter to her son and daughter-in-law, who had just left her, when she took the stroke that killed her.)

Keeping herself

At the age of 14, Millie had to "keep" herself which meant getting a job, and that meant in her family circumstances, going away into private service. She left the Waverley Station with 6d in her purse, a stamp for a letter to her mother, and only the clothes she stood in, in order to skivvy for a Doctor Weatherhead in the unknown–to–her town of Galashiels. She would wash her underwear every night and sometimes have to put it on damp the next morning. When the housekeeper realised Millie was in such a bad way she spoke to the doctor and he gave her a small advance in her wages. The first to get up every morning (to set the fires) and the last to get into bed, under the direction of the housekeeper, Millie did relish her day off, sometimes to visit her mother at the Kirna in Walkerburn, and then to the dancing at Galashiels Volunteer Hall!

The One for Millie

A boy a year older at James Clark's had shown great interest in
Millie and when he was old enough to have a motorbike, down
he came to Galashiels to visit. Mind you, he was very different
from my mother – the dour, silent type, and he did not dance!
However, there was a pillion on the bike and William did belong
to – was a founder member of the Melville Motor Cycle club, with
speed-drives along the Dolphinton straight and picnics when they
had their stops. This was a real courtship ("winching") all right!

A tragedy kept secret

But something terribly destructive happened to my mother
when she was seventeen during her time in Galashiels,
something she could never talk about. The facts we do know are
that the housekeeper realised she was ill and gave her the money
for the train fare to Edinburgh, where her older step-sister,
Lily took her in – and Millie was wary of creepy husband! She
was admitted to the Royal Infirmary under Professor Norman
Dott, where her weight fell to just over 5 stones and, including
surgery across her neck for goitre, her stay lasted 13 months.

I have a reference given by Dr Weatherhead, testifying that
Millie had served him well for more than 3 years and he was
sorry to lose her. This was no doubt important when, after her
discharge from hospital, Millie got a maid's job in the Duke of
Roxburgh's Ednam House in Kelso.

Saved by marriage

My mother was saved for a better though never trouble-free
life at nineteen when she married my father, who was by then,

twenty-one, had just finished his apprenticeship and was now on a tradesman's wage. The marriage service was conducted on 29th March 1928 by the Reverend Doctor Gardiner of Greyfriars, no doubt facilitated by my church-committed Nana. (My father had become a sergeant in St Giles' Boys' Brigade: just when he became atheist – I don't know.)

The couple first got a room in the West Bow and then managed to get their first home, in which their first child was born, 22nd July 1929, at 155 Causewayside.

Millie had remained very weak and Nana arranged for John ("Jackie") to be looked after by a friend in Prestonpans for some months. This last detail I did not learn until I was in my 50s, decades after my wife and I in preparation for parenting in our turn had read John Bowlby's classic "Childcare and the Growth of Love", with its emphasis that unchanging security and affection for at least the first 18 months were determinative factors for a child's future life. (I began to wonder if my infant experiences accounted for some of my adult deficiencies!)

More importantly, such a start to adult life for my mother certainly added to the strains and she coped with bringing up a family of four, on her own in time of war, and then with teenage trials.

When Millie became an old age pensioner – no private pension, of course – and a widow, she would often reflect that she was better off than when she had four young children. Back then, the housekeeping money from my father was 26/- a week and 1/- of that had to be saved every week because there was no wage for the "holiday" week at Hogmanay or the Trades Week "holiday", six months later. (Mind you, her adult children helped discreetly!)

But I remember that in the bad old days of the 1930's, two men used to go round the doors of the slum property every Friday night asking for condensed milk for the babies suffering in the Spanish civil war, and my mother had her tin ready.

The two "black sheep" – and a working-class saint

During the war, my mother gave a home to her father, and this was not long after a distant member of the family had reported seeing him stealing money for booze from a drunken Canadian Air Force Officer lying in Princes Street.

Then in 1953, the day before my wedding, when the father that her husband and his brothers hated, and never did forgive, was charged with a heinous crime, she went up to the police headquarters to plead that the trial be kept out of the papers in order to protect her respectable children – and thereafter still visited him in his secure block at Greenlea Old Peoples Home (Edinburgh's Poorhouse).

When a young grandson, desperately searching for new friends in order to get away from the local bullies whose terrorising he'd kept from the family for years fell in with a chapter of Hell's Angels and their "protecting" ended up with him in court and put on remand, frail Millie got the bus to the jail and put the palms of her hands up against his on the dividing glass screen in the visiting hall.

She was clearly a good Christian woman, my mother, not just the church attender and office–bearer at Canongate and then Stockbridge St Bernard's that some outsiders would only see.

Summing up her life at the funeral, I paid tribute saying again and again "Millie coped" – not just a refrain, but a mantra, a eucharist. Ordinary working-class Edinburgh women are not the kind who have obituaries written about them, are they?

Like all the saints, even St Peter himself, my Mother was not faultless. But she was a saint. Halleluiah!

HOUSING FOR THE EDINBURGH WORKING-CLASS:

Getting a house in 1929

We hear a great deal in the media these days about the difficulty young couples have in getting a house – or on the housing ladder – and sad it is. But my father only got a house in 1929 because he wrote to a Property Agent saying he was a young tradesman who would improve any property and also because my grandfather Kellet gave the £20 'key money' (out of a small legacy he had received) to my very young, very underweight, very pregnant mother.

These were the years of The Great Depression of the 1920s and 1930s. The first Labour government had passed the Rent Restriction Act, so that rents could not be raised and poor people would benefit. The unintended consequence was that landlords wouldn't pay for essential repairs.

In the 1950's the Edinburgh Evening News headlined a story that a whole tenement in the South Side (Beaumont Place) was on the market for sale at just one penny! It seemed that the headline writer didn't know that the 'generous' benefactor had bought the property only very recently, had managed – in that time of post-war shortages – to sell two of the little flats, and now would make a considerable profit if he could escape the responsibility for the urgent repairs required in the rest of the ruinous building.

Many years later, a Presbytery Elder of Wardie Kirk told me that as an apprentice lawyer one of his weekly duties was to go round and collect rents in Marchmont, remembering to take a pad and to write down before the tenants all the repairs reported to him, and then not to forget to drop the notes into the waste paper basket hanging on the lamppost at his bus stop for home.

Causewayside – part of the site where the National Library of Scotland map section is now

The house my father got in 1929 was at 155 Causewayside. The brass plate for 155 was actually half way up our pend on a door in a high wall that hid the garden and the big house that we never saw. Built into the back of this middle-class house was an outside stair that led up to a number of tiny houses – slum flats, as we would say now. My guess is that this substandard property was built to provide an income for the owner of the big house.

The 'house' my father got was one of three on the top floor: a room and kitchen, with coomb ceilings, an iron sink and cold water tap on the common landing outside the door (required to serve three families) and the toilet (for all six houses in the block) on the floor below. Needless to say, my father did improve the property, and when another, slightly roomier dilapidated house on the floor below became available, he was offered it, and immediately put in an inside tap and sink himself. Towards the end of his days, my father once remarked that this move, from the low-coombed ceiling, but with the same toilet, was the biggest change of house ever. That is when I realised how bad things had been for Edinburgh working-class family life in those early days.

GOD AND THE DEVIL

A good mother-in-law with a devil for her husband

Comedians make 'jokes' about mothers-in-law and the Great British public laugh as if they know the relationship well. But my Kellet grandmother and my mother were best friends, mutually supportive and admiring, sharing life almost daily, and this in spite of what might be summed up as the devil's work.

No matter the seriousness of the disappointments and betrayals that came from her husband, the grandmother in this case – my Nana – remained a good woman by anybody's standards. Born in 1881, she came to Edinburgh from Alyth in Perthshire, and attended Canongate School. But with the name Mary Gardiner Lockerbie, her antecedents may have been Doonhamers.

Her family had a dairy at 1 West Newington Place. In 1902, age twenty-one, she married Jack, Watchmaker and Jeweller. With her husband spending so much money in pubs, her expectations were shattered, the business went, and a succession of homes were given up until the family, with four sons, were in the two rooms which could be found at the lowest rent. But Nana proved herself both a Mary and also a Martha!

Sundays

Every Sunday, Nana would put on her posh (old) fox fur, taking care to hide her poverty and unhappiness during morning service in Greyfriars church. She was always terribly aware that there were even more miserable souls all around the area, so somehow, Nana managed to take her turn helping to provide the open Sunday breakfast for homeless people who crowded the Grassmarket. She would also have with her a stick of pipe tobacco for one of the old soldiers damaged by the Great War.

Under my Nana's influence, my parents were married in March 1928 in Dr Gardiner's Manse and I was baptised as an infant in Greyfriars.

Saturdays

On a Saturday afternoon, Nana and my mother, with the children, would be out buying eggs and salad vegetables from the street barrow in Infirmary Street for the family tea when "the men" – my father and his brothers – came home from the football match. (They were Hearts supporters but, as was the common practice in those days, they watched the Hibs every second week.)

The pictures

Nana was very good with her hands – crocheting and knitting. In those days working-class people went to the cinema once or twice a week. Believe it or not, many women knitted while watching the pictures – click, click, click – while the men smoked and created a fug. And Nana was so skilled she could turn a sock in the dark.

Helping daughter-in-law and grandson

When I won competitive bursaries to secondary school at both George Heriot's and The Royal High, I knew nothing of either school, except that my Nana had been a waitress in the dining room at Heriot's, so I went there for my education. The lunch-hour turned out to be only 35 minutes, so I had no time to go home and Nana – living nearby – provided sausage and mash, or whatever, every day.

The heart attack

When I was away on National Service in Egypt, I got a letter from my mother to say that Nana had died from a heart attack. Now, over the years, Nana had often stopped when going up a wee brae, saying that she was 'puggled'. But a day came when Nana saw a young woman struggling up Cockburn Street with a pram and a big parcel, and to make things easier for the young mother, Nana had carried the parcel.

"Typical of my mother," wrote my Uncle Ian to me many years later.

VERY SCOTTISH AND TYPICALLY "MONGREL"

"The Gael and the Pict, the Angles and the Danes – from Galway, China, Pakistan, England… They are all Scotland's story and they're all worth the same." (The Proclaimers)

My Kellet Grandfather got his surname from an English antecedent, a travelling tinker (that is, a metal worker) who came up to Scotland and was in the normal way given the surname of the birth place he'd come from in North Lancashire / South Cumberland. I was told that the first pawn shops in Leith were founded or managed by Kellets. One family produced the very famous all-in Wrestling Champion, Les Kellet – a referee – (because he is now "too old") – when my father took me to see our relative perform in the Leith Eldorado. Back Les came to the ring when television gave the sport mass audiences and he became an enormous star. My own direct antecedent, my father's grandfather opened an Ironmongery at 61 & 63 Broughton Street that became well known in Edinburgh as "the shop with the kettle hanging down in front of the doorway."

Heirlooms

I have two 'heirlooms' from the business. A two-handled ornamental tray in polished copper made by my great great grandfather will go to my son Malcolm. A 'piggy' hot water bottle bearing the business name "William J Kellet", Broughton Street has been passed to my son William.

The family business "black sheep"

This Broughton Street business was particularly successful. They had the contract for looking after all the paraffin lamps that hung from the houses in the new town, cleaning the wick and filling up with paraffin. The family, living above the shop (no.59), became wealthy. My grandfather, born in 1871 or 1874, was sent to Edinburgh's "Model School" in Johnston Terrace, paying for each day's education every morning (2/6d per week). At 21, he was set up as a Watchmaker and Jeweller in Chambers Street. But, because of drunken ways – perhaps partly due to World War One experiences with the Rifle Brigade in Palestine – this Prodigal Son did not receive his father's blessing and the business went to the upright son instead. My Kellet Grandfather was called the black sheep of the family – as indeed was my other grandfather.

In 1981, his oldest son, Ian, confirmed to me that he was, "a rascal and a black sheep all right not even a loveable one. He was a drunkard and a disgrace to a perfectly decent family and I don't say that pompously. I personally had no liking, admiration or love for him. He treated my mother abominably and I think it should be known throughout the family."

My grandfather moved his wife and family four times, and at all times downhill. So my father was brought up in the awful slum that was 5 Society Buildings, Brown Square – a site now built on by the National Museum of Scotland, Chambers Street.

Burke and Hare

Incidentally, my father kept his motorbike in the cellar of the Friendly Society building which had a plate on the wall to say that Burke and Hare kept their bodies from Greyfriars Churchyard there until the deals were done with the Royal Infirmary pathologists.

Four boys shared the one small bedroom: the window was kept half-open day and night all year round. A pulley for hanging out the washing stretched out from the window. Three families shared one toilet on the landing: old newspapers were torn into squares for toilet paper. Dossers used the gas for the light in the stair to fortify the meths they drank.

"Shoat!"

In those days of mass unemployment, men played pitch – and – toss with pennies at the foot of the stair while others sat round a table gambling with cards. These men would pay two wee boys to stand at the entries to the square in Chambers Street and Lindsay Place and to shout "Shoat" when the mounted police came on their periodic raids.

The all prevailing smell of "Snow Fire"

I once asked my father why he worked as a grate-builder, an awful job which demanded in winter days in freezing rooms, having to start by breaking the ice in which the Dutch tiles had been left steeping, and coming home with sore hacks over his hands, burnt into by lime and cement. He replied that he was lucky to get any job, "your grandfather met a man in the pub."

Thus it was that every night after work, he would rub olive oil and sugar on to his hands and fingers, trying to clean out the hacks, and then rubbing in "snowfire" to try and soothe them.

MY OWN "TALES OF A GRANDFATHER" (NO. 2)

Teuchter Mackay

If you happen to know the Proclaimers' popular and inspiring song that helps everyone in our country to realise that immigrants have always been coming to Scotland and are parts of our story – in fact have often built up businesses that have become a boon for us – you may recollect that after citing the Irish, the Pict, the Gael, Pakistan and from afar, they slipped in a line about a Mackay coming south.

Well, it so happened that my great grandfather, John Strachan Mortimer Mackay, born in 1856 or 1858 – one of many, many John Mackays – came south to 19th Century Edinburgh from Rogart in Sutherland as a boy. His parents had a wee croft with fishing, and his mother saved hard and kept poultry so that the children could be educated. John passed the "Qualifying" two years' early at nine, but ran off to sea. When a day came that he had a fight with the laird's son, he realised he really had to leave his home district immediately, even though this meant walking all the way to a big city, where he knew not a soul.

Lucky in love, and Edinburgh's Chief Scaffie

The tale my mother had heard was that John Mackay was lucky to get a job in the Lighting and Cleansing Department of Edinburgh Corporation and eventually rose to become

Chief Scaffie. When, late in life, my mother managed to find still alive the youngest sister of her father, hoping to discover more, she was instantly corrected by "the very prim and proper Baptist lady" – Mrs. Flora Gascoyne. "Your father was the Cleansing Superintendent. And I have to tell you that my mother always said that your father was a guid laddie spilet!"

I myself, however, have since been told different stories. First, great grandfather John served his time as a baker on the corner of Hamilton Place. There he made shortbread for Queen Victoria, packing and sending it to the palace every month.

Secondly, that his brother–in–law Vallance was a Quantity Surveyor and got him a job as an inspector in the Lighting and Cleansing Department. On his retiral, Cameron's in the Lawnmarket offered him a job and he worked part-time baking shortbread and cakes and serving the Royals.

Thirdly, that one day he went up on the roof to clear snow that was interfering with the fire, and fell. When in hospital, he bought a shop in the High Street, just down from Patrick Thompsons (pre-1914), where he and his wife sold sweets, fruit and vegetables, supplying the castle and also troops billeted in the bridges… and "made a fortune."

This John Mackay was certainly lucky in love. His wife–to–be was actually "full-blooded Spanish." Her birth father was captain of a Spanish ship which foundered in the Firth of Forth, killing both parents, but not the new baby they'd brought on the voyage. She was adopted by a West Lothian family: Jim Vallance owned the first shale oil refining works (near Broxburn) and also owned property in South Edinburgh.

"I object"

Now, when in the 1870s John came to be married in Bristo church on the corner of Bristo Street and Forrest Road, both just 18, a terrible thing happened, something I'd always dreaded might happen when I was conducting weddings myself decades later. As soon as the minister uttered the words, "If anyone can show just cause why they may not lawfully be joined together in marriage, let him speak or forever hold his peace," the Bride's father shouted from the back of the church that he objected: his daughter was a heiress to a large fortune and she would not get it if she married this penniless teuchter!

Well, the minister ("wee Morrison") happened to be a friend of my great grandfather, but even if he hadn't this was no justification for cancelling the marriage.

A typical working-class family?

The determined young couple set up home in Guthrie Street and later in St Giles Street. They had thirteen children, of whom three died in infancy, while the others grew to become good singers. Daughter Jean trained and sang soprano in Italian and Spanish, then emigrated to the United States of America. Daughter Nellie also became a professional singer, singing "I dreamt that I dwelt in marble halls" when the St Andrew's Square Theatre (later cinema) was opened.

Youngest lamplighter

With a father like he had, the first-born son, my grandfather John Mackay (Junior) became at 13, with the help of a specially extended stick, the youngest Leerie in Edinburgh.

"Johnnie" was his mother's favourite – "very clever, a great laddie" – but later "a wasted boy." He fell out with his parents, and his daughter Millie, my mother, never met them.

I can't be sure what all went so wrong that his youngest sister Flora was to call him "the black sheep of the family and a drunkard and a rogue." But he did serve with the Royal Marines in the Great War – and volunteered again as a cook in the Royal Engineers, going to France for a second time after having received a bullet in the knee and being discharged. He'd sometimes speak to me of the generous tots of rum issued before front-line battles. Perhaps his time touring the halls, singing and playing the mandolin, developed his dependence on booze and helped bring him down; though I also remember him telling me of his dislike of Will Fyfe who modelled himself on Sir Harry Lauder, but turned to smut to increase his audience!

Years later my Grandfather Mackay passed his Spanish mandolin skills to his youngest daughter, Peggy; and eventually gave me his Basque blood-group along with my (one time) Spanish blue eyes!

"Bah-bah black sheep"

Drink and debt eventually forced my grandfather to run away. He became a miner at Wheatley Hill in the Durham coalfields, met Mrs Mary Jane Pearson (née Oates) of 3 Gothea Street, with daughters Sally and Lily, and brought them to Musselburgh (9 Mitchell Street) and the Carberry Pit. Mildred, my mother, was born on 6th May 1908 and daughter Peggy was born on 4th August 1912 after moving to an area house in St James Square.

My grandmother Mary's life was so bad she ran back

to Durham with baby Peggy and thereafter found work as a cook /housekeeper to a Ballantyne family at the Kirna, Walkerburn, Peeblesshire.

Have you any wool?

My grandfather was to tell me that he had to lie stretched out while wielding his pick-axe in a seam only twenty inches high at Carberry, and on one occasion a huge chunk of rock fell on his skull; lots of blood and bruising, but no medical treatment. My mother told me that some weeks before pay day came the hot meal was just fried bread. Such "facts of life" were very important for my understanding and eventual development as a socialist.

More tragedy

John Mackay eventually married Jessie Kerr – a servant girl – from Moffat, and their son John died in infancy when she was thirty-six. Jessie became ill and was admitted to Bangour Mental Hospital where her husband visited her until her death in 1938. Thereafter, John started work in Greig's Bar, Picardy Place, took to drinking heavily again and ended up as a grave digger in the Eastern Cemetery.

My mother took him in to 4 Waverly Park Terrace after my father joined the Royal Air Force in World War Two. My grandfather's rent money would obviously have helped my mother with four children to keep.

Every Sunday morning while she lived, my Grandfather Mackay took Sunday papers up to his mother in St Giles Street and played dominoes with his two brothers.

Lessons from Grandfather John (Mackay)

When I was very young, I would sometimes jump into his chair by the coal fire when he left the room, perhaps to go to the bathroom and he would make me question myself on his return by saying, "Would you take my grave as quick?" And something else to ponder, when I was given an autograph book, he wrote in it, "Needles and pins, needles and pins. When you get married all trouble begins."

Among his grandfather tales was that scientists would not say that coal came from peat if they had been down the coal face, and that Edward VIII was the right King for the working–classes, but the bosses wouldn't allow that!

I learned a lot more from him; playing dominoes, getting books from the library, how to sole and heel family shoes, how to use the sandpaper strip on a matchbox to rub down hard skin on the feet – in case I too would end up in the trenches one day? – the importance of listening to the news on the wireless, and laughing out loud at Tommy Handley.

He taught me my party–piece, the old Sir Harry Lauder war time song –

> *"When the war is over and the fighting's done*
> *and the flags are flying high,*
> *The bells are ringing and the boys are singing songs of victory,*
> *We'll all gather round the big camp fire*
> *And the old Mother kisses her son*
> *All the lassies will be loving all the laddies,*
> *The laddies have fought and won."*

Grandfather Mackay died after he came home from playing dominoes and downing pints in the pub, having had to walk through snow in gym shoes – worn because of his sore, swollen feet – and caught pneumonia. Next day, he sat up in bed, said he was getting better, drank a bottle of beer, and died.

It's a pity you only "know" grandfathers when they are old and that earlier you are too young to know what to ask.

"The black sheep of the family??"

What an awful label this is on many grounds, including racial ones in our day and age! It doesn't seem to register in public society that the reasons farmers didn't want an odd black sheep was that their livelihood depended on the sale of white wool. But farmers always knew that a black sheep also produced very good meat too!

THE GREAT DEPRESSION AND WORLD WAR TWO

The mass unemployment affected our family too. My mother's step-sister's husband, Jimmy Boa, didn't have a trade and Uncle Jimmy was unemployed for a long time. My father told me that Uncle Jimmy used to pray for snow in the winter so that he could hurry up early to Ravelston Dykes with his spade and clear the snow, hoping to be paid.

It was, in fact, my father who got Jimmy Boa a job wrapping parcels in the front shop of James Gray and Son in George Street.

In those days, vacancies were not often advertised. The companies would rely on an employee recommending someone and then would hold that employee responsible for the good behaviour of the new employee.

Front shop / Workshop "bone of contention"

A year or two after WW2 started, my father decided he really had to give up his Reserved Occupation status and "do his bit" so he volunteered for the Royal Air Force. Too old for aircrew, he trained as a blacksmith / welder and served as a Leading Aircraftman in England, Belgium, The Netherlands and Hamburg. It was a bone of contention for my father that Mr R.E. Douglas, the City Treasurer who owned James Gray and Son, told people that he made up the wages of staff who volunteered for war service but the whole truth was that he made up the wages of the men from the Shop in George Street (like my uncle Jimmy) but not for the workers from the workshop in Glenogle Road, like my father.

Uncle Jimmy Boa served as an army driver and came under such stress in the failed struggle to get through and relieve the troops at Arnhem that he became morose and had to opt out of family life.

Back to Waverley Park Terrace

From the time we moved into Waverley Park Terrace my father began to improve the house, as he had the two previous houses. The old fashioned black and steel range which demanded so much cleaning and polishing was removed and a modern fireplace built, with the hot water tank behind. (Mind you, in the Auld Reekie tradition, the fire was still "backed up" last thing at night with the day's potato peelings!)The old bath, wash hand basin and toilet were replaced and the bathroom walls were transformed by Dutch tiles which my father had picked up as scrap. I remember he told me that he could do any tradesman's job because when tradesmen went round the houses they passed on their skills to each other. He could do any job that is, except smoult a lead pipe so for this job he contacted his friend Bob, a plumber, who had been brought up with him in Society Buildings. I watched the care Bob took wrapping cloth round the hot melted lead laid on the waste pipe under the bath to smoult it together.

My father remained close friends with Bob Watson all his days, and told me that Bob, a good man, had served his apprenticeship as a plumber in Forrest Road. But he was also an amateur boxer and his face got bashed about quite a bit. There came a day when – wrongly – he was charged with having stolen some plumbers' fittings. When he appeared before the judge – "with His face", my mother and father said – there was no chance that Bob would avoid being sent to jail.

The air raid shelter

Another thing I remember about Waverley Park Terrace is an event that took place in 1940. The siren went during the night because German Bombers were on the way overhead-on the way to Clydebank, we learned later. A shelter had been built in the back of the neighbouring stair, number six. This shelter was a brick wall building with a concrete roof and floor, no windows at all. All of us from no.4 and no. 6 crowded into this shelter until the all-clear sounded.

A good family house-flitting – and a deceit

After the war, my father continued to improve the family house. He had the coal cellar removed. Now the coal cellar in such tenement houses was actually a little room cut out of what was called "the kitchen", and thereby leaving a bed-recess behind it. It was into this, every week, that the coalman, with the door necessarily open, would tip his bag or bags of coal, and black dust would go everywhere. So my father decided to dispense with the coal fire, and had to arrange approval from the Dean of Guild for the coal cellar to be removed and a steel beam to be fitted as this was the ground floor of a tenement. The small bedroom in the house came off a room designed as the parlour but always used as the main bedroom. My father changed things so that we didn't have to go through someone else's bedroom to get to the small bedroom (and vice versa). He opened a new doorway from the hallway direct to the small bedroom. He also put a trap door into the floor of the scullery so that he could store things on the ground underneath. All this made our home in Waverley Park Terrace a very good family house.

When their four children were married and away, William and Millie could realise their dream of a main door house, with a small garden with which my father – now workshop general foreman/ manager– could escape to from the workshop in Glenogle Road during his half hour lunch break.

Well, the time came when the nearest Stockbridge Colonies house to James Gray and Son, Glenogle Road, became available. My father put in a bid to purchase it and arranged to sell the family house at Waverley Park Terrace.

Now, one of the couples enquiring to buy the house pled with them to have the house for a lower price than the other offers that had come in because they had a son with asthma and they wanted him to be close to the King's Park for his health. So my mother and father sold their house at the reduced price to let this family and their wee boy have a better life. They had just enough money to buy the (smaller) house in Glenogle Place, and they were content. But as my father began to redecorate the hallway of their new home he discovered dry rot. To their consternation, cancelling many plans they had for their old age together, they had to take out another mortgage. Meanwhile, just 18 months after the young couple with the boy with asthma had moved into Waverley Park Terrace, they sold it for the market price and made a big profit.

SON AND NEPHEW TO... THE BROTHERS KELLET

All four brothers played a big part in my early life. The final thing to tell about my father is especially important to me, but it is sad and actually shameful so I will leave that until last.

Uncle Ian and King Edward VIII

Ian Henry Fraser Kellet, the eldest, became the most prosperous of the four brothers. He had started work at 14 as a telegram boy for the General Post Office and, as I only learned from Uncle Charlie when attending his funeral in Bath, had come first in the annual all-Britain Competition Exam to become an apprentice engineer, before being promoted down south to Whitehall. Also after his death, a family friend in Edinburgh since their youth together, told me that in the 1930s Uncle Ian had laid the telephone cable from London to France that enabled King Edward VIII to talk to Mrs Simpson – and had been decorated with both an MBE and an OBE.

The news revealed in May 2013 by the publication of Secret Papers that the Home Secretary in the 1930s "instructed the GPO to covertly monitor the King's telephone calls" makes me wish I'd known earlier and been able to quiz him!

With the coming of the Second World War, Ian was transferred to the Admiralty and moved from Whitehall to Bath with responsibility for setting up and keeping effective all the communication systems that were now essential for the War effort. On his frequent visits to Scotland – "on government business, so we don't ask questions" – he always stayed with us and was extremely patient with me and my talk.

When very young and my father was away I showed Uncle Ian a "throwing knife" – a rare and desirable possession for a young lad in those days. Uncle Ian handed it back saying it was just a paper knife. But I had never heard of such a thing and would not be convinced! Also, I would not accept from him that a Kellet could be a Hibs supporter, and – in later years – found it impossible to understand his response to my politics that, "everyone should be a socialist when they are young, before becoming a conservative in time!"

(It took me many years to hear from a French teacher and see the wisdom of "N'insistez pas!")

Keeping mum in Germany – and Scottish education

Immediately the Second World War ended in 1945, the Allies – as is well known – competed in a dash to seize the colossal achievements of Germany's inventiveness. The Americans and Russians grabbed all the rocket scientists they could. From Britain's Leith–born German speaking Fleet Air Arm Captain Eric Brown ("The greatest pilot ever?") we have learned that he was sent to interview Goering and to bring back supersonic wind-tunnels and aircraft.

Only in 2015 did I learn from my cousin Graham in Sunbury-on-Thames that when the Admiralty put his father into uniform as a lieutenant commander and sent him to Germany too, they tasked him with bringing back any useful telecoms. And when Ian was allocated an interpreter (Polish, as it happens), he chose not to tell him that he actually had a good knowledge of German – a ploy that proved to be "rather useful".

My English-educated cousin Graham is certainly impressed not just by his father but by the effectiveness of second-language teaching in Scotland!

I was a minister by the time Uncle Ian died. When my cousin Charlie drove his father, Uncle Graham and myself to the crematorium at Bath, I went into the vestry to see who was conducting the service. I met a very nice Church of England priest – a retired canon indeed – who said he knew nothing at all about Uncle Ian and was just the man on duty for the day. Afterwards I wrote to the parish priest for Ian's nearby village of Bruton; but they do things differently in the Church of England!

Uncle Graham and Dunkirk

Graham was one of the young men who played cards in Brown Square, gamblers having to watch for the mounted police. He was also one of the generation who "misspent" their youth in the billiard room. But, a coach-painter when he could get work, he helped my father build a beautiful pedal-car for my 4th birthday. In the sea cadets, pre-war, he was called up for the Royal Navy in 1939, but soon discharged because of a duodenal ulcer. So he joined the army and became one of the thousands on the beaches at Dunkirk, telling me later that the truth was nothing like BBC was reporting at the time for home consumption.

When in 1957 I went as student assistant to St Bride's church (handy for Tynecastle!), I found that Uncle Graham and Auntie Margaret – from Coatfield Lane in South Leith – were members and my young cousin Billy was in my Bible class.

When word got out in 1969 that I was going to become Minister at South Leith, Uncle Graham phoned to congratulate me, saying he could hardly believe it, because he knew from his courting days that people queued up to get into South Leith Parish church for communion! Years later I felt honoured to be asked to help the family by conducting Billy's funeral after an untimely death.

Uncle Charlie and "walking on the water"

Charlie, the youngest, was the most gregarious and socially confident of the brothers. My earliest memory is of his coming home to 5 Society Buildings, really dirty and greasy from his work as an apprentice turner, with an old tie round his boiler-suit waist. Next time I saw Uncle Charlie he was very different. This was still in the 1930s, the Royal Scots "Dandy Ninth" parading in their kilts for the Annual TA camp, and Uncle Charlie already a sergeant.

But decades later, one Saturday at Tynecastle Park – and by that time he was responsible for £8m of plant at Edinburgh's biggest employer of labour – I heard him teasing his big "engineer" brother Ian that you can't really call yourself an engineer if you're not getting your face dirty!

I once asked Uncle Charlie why he had taken on the onerous burden of Shop Steward in the Rubber Mill and his reply was instant: "Because otherwise a communist would have been elected." A reader of the *New Statesman*, I told him on a later occasion that the long out-of-print story of working men, "The Ragged Trousered Philanthropists" was to be republished and asked if he'd heard of it. "Ah, Jackie, we all read that when we were young."

A 1953 working-class wedding

When Ena and I were married in Canongate Kirk on 14th August 1953, Ronald Selby Wright conducted the service, and the crowd outside afterwards stopped the traffic! Ena had saved up to pay for the reception, in – of course – the CO-OP hall and my father – in the working-class tradition – provided a free bar.

We'd asked Uncle Charlie to be our MC after the dinner. He was a natural, engaged everyone, and sang "One finger, one thumb keep moving." Penry Jones sang, "My baby has fallen down the plug-hole." As Ena and I went out to leave, George Wilkie tugged my shoes off and hoisted me on top of the taxi – definitely not a working-class practice! – and wouldn't help me down until I sang, "I'm the saftest o' the family."

Uncle Charlie on politics and the church

It was on Iona in 1953 that I realised I'd been called to the ministry. My mother told me that at Tynecastle the next Saturday – when I couldn't be there, Uncle Charlie (characteristically) quizzed my father, "What's this I hear about Jackie?" My father –also characteristically – responded: "Well, you've heard."

Uncle Charlie, "I thought he was interested in politics?"

No response from my father.

Disciplinarian carried eight miles by his men

One evening in the 1970's, a phone call from an undertaker took me to an old lady I didn't know in Constitution Street whose husband had just died. Shortly afterwards, her daughter and son-in-law from West Lothian got to the house. The man asked if I had a brother in the Royal Scots and I learned that he'd served with Uncle Charlie.

"What a disciplinarian!" he said. "When the battalion was in Gibraltar he put me on a charge for having a tiny bit of rust in my mess tin. He was so severe indeed that we made up our minds that when we got into battle, he wouldn't get away with it, one way or another."

"After our first spell in the Italian Campaign, we were sent to Palestine, supposedly for a rest. One day, this exchange took place: one of the lads said, 'That's the sea of Galilee, you know.' Another reacted, "What's the Sea of Galilee, then?"

"That's where Jesus walked on the water."

"Well don't tell that bugger Kellet or he'll be having us walk on the water too!"

"Now here's the important thing. Your uncle Charlie was leading a charge up a mountain when he was hit by mortar fire. Four of us carried him on a stretcher 8 miles through the snow and mountains to the field ambulance unit. His wife wrote to the CO for our names and sent each of us a letter of thanks and a home-made cake!"

My father dies: "Oh my God!"

"Oh my God" was the instant reaction of my uncle Charlie and other family members when I telephoned round that January Saturday morning in 1975 when my father died unexpectedly. This response was in a totally different nature to the common laughing OMG of today's youth culture. And I myself, sad to say, despite so much involvement over thirteen years of Parish Ministry with unexpected death and stunned bereavement having become a norm in my daily life, was caught totally unprepared.

New Year's Day was a particularly important time for our family. Without exception, after the annual Hearts/ Hibs match, we all gathered in my parents' home for the traditional dinner and a real get-together. As the number of grandchildren grew, my father even built an extension to the dining table that took in the space at the oriel window and ensured sufficient places for all of us to sit round the table. But, towards the end of 1974 my father caught the flu and our great event had to be cancelled.

Ena and I with our children, as did others, looked in on New Year's Day for a wee while. My dad, up to use the bathroom no doubt, came to the living room door wanting to wish us a happy new year – and insisted we kept our distance.

Ena said privately to me that my father looked to be dying, but, having seen so many people look like death and recover quickly to normal after getting antibiotics, I thought I knew better. Going into the bedroom before leaving, I saw the necessary glass of water by the bed but discovered nothing had been drunk from it all day, so sought to persuade my dad to drink from it and drink a lot. It was obviously essential to get the doctor and my mother agreed. Next morning I phoned to check how Dad was and was distressed that my mother had not called the doctor, "because your father says no, not to trouble him at this time of year." Anger must have been felt, as well as concern, for I told my mother that the person who is ill is the last person to make such a decision. "If the doctor hasn't come by 5.30pm I will contact him myself."

Ena and I visited again together at that time to find the GP had been and Dad was in the Northern General Hospital, so we drove there. Ena stayed in the car until I checked whether she'd be admitted too, as this was not a public visiting time. I discovered that Dad was being examined and getting tests for pneumonia so I couldn't see him just then. There happened to be fixed commitments for me with other people in the church halls on a Friday evening so we agreed I'd go back afterwards.

It was 11pm when I finished work and drove back to the hospital. My father was distressed and said, "I'm finished." But he had started the antibiotics, he was getting oxygen and he was not one of the obviously dangerously ill patients in the ward who each had a personal nurse beside the bed.

I went instantly to look for the doctor in charge. He assured me that my father would be all right now as long as he swallowed the tablets, kept the oxygen mask on and drank plenty water. I conveyed this message, repeating the doctor's reassurance to my troubled father, and shortly afterwards left for home.

Now, at 6.30am the Manse phone rang. It was my sister Jean. She had been so worried and thoughtful for my mother, she'd arranged that if there was any change in my father's condition, the hospital would phone her and not our mother. My father had died from a heart attack at 3.15 – less than four hours after I had left! The doctor would be able to give me the death certificate at 10am.

Ena was at least as upset as I was. But I had to phone some people right away. It was a great shock to everyone, of course. I vividly remember Uncle Charlie's, "Oh my God!" Jim Marshall, my associate minister, immediately said that he would preach for me the next morning: but I'd often asked myself why so many newly bereaved people gave church a miss when the support that comes from public worship and a loving congregation was there for them, guaranteed.

We drove to see my mother and I continued to the Northern General Hospital. Sadly, my brain and any graciousness I might have had stopped working. The doctor – the same young man of the previous night – asked me to allow a post mortem. I found myself totally taken aback and gave a knee-jerk "No!"

In the years of looking back, I do recall that today's touchy-feely relationships were quite unknown in Scottish working-class families then, even when the father /son bond was absolutely strong. But I know I should have found some warm way to express far more effectively my understanding and love and support. And, of course, I would certainly have stayed very much longer – as I did for many others – had I allowed myself even the slightest suspicion that my father was going to die from this illness.

I well understand why the plea from Charles Gounod's song "Repentir" of 1893 continues to be remembered. "Pardon my Frailty": we all need it. Over the Saturday night/Sunday morning, with Ena bringing coffee and soup, I wrote a sermon on "Oh My God!"

The funeral was conducted very sensitively by my mother's minister at St Bernard's, Stockbridge; George Young.

That day was Malcolm's 17th Birthday.

A better ending

Soon after I arrived in South Leith in 1969, one of our elders had told me that his father, a retired minister whom I'd not yet visited, was dying. I went to the home right away. The good man was in bed, unable to speak or move, very clearly near his end. I sat on the chair beside him my right hand touching over his for some minutes, until I was sure there could be no response. I stood up and leant over close, lifting my right hand to lie on the dying man's forehead and putting his left hand over my left hand before pronouncing into his ear the Aaronic Blessing he would have known so well:

The Lord bless thee and keep thee;
The Lord make his face to shine upon thee, and be gracious unto thee:
The Lord lift up his countenance upon thee, and give thee peace.

As I turned to leave, I realised that Alex Anderson, then the librarian at Heriot Watt University, had been standing near the door behind me. "I am very very grateful" he said, "I have been wanting to do that myself to my father for a long time, but could not."

A SHOCK WHEN STARTING NATIONAL SERVICE – AND A LESSON FOR LIFE

"This Man's Back Is Filthy, Sergeant!"

Not just a surprise but humiliation.

We were 18-year-old recruits ordered to report for six weeks' basic training under the Royal Scots at Penicuik, all lined up for inspection by the Medical Officer, our chests bare (freezing December of 1947), and our PT shorts ready to be dropped on command. When my turn came and my back had to be looked at, the MO raised his voice: "This man's back is filthy, sergeant," and the sergeant bawled at me to go straight for the shower and get it clean, all before the whole platoon of 20 or 30.

It took actually some days of shock before I realised how my back had become dirty. On our first day we had been issued with all our army kit and instructions to stamp our army number (21063163) on every item, using metal numbers and thick black ink made available. Our second set of clothing was to be displayed on our bed after reveille in a specified order ready for inspection. The spare white vest was to be right in the middle and I had spent time applying the ink thickly to make the number stand out. It was now evident the thick ink had not been able to dry properly before I started to wear the vest. I don't know if anyone else guessed what had made my back "filthy."

Maybe this is when I began to learn that perfection is sometimes impossible and the most conscientious of us should be happy to settle for improvement…

INTO THE ARMY – SURPRISES AFTER THE WAR

Responding to my call up to the army for National Service at the age of 18 brought hardly any surprises at all. On 4th Dec 1947, at Glencorse camp, where six weeks' basic training had to be done under the Royal Scots, conditions all round were certainly miserable. The Nissen Hut was ancient and ice-cold. The twenty to thirty iron beds had obviously been used by recruits for decades. The rough dark grey blankets and lumpy pillows looked anything but clean: I think we may have got a pillow slip before nightfall, but no sheets.

Because of the national fuel crisis there was no coal for the stove in the middle of the hut, but two men aged about thirty who had re-enlisted as regulars to be able to afford a divorce and had arrived two days earlier crept out in the blackness to the back of the officers' mess where they collected cinders out of the ashes that had been thrown out of the back door so that we could huddle round and heat our knives for the requirement to smooth and polish the marled leather toecaps on our new boots.

"Reveille"

Reveille came at 6am when two of the camp staff who had been patrolling all night on guard duty, banged their pick-helves on the metal bins outside, opened the door wide and yelled at us the crudest of wake up calls. And then we were out in our vests through the blackness to the ablutions block so as to wash and (whether our young faces needed

115

it or not) to shave, the water taps running uncontrollably with icy water.

No surprises there, then. Not to young lads who had grown up in the war years, with all the unpleasant experiences we had had to accept – including fathers and older brothers risking their lives through great dangers far from home. But one event which even we innocents just took in our stride at the time will no doubt surprise generations today who just cannot know that the life they take as normal is so very different from what was the case only a few decades ago.

The Medical Officer too embarrassed to speak to us

One day soon after our arrival we were marched to a hall for a lecture by the Medical Officer. He turned out to be a newly qualified doctor, and therefore some six years older than us, but having to do his stint of National Service too. The lecture turned out to be on sex in the army and the poor young man, so red in the face and hesitant with words for quite some time, proved too embarrassed to cope. Our long–serving sergeant had to make some excuse for his "superior officer" having to be elsewhere and then proceeded to tell us about his experiences in West Africa and all over, describing in detail the effects of various venereal diseases, the precautions to be taken and the availability of convenient PTCs – Prophylactic Treatment Centres.

The real surprises of army life – and surprising still – came in Egypt

Disembarking from our troopship in Port Said and walking to the train for the new Middle East Land Forces Base down the Suez Canal at Port Tewfik, I was taken aback and actually considerably distressed to see how many Egyptians had seriously red and obviously sore eye defects. (I was to learn later that Egyptian mothers had to carry their babies on their backs, while bent low working away in the fields. The wind would blow sand into the babies' eyes, the tiny hands would instinctively come up to rub them, and the children's sight would be damaged for ever.)

German prisoners of war

The second, and in this case totally incomprehensible surprise, came the first night when a German prisoner of war came into our tent selling cigarette cases made out of old mess-tins and greetings cards for sending home all beautifully painted with forget-me-nots. DOES ANYONE TODAY KNOW THAT BRITAIN WAS STILL KEEPING GERMAN PRISONERS OF WAR IN EGYPT THREE YEARS AFTER VE-DAY?

156 Transit Camp, Port Said

A few days later, some of us found ourselves posted to the staff of the army's transit camp in Port Fouad, just across the Suez Canal from Port Said. It became clear that the army had selected national servicemen with Scottish Highers or English A levels to replace war –service soldiers who had chosen to stay on temporarily after their scheduled demobilisation date. The evacuation of Palestine was now an urgent and immense undertaking.

At 6 o'clock on our first morning, I was wakened by a hand on my shoulder through the mosquito net, and a German prisoner of war saying "cha" while he filled my mug from the pail he was carrying with hot tea – sweet with sugar and evaporated milk. At breakfast, I realised that the food – so wonderful after the war time rationing still applying at home – was cooked and served by German prisoners of war (some of them ex paratroopers).

The biggest surprise was that German prisoners of war outnumbered the rest of the staff in the Movement Office, of all places, recording the details of all troops coming in for transfer elsewhere in the Mediterranean and Africa, the Far East and the UK. Before the prisoners of war were eventually released home, the German chief clerk had to write down for us what the British Army's procedures were. We and the local successor–clerks had to keep consulting what we called "Bert's Bible"!

Reverting to peace time procedures

A day came when pre–war army disciplinary practice was to be resumed. There would be a General Inspection from on–high and also a Garrison Sports Day.

No flies on us

The camp's written "Order of the Day" began with a message from the Commandant: "There will be no flies in camp this day."

Now Colonel Catt, of the Gordons, was commonly thought of as not just over-the-top but off-his-head. He could be heard from one end of the camp to the other when screaming for the Regimental Sergeant Major whenever any transient soldier who unwittingly passed him did not perform his salute immaculately. Once when I had become

Embarkation Sergeant, Captain Andrew Paul of the Argyll and Sutherland Highlanders, our Embarkation Officer, came into the Movements Office from a "meeting" with the Commandant, muttering angrily, "At least my kilt disnae have a yellow streak in it!"

But in Colonel Catt's time all buildings had a little blackboard over the door showing when "last DDT". Two soldiers had the job of spraying all the buildings inside and out and making sure that the date chalked in was less than fourteen days back. In those years, no one knew the harm DDT was causing, but killing flies was a priority for our Commandant (and all of us). Just imagine it: the heat, dust and widespread disease of an Egypt without twentieth century sewage systems. "There will be no flies in camp this day"!

Not just mad dogs and Englishmen

Another event was the revival of the annual Sports Day. Having run round the King's Park three times a week while training for the Boys' Brigade cross country race – no one even thought of attempting marathons those days! – I responded to the appeal for volunteers to represent our unit. On the big day, I ran round the football stadium in Port Said twelve times, just as a sandstorm was picking up.

Having come in third – due to thrawnness, not fitness or athleticism – I found myself entered for the All-Egypt Sports Day at Moascar. Three of us were sent down the canal on a weekend pass. I have no better explanation than stupid stubbornness or madness for coming in fifth, while a number of physical education instructors found the heat too much for them.

"The Red Sea"

On the Sunday afternoon, I found that two of my corporal colleagues who had been at English public schools and knew their way about things abroad had hired a felucca for us. Unaccomplished in the water as I was, I remember diving and swimming in Lake Timsah.

Many years later, after I had learned that the Hebrew Old Testament had been wrongly translated in the Authorised Version to say that Moses and the Israelites had crossed the Red Sea instead of the Sea of Reeds, I wondered if we had been on part of the crossing Moses actually made.

The sergeants' mess

Given extra responsibility and promoted sergeant, I found myself the only slim young man in the mess. A busty staff-sergeant maybe in his late thirties determined to get me into shape and would not let me leave after lunch without having sat opposite him and drunk a bottle of Guinness!

18 months in Egypt and it never occurred to me – to any of us – to start learning Arabic.

THRIVING THROUGH THE
IONA COMMUNITY

ECCLESIASTES 3 v 8:
"A TIME TO HATE" (??)

The First Man I Ever Hated – And The Last

I want to tell you about the first man I ever hated. I can't forget him. He was the father of the first girl I ever loved. She, my Jeannie with the light brown hair, though she called it "moosie broon," was just 14 when I met her in the Christian Workers' League, sponsored by the Iona Community in Edinburgh's Canongate. I was nearly 18, still a schoolboy, but so full of self–confidence and so smitten that we started to go out together every day in the week. Of course, I would walk Jeannie home and, of course, we did not want to leave each other any earlier than we really had to, but for a long time Jeannie did not allow me to come into her stair before saying "Goodnight."

This troubled me, because Jeannie lived four flats up, there was no door at street level, and any drunk from one of the drinking dens next door and across the road could have lurked in the dark lavatory landings. I also realised that Jeannie gradually got apprehensive as we drew near her stair.

It took quite a while before she could explain, could bring herself to confide in me that her father got drunk every night and sometimes his roaring at her poor distressed mother could be heard all the way down the stair. Things could become especially bad for the family when he thought his wife had some money left from the housekeeping and she was screaming "No!" Jeannie didn't want me to know, or to be upset. She hoped that her father would be asleep by the time she got into the house. To go in, in the middle of a row, was to provide an excuse for another chapter of harangue and abuse. Things would quieten down eventually, and then it was safe to creep into bed with her mother and wee sister.

Gradually I learned of the occasion when Jeannie stood in front of her mother to try and protect her. A pot of brown paint was thrown all over both of them. There was no hot water tap and privacy for washing was always a problem. Some nights the family huddled in the stair or else ran away to their grannie's tiny house.

With this knowledge, I would not leave Jeannie until very late and only after we had checked at the top flat door to make sure the household was quiet. I would then stand across the road until Jeannie would wave down from the window that she was safe, before I walked home. (On one occasion, two policemen who must have watched from a neighbouring close what seemed like very suspicious behaviour suddenly confronted me with alarming questions!)

In those days, mothers with three children were totally dependent on their husband's wages and could not just run away. Jeannie's mother had become a nervous wreck and teenager Jeannie could have ended up the same way quite soon. So she advertised for "digs". A smiling landlady responded and volunteered that her other lodger would be pleased to drop Jeannie off every morning on the way to his work. The "other lodger" quickly revealed himself as a dirty old man.

James Barker was the first man I ever hated

It had never occurred to us that Jeannie's mother would be heart-broken by her departure. Jeannie's young brother, Ronnie, was in Korea on National Service with the Royal Scots by this time. For young sister, June – now an apprentice bookbinder and growing into adulthood – life would continue to be troublesome.

Trying my best as I thought I did ask Mr Barker permission to marry his daughter. And then Jeannie asked him to come to the wedding and "give her away". But on the big day, he pawned the new suit bought for him and did not turn up. Ten years passed from the time I first met Jimmie Barker, when booze took its ultimate toll. The pain was obvious: his skin and white of his eyes had gone yellow. At the Royal Infirmary they cut him open, confirmed there was nothing they could do about the cancer, and sent him home to die.

Visiting the house, we were told by Jeannie's mother that he'd given strict instructions that no one was to be allowed into his – the only – bedroom. Then, all of a sudden, we heard him getting out of bed. There was a banging on the door, and he yelled out, "I'm coming through. Do not look. Face the fireplace until I get back."

We sat still and silent. But I glanced to see the tottering figure emerge, stagger against the wall with the weight of the pail of urine he was carrying, and somehow make his way past the coal cellar and out to the landing. We were all intensely aware of the struggle down the stairs to the common lavatory, and then, eventually, the agonising clamber back.

On our next visit, the district nurse was due. Hardly had she got in than she looked back into the kitchen and asked if someone could help her turn the patient. I made the move. The man's body had shrunk to a skeleton, the bones prominent above the yellow skin. And then I saw them: three jagged lumps protruding grotesquely; one on the temple, one below the shoulder, one on a leg. Shrapnel!

Jimmie Barker's early life – never talked about – flashed up from memory now ten years old; buried in the trenches at the Somme, twice.

And in the Second World War, hadn't he volunteered for the Merchant Navy, suffered the dangers and hardship of the Arctic convoys to Murmansk and been torpedoed (also a second ship torpedoed under him in the Thames, kept very secret of course).

The Christian prig in me was exposed. And James Barker became the last man I ever hated.

A surprise from Ronnie

Jeannie and I visited Ronnie in Toronto when he became seriously ill decades later. He started to talk about the reasons for emigrating after he came home from Korea. "I had to get out of that house because there was going to be a murder and I wasn't sure who was going to be the murderer and who the victim."

"My father never spoke to me. But then, two days before I left, he suddenly said to me, 'Don't go! I've been over there. After the first war, there was so much unemployment here. Some of us crossed the Atlantic to try and get a job but it was impossible to get a job there either. I travelled from the North down the coast to Mexico – desperate for work – failing to find it. Eventually I managed to join the crew of a ship coming home.'"

None of us had heard any of this before.

Surprise from June (to Jeannie)

"I always remember you as the quiet one and I was the cheeky one. I set up cheek all the time and Dad chased me round the table. One time I slipped and cut my head. Dad was down on his knees beside me wanting to help."

It has always been very difficult indeed for the "poor in spirit" to get the blessing Jesus willed, hasn't it?

"THE CLUB IN THE CANONGATE" – THE CHRISTIAN WORKERS' LEAGUE

The most important decision I made in my life was to join the Christian Workers' League. It was definitely the most important decision because it was there that I met the girl whom I was going to love, cherish, understand, challenge and be an example to me for the rest of my life, that is, for 66 years to date. I joined the Christian Workers' League in 1947 when I was still at school, having been encouraged to do so by boys who came to Waverley Park Terrace, really interested in my young sister and her friends. The other reason why this decision at the age of seventeen was so crucial in my life is that it turned out to be the first stepping stone on a journey that I was going to take in the church for the rest of my life.

Ena Barker (baptised Jeannie) arrived at the club at 179 Canongate with a friend from the neighbouring stair having been encouraged by her mother that it was time she joined a youth group. I took to her right away, She was still only 14, but I fell for her unsophisticated, shy, sometimes quivering lip with the most dazzling smile I'd ever seen. Very soon, she was agreeing to meet me every day after school, and after her work as an apprentice upholstery sewer. The arrangement I made was that we would leave the house at the same time and walk towards each other, she down from 3 High Street and me up from 4 Waverley Park Terrace. An important time in our relationship happened almost immediately when we went with the club one Sunday afternoon to Hillend Park and she and I were sent to collect the water from the tap. Another significant time was when as a club we went to Temple Village in the September, staying in the primary school, cooking for ourselves and, on the Saturday evening, walking together through the rain to Roslin church. A former assistant minister at Canongate, whom we knew, was now minister, and there was a dance. He indeed was among the fiddlers playing on the platform and we found ourselves in a Grand Auld Duke of York. When we were caught together in order to kiss in the normal way as part of the fun, that actually seemed to seal the commitment we had for each other. I don't know when I would ever have been able to kiss Ena had it not been that Grand Auld Duke of York.

"One flesh"

Ever since those very early days, I have felt Ena and I are one person; not just "one flesh" after we married as the world understands/misunderstands that biblical term, but actually very like a coin with two different faces seen from the outside, and yet clearly one single coin.

Christian Workers' League

The Christian Workers' League originated with a Roman Catholic priest in Belgium who was distressed – as the church all over in France, in Italy and in Britain was – that working-class men were missing from active membership in the church. So Canon Cardjin formed groups called 'Juenes Ouvriers Chretiens for boys over the age of 13. This movement was so popular and so effective that it came into being in England as the Young Christian Workers (a Roman Catholic organisation, of course.)

It so happened that John Summers, a member of the Iona Community, (a very puckha member, with a very middle-class upbringing and schooling behind him) attended a conference down south about the Young Christian Workers and he put it to George MacLeod that the Iona Community should have a similar group, a similar movement as part of its concern for the working classes in Scotland. This led to the beginning of the Christian Workers' League in the Canongate, then one of the least salubrious, slummiest, most undesirable parts of the City of Edinburgh. Started first in Milton House School, there came permission to use and decorate a tenement stair with two or three floors at 179 Canongate that had been condemned. Permission to use it was for the duration of the war, so long as it was safe, after which it would be reconstructed or demolished.

"Democracy" meant girls, too!

The Christian Workers' League was created to help young people, young boys, young men find the life more abundant of which the gospel speaks; to become purposeful, fulfilled and to campaign for the better world that everyone needed. It was to be a very democratic organisation where members, not the adult advisors, were to make the decisions. To John Summers' consternation, one of the first decisions they made in the Canongate was to invite girls! At that time, there were no mixed church youth clubs in Edinburgh. (I think John tried to insist that boys and girls didn't hold hands when in the club!)

"Action night"

The big Christian Workers' League event in the week was Friday night, Action Night. To belong to the Christian

Workers' League you had to attend Action Night; other activities were optional. But the great fun night of the week was a joint meeting with the youth fellowship of Canongate church on Sunday. There we had a lot of laughs and learned a great deal about the world. I remember Reggie Barrett-Ayres, music master in Iona Abbey (and Head of Music at Aberdeen University), come one evening and ask what was a favourite classic song. When the answer came, "Drink to me only with thine eyes", he proceeded to the old piano and played the tune in five or six different styles, including a jazz version!

George MacLeod – the bomb

George MacLeod came to speak to us and I still remember his performance of "A wee cock sparra." I also remember what produced a big laugh, but always had the kind of serious message that George wanted to convey, was his story about an atom bomb in a bomber sent to bomb China – which was what a number of senior American Generals wanted to happen at the time. When over Peking, the bomb refused to be dislodged from the plane, so they circulated for a while and tried all sorts of things to get the bomb to drop from the plane. They finally decided the bomb was stuck. Realising that they were running out of fuel, the crew started screaming to the captain, "What can we do?" Breaking his silence the pilot responded: "Say after me, Our Father…"

South Africa and being black

I remember, too, in 1947, a black South African medical student telling us about life in South Africa and how astonished we were to hear (long before the days of official apartheid) that – under

General Smuts, such a great favourite with the British public for his war efforts in aid of our struggle for freedom, there was such hard and rigid racial discrimination in his country.

The Deaconess

A particularly significant speaker was a Mrs McGillivray, a deaconess who seemed to have a roving responsibility in the church, and she was calling for people to help poor souls in our society. As a result, Ena and Joan Low, one of our advisors – a primary school teacher later to be senior Primary Advisor for Lothian Region – went every week to see how they could help a very old man. Ena would scrub the floor for him (the floor was filthy). The one thing she couldn't bring herself to do was to cut the man's toenails!

Emergency help

Another two members of the club started to look after an old lady (Annie Hodge) and her husband who lived in Candlemaker Row, coping with terrible illness. I remember this particularly because the man died. By this time, I was a student for the ministry and I was approached to conduct the funeral. It was a frightening prospect for me. Anyway about 1 o'clock in the morning there was a loud banging on our door in Candlemakers' Hall, where Ena and I were renting the first floor. Down I went in my pyjamas, and there was Annie Hodge shouting, "I can't stay there any longer! I'll have to sleep here." Now we only had one single room, with our three-quarter sized bed in it. We ended up taking the mattress off the base, giving Annie the choice of what to sleep on and the three of us spent a noisy night attempting to sleep.

The scourge of tuberculosis

Even more important for us, was that Mrs McGillivray told us about a young woman she'd started to visit in a TB ward, in the City Hospital. Now, by this time, the fear of TB was gripping Edinburgh (1950). The incidence in the capital made it one of the worst in Europe. The city's TB service deployed 400 beds and there was a waiting list a year long. But the girl Marjory was divorced and fading away, not just with the illness but with absolute desperation, as she was friendless and no one visited her. So, Ena and I decided to go the next Sunday afternoon. We went, though considerable concern was expressed to us that this was a very dangerous thing for young people to do. We felt we were called to do it, so we went anyway. She was absolutely thrilled. We were inexperienced hospital visitors, being so young, but there was no difficulty beginning and sustaining a good conversation. We said we would be back next Sunday. Next Sunday arrived and of course we turned up as promised. And there was Marjory sitting in bed with a fresh cardigan on, lipstick on her lips, sitting up expectantly. She was overjoyed to see us. And once again we felt we had an easy and useful and even happy time together. But this was about the time when Professor John Crofton was appointed to take overall responsibility for dealing with Edinburgh's bad TB record. He introduced tighter discipline in the wards, and we were told we could no longer visit. Sadly, Marjory died soon after.

Action night and see/judge/act

The procedure on Friday night/action night ensured a serious evening for us all. We divided into small groups of four or six and were each handed (by the General Advisor, George

Wilkie) an octavo duplicated Bible Passage. Underneath, there were questions, and for a fixed time of 20 minutes we would study the particular passage. It was required that each person in the group speak in some way. The adult Advisor to each group would not speak at all. I think I can sum up the kind of questions into three:

- *What did the passage mean at the time?*
- *What does this passage mean for the church today?*
- *What does this passage mean for me and my life?*

There were no "correct answers" provided for us.

Thereafter, we moved onto the investigation. Now, each week we were issued with another piece of octavo-sized paper with an investigation which we had to deal with in the seven days before we would meet again. There were investigations on e.g. choice of work, training for work, relations with the boss, attitude to parents, and conditions at work. The directions on the paper said that no names were wanted. "You" means you yourself or, better, ask a friend for the facts requested. Opinions are not wanted. The replies must be written in your notebook. The SEE section listed the facts to be sought. The JUDGE section was sometimes related to the Bible study and demanded discussion. The ACT section meant that we couldn't leave the meeting without deciding what action to take.

Results for life at work

I remember Ena (apprentice upholstery sewer) being very upset by the conditions in her workplace. There was a great deal of filth in and around Patrick Thompson's sewing room and, as the youngest apprentice, she had to go down stairs to fill the kettle at a sink that was never cleaned. The toilet was never cleaned either. And Ena said there was always a man hanging around who gave her the creeps. So, she decided (as a result of the Investigation and Action) to raise this with her colleagues and it was agreed that two of them would go and speak to the manager. Ena and an older upholstery sewer duly arrived at the manager's office and they began to explain why they were there. When they were more or less finished, the older lady said, "we're not here to make any trouble," and Ena (young girl though she was) said, "well, yes, we are," as the older woman began to retreat.

The range of investigations and actions was much greater than I can describe here. The Secretary of State for Scotland must have introduced Day Release for apprentices because of the number of letters of complaint he got from the Christian Workers' League!

Action for football pitches

Another piece of action I remember taking part in occurred when I was on embarkation leave from National Service. CWL had complained vigorously about the shortage of football pitches and I joined with Ena when a large group of us went to rake over Edinburgh Corporation ground that was to become football pitches. I remember the large amount of broken glass that was there all over the ground, along with big stones, which we duly raked away to prepare for grass to be sown and pitches developed. This Action we shared with the Young Communist League in Edinburgh.

Christian Workers' League – thriving and spreading

The Christian Workers' League was really a very successful movement. George MacLeod and Deputy Leader of the Iona

Community Ralph Morton encouraged the "New Men" – Probationers and Ministers – to introduce it in their churches. George Wilkie (General Advisor) sent Canongate Members out as missionaries to Youth Fellowships in Edinburgh and the Borders. By the time George Wilkie moved to take up a charge of his own (a church extension parish in Port Glasgow), branches had formed in West Pilton, Coalburn, Hamilton, Hillington and Polmadie in Glasgow, Dumfries, Gorebridge, Fallin and North Leith.

St George's West

One of our experiences was going to St George's West, where the great Murdo Ewen MacDonald was minister. There were lots of people at this evening service, but some seats were still vacant towards the front, so we went into a long pew there, about the third pew from the front. Just when the service was about to begin, the two front rows filled up, and when the first hymn was announced, we suddenly realised that this was the choir, because they turned round to sing and we were standing there with our hymn books in our hands, inches from the row in front. Beside me, Ena found it very difficult to control her giggles.

West Pilton

The visit we made to the Old Kirk at West Pilton was of startling significance. We arrived to talk to the youth group and found ourselves at a disco. It turned out that the evening concluded with a (compulsory) epilogue, conducted by the assistant minister, James Currie (later of St James, Pollock.) During his short act of worship, there was quite a bit of giggling and chattering, along with a number of comments from teenagers in the front row. Immediately James Currie had pronounced the benediction, he stepped forward to one end of the front row and slapped every single face right along! You don't do that sort of thing nowadays of course…

But that was the night when we met Peter the Coalman.

THE WORKERS MEET "THE POSH BOYS"

I remember a CWL weekend conference away at Cambusbarron or Wiston Lodge when we were surprised to find a group of Fettes boys joining us. Now, a proud and healthy principle of CWL life was that we were "democratic" young people growing to maturity by making all the decisions free from adult control. But I, though "National President" at the time, and Peggy Bee, our National Secretary, knew nothing at all about this joint meeting in advance!

Fettes and Fettesians lived in a different world from us, of course, but we all got on surprisingly well in the special circumstances that we were in. The class gulf, however, was suddenly very real during the Saturday night dance. My wife, Ena, asked a boy what he was going to do when he left school and he replied, "I'm going to be a manager." This confident assertion was relayed among us and, in our working-class naivety, we were all absolutely astonished. We took it for granted that managers had to work long and hard to find that they'd earned such an appointment.

In later years, I learned that a number of Iona Community (middle or upper class) leaders had close relationships with Fettes. This Conference took place when the saintly (and hard-headed) Ralph Morton, Deputy Leader of the Iona Community, was looking after CWL for an interim period. Ralph had two sons at the school and his daughter married the then chaplain, Bill Aitken.

Did Ralph and Bill think that the Posh Boys needed to spend time with "workers?" Did they think that we needed the shock of confronting the class divide? Were the Fettes boys alerted in advance?

Is it just possible that a very young Tony Blair might have been there? (Might this have been his first encounter with the Christian socialism he later claimed as his own creed?) What about the equally pukkha Ian Mackenzie who as Head of BBC Scotland's Religious Department, later picked me out to join a TV quiz panel?

The Ten Commandments for socialists

This seems an appropriate point to tell people today about the long forgotten and sadly neglected "Socialist Ten Commandments".

When Aneurin Bevan was a young man and determined that the harsh unjust life of Welsh Miners must be transformed he asked himself, "Where does power lie?"

Twenty years later young people in Edinburgh's Canongate CWL "investigating" their parents' and neighbours' quite appalling lot, and the prospect of their own almost certain future, found themselves asking the same question. And more than a few of us reached the same conclusion: we had to get involved in politics, and hope lies with the Labour Party.

Now, the Labour Party for me meant Holyrood Ward, meeting in the St Cuthbert's Co-operative Society's hall at 4 West Richmond Street. On my first attendance I saw sitting on the floor in the corner just inside the door a big old cardboard box which happened to be filled with copies of the Socialist Sunday School Hymn Book. This movement for working-class children had faded away by 1950, but I've always been disappointed with myself for not "saving" one of the books right away and certainly before the building was demolished. In recent years, however, a friend picked up from the Oxfam shop in Stockbridge a copy of a post card produced c1912 by the Bolton Socialist club (founded 1886) which lists the Socialist Ten Commandments used in all the socialist Sunday schools and committed to memory by the children. We could all do with following them now, socialist or no, Christian, Jew, Muslim or "secularist!"

Socialist Ten Commandments

Used in all the socialist Sunday schools and committed to memory by the children.

1. Love your School Companions, who will be your co-workers in life.

2. Love learning, which the food of the mind is, be as grateful to your teachers as to your parents.

3. Make every day Holy by good and useful deeds, and kindly actions.

4. Honour good Men and Women; be courteous to all, bow down to none.

5. Do not Hate or speak evil of any one; do not be revengeful, but stand up for your rights and resist oppression.

6. Do not be Cowardly. Be a friend to the weak, and love justice.

7. Remember that all Good Things of the earth are produced by labour. Whoever enjoys them without working for them is stealing the bread of the workers.

8. Observe and Think in order to discover the truth. Do not believe what is contrary to reason, and never deceive yourself or others.

9. Do not think that they who love their own country

must hate and despise other nations, or wish for war, which is a remnant of barbarism.

10. Look forward to the day when all men and women will be free citizens of one community, and live together as equals in peace and righteousness.

Socialist Party, 16 Wood St, Bolton.

Post script

Since writing the above, I have uncovered a faded photograph of the first CWL General Assembly in early 1947. It shows 54 people present, members and adult advisors. The young man on the left of the back row is Hugh Morton, a pupil at Fettes who later became a High Court Judge and Labour Peer.

SEE-JUDGE-ACT A PATTERN FOR THE WHOLE OF LIFE – AND THREE GODSENDS

Planning a family

This discipline of seeing facts before coming to a judgement, making a judgement based on what the Bible teaches, and then always taking action about it is something that has stayed with Ena and me throughout our married life. A particularly important effect of this way of living life came through the way we tried to organise our family. Some years before we married – that is, before I was 24 and Ena was 21 – we began to talk about what family we would have. We decided that we would have four children, because no single child could be happy without brothers and/or sisters for the whole of their life. And then one evening, watching black and white TV in my parents' home, we saw a prominent theatre personality being interviewed, and questioned about the fact that he and his wife had adopted a child of mixed race. The interviewee made it clear this was important because white children available for adoption were being snapped up but the black, brown and mixed race children were being left without parents, without family.

After checking upon the facts, we decided (with all the confidence of youth!) that we would have our first child by the normal method, and then after two years we would enquire if there were indeed still children needing to be adopted. Two years on, we would have a third child "naturally," and two years later would have a fourth child by adoption.

Things never work out as you plan of course – who was it who said "Life is what happens to you when you're busy planning something else"? But Ena did give birth to child no.1, Malcolm (Servant of Columba) in January 1958 and before the full two years were up we were in Edinburgh on holiday and asked to see the person responsible for adoption in 121 George Street, the Kirk's Central Offices.

Lorna Joan

Do you believe in Providence? Miss Mairi MacDonald responded, "Just this morning I have heard from a young woman who's already had a baby outwith marriage and had her adopted, and, lo and behold, she is pregnant again. She won't be able to look after the child and realises that the best thing to do again would be to arrange adoption. Would you be interested? The baby is the product of a drunken evening between this Glasgow working–class girl and a medical student from Ghana." Well, Ena and I decided we would wait for the birth of this baby. So we did wait almost the length of the pregnancy, not knowing whether this would be a boy or a girl, but certain we were going to adopt this child. The baby was born, a girl, in the then Church of Scotland Mother and Baby Home in Glasgow. A friend of ours in the Iona Community, Tom McAlpine, drove from Hamilton to pick us up in Edinburgh and took Ena, 2-year-old Malcolm and myself through to Hamilton. Tom and his wife Jean gave us lunch. (We were early for the appointment so I helped Tom paint his old Ford car. He'd previously covered over the rusty bits with red-lead paint and now we applied Valspar black paint.) When the time came, he drove us to the Mother and Baby home.

The baby girl was brought down to us and we saw our Lorna Joan for the first time. We had told Malcolm how he would become an older brother, and instantly he sat down on the floor. The first person to receive our daughter into his arms was our 2-year-old son.

Lorna arrived with lots of woollen baby clothes that had carefully been knitted by her first mother. The Matron of the Home told us how, "We're not allowed for the mother to see you, or for you to see the mother, but I can tell you privately that very often the mothers look out of a window in a stairway to watch who is taking their baby away. The dread is that it might be a very old couple, so maybe you could just turn at the gate so that she can see you." So, of course, we did that. Our friend Tom then took us to his home in Hamilton and to our prefab in Pennywell before driving himself home. We now had Lorna in our family – a Godsend.

Arrival of William Mark

Ena and I gradually realised that the third presumed–for baby wasn't arriving and that a considerably longer time than we expected for our third child had passed. So, when we were on holiday again in Edinburgh, we went back up to 121 George Street to ask if there might be toddlers who had no family or hope for adoption. And once again – not a coincidence, surely, but Providence at work – the same lady said that just that week a young boy had been left with them because his natural mother, originally from Jamaica, was being offered marriage by a Jamaican man who didn't want to take the child. So, in Glasgow, this little boy had been left in the care of the Church of Scotland.

Miss MacDonald insisted we go and see him, although we were very wary of seeming to inspect the child to see if we might find him attractive, and demurred. But Miss MacDonald persisted. The toddler was being fostered in a housing area near Dalkeith and she drove us there. We duly were admitted into the house, and the foster-mother said, "Oh, he's out playing in the garden and he's black as coal." She shouted for him and in he ran, his legs crooked and his face was "black as coal" all right, but it wasn't just the coal that made him black. In no time at all, we managed to arrange for us to have William into our family.

On the date suggested (in autumn 1964) we drove from Dundee to my parents' home in Stockbridge and Miss MacDonald arrived with our new son. His only possessions were a small aged bag, carrying a plastic mug and a rather worn little teddy. Unsurprisingly, the lively little boy we'd seen so briefly was totally inhibited by four adults and two children he'd never really seen before, in a strange house. He sat on the settee and would not move or speak. My father (normally quiet) suddenly said, "Pinky and Perky will be on." He left William's side and switched on the TV. Ena and I had never heard of Pinky and Perky, but suddenly William jumped off the settee, went right up to within inches of the TV set, and started to dance in front of it. He was our son already! A third Godsend.

Family life develops

"It is through children that the soul is cured." – Dostoevsky

Instantly, family life changed in unexpected ways. Local school children started arriving at our kitchen door "to chum Malcolm to school." In they would come and stand round the table while we were finishing our porridge – their eyes on William in his high chair. As they left for school, they would all pat his black crop of curly hair. And William naturally loved all the attention in his new family life, beaming away with his white teeth so perfect.

(Sadly, Pip, our wee cross-shepherd pet dog's excitement turned to aggression – jealousy? – and he began jumping up at William in his high chair. So we accepted the advice of our "county of Angus" elder and friend, Tom Penney, that Pip was really a working dog and he arranged a place for Pip on a farm.)

Our GP, Dr Langlands – an elder with Hugh Douglas at Dundee Parish Church (St. Mary's) – arranged an appointment for us at the city's orthopaedic clinic, where William was stretched out along the top of a wooden table and Ena was taught how to twist his legs twice a day to help get them straight: 4-year-old Lorna would talk of William being "torched".

As time with us passed, the small brown marks on William's body – cause unknown? – gradually disappeared.

The soles of both William's shoes had to be built up along the side to help with the straightening process. Then a stage came when the build-ups were not necessary but William had to wear his shoes on the wrong feet. The next Sunday morning Mrs Jessie Lettice, the Primary Leader in Sunday School changed them round because "Ena must have had an awful rush this morning".

Within a few years no one could have guessed from William's gait and his physique that he had ever had such problems.

Legal arrangements

This time we had to arrange the adoption ourselves. I was a minister in Dundee, in a new housing parish, and we didn't have any spare money. So I enquired about the necessary legal adoption forms and completed the paperwork formalities. I submitted them to the court in Dundee and, sometime later, a letter arrived from the sheriff to say he had received the papers but before he could sign them he would have to see me on a certain date as he had questions to ask.

Now, I was so serious about my work and all that could be done in the early days of Menzieshill scheme that I resented having to go elsewhere on a Saturday morning. I was not in the most gracious of moods when I arrived down at the sheriff's chambers, as instructed, and was shown in to see him. The sheriff had the papers in front of him and said, "Well, Mr Kellet, you are here because I have really just one important question to ask you: will you undertake to tell the child he is adopted?" With an edge to my voice, I responded instantly, "He is black," and gave the sheriff the hardest stare he probably ever had in his life. Clearly he had not read the papers before him.

The need for adopters

Over the years, Ena and I have always been upset when we've heard on the media someone lamenting as a tragic fact that they were unable to have a child when there are so many children desperate for a family.

The need for foster parents too

In 2013 Glasgow advertised its need for 1800 Foster Carers, many long-term, all of whom would be paid.

POSTLUDE
See – Judge–Act as a pattern for the whole life

Tommy was one of the first boys in the Canongate to join CWL.
After National Service in the Far East, he graduated from Edinburgh University and departed "to do his bit" for some years in West Africa, where Canongate CWL's founder had

gone. Back home he became a primary school Head Teacher and sang in his local church choir (Lochend).

For some reason I never learned, Tommy stopped attending church after a change of address, but he continued to relish annual CWL members' meetings.

When the love of his life died, we attended the funeral, of course.

No minister, but Tommy himself standing at the front in the undertaker's parlour. With the coffin in front of him, he conducted the service himself and concluded by singing, "My Sweet Embraceable You!"

SEE-JUDGE-ACT did give us all great confidence not to accept social norms but to do what we judged was right and good.

Incidentally, Tommy was one of the early CWL-ers who knew Sean Connery's Grannie in the Canongate.

"YOU GOT HER ON SATURDAY??"

The presence of our baby daughter with us caused considerable instant confusion when we met kindly strangers and even very well educated friends.

At the New College Students Annual Dinner in 1960, Duncan Forrester and I got to know each other a bit better because he was the chosen speaker for the final year, while I represented the 2nd year, and some said afterwards that the two addresses were "interchangeable".

Now just a few years later, Duncan was appointed Professor of Practical Theology, but already as a divinity student he was vigorously advocating to us all – necessarily to some of the staff too! – the importance of realistic political action and the merits of the neglected Reinhold Niebuhr and the despised Machiavelli.

From my less wide-ranging experience it was Bonhoeffer that I was prompted to try and introduce to the suffocating dogmatic obsession with Barth and Bultmann.

So it was an absolute delight when this knowledgeable and firmly grounded young theologian surprised us by arriving down at our Pennywell Prefab on Sunday afternoon of the next week.

I'll never forget Duncan's face when Ena invited him out into the garden, "Come and see what we've got!" There stood the pram, Lorna fast asleep and Ena turning down the protective net. And there stood Duncan, taken aback physically, totally at a loss, unable to grasp this reality.

"This is yours? Arrived on Saturday? But only on Thursday…" And I knew he was seeing Ena at the dinner, very slim and in her little black dress! The notion of adoption was beyond his ken.

"One like Mummy and one like Daddy"

That summer we rented a wee flat in Walkerburn for a week's holiday. One day we took the train down the Tweed Valley to Galashiels. Right away I led 2yr old toddler Malcolm to see the panorama from the observation car at the rear while Ena nursed his infant sister in her arms.

Getting close to Gala, we walked back along the central corridor of the near empty train, Malcolm running ahead. I arrived at our carriage door just as a kindly face was greeting Malcolm, saying, "Oh I see: one like Mummy and one like Daddy!" (Ena had noticed how the lady had kept glancing over at her and the baby while we were "away"). And then the fellow passenger looked up beyond Malcolm to me as my Peele Wally presence arrived and she was totally nonplussed!

"LOOK WHAT YOU'VE DONE TO MY MUMMY"

We were very late leaving when we drove off on holiday, and I was soon to regret this. Two-year-old William, the baby of the family (and not very long with us) had been sick and upset all morning. My wife said we should wait until he was better before travelling. We might even have delayed our departure till next day but we were exchanging houses with my sister and brother–in–law in Edinburgh and they were due in Dundee early afternoon. So eventually, in the circumstances, we decided William was well enough and set off – realising that we would now be facing traffic coming from Edinburgh on the Trades Weeks Holiday Saturday.

Inevitably, given the then norm, I wondered about our passage through the twisting miles of the commonly dreaded Glenfarg. The boot of our Morris Minor saloon was very small and most of the luggage for the five of us had to be strapped to our roof-rack. The two older children got into the back seat with some things to interest them – and the usual reminders to be "good passengers!" My wife took William into the front seat with her, sitting him on her knee so as to comfort him. These were the days before seat belts were common, far less compulsory. Traffic driving north on this the busiest day of the year for these roads was just as heavy as expected.

Coming into Glenfarg we could sense the frustration of some of the drivers because they were indicating their wish to overtake the "slow" stream in front of them when the road was choc-a-bloc and there was actually no space and no long view.

A reasonably careful and not fearful driver myself, I nevertheless expressed a certain relief to my wife when eventually we began to drive up from the glen towards the village: the safety of one's family does depend on other drivers too.

The thirty mile an hour sign duly appeared and I slowed down. But the vehicles in front of us didn't and suddenly there was quite a space in front of our car. The line of traffic coming north towards us on the other lane remained continuous. We came round the final bend before the village and there on the straight a large black car was on our side of the road and hurtling towards us, the driver obviously having come this way before and thinking he could use the space to overtake his line of traffic before getting stuck in the queue through the twists and bends of the glen.

Startled as I was, and with only a split-second to work out the best option, I saw two other cars move out to follow the overtaking Hillman. Three cars were now in a line about to crash into us. There was no space on road or pavement for me to try and avoid the collision and beyond the iron railing beside the roadside on my left the ground looked as if it fell down steeply. My wife took in the situation as quickly as I did – "we're going to be killed!"

I shouted to everyone to hold on tight, braced myself, and jammed my feet down for the emergency stop, all the time hoping the driver facing us would do the same instantly and there would be enough space for us to stop safely or have minimum impact. Our car did stop but the big car hit us head on.

Blood was pouring down my face. I turned to see how Ena was. She'd huddled William down into her, so her face had hit the metal drawer and windscreen. She was yelling out that William was alright and already checking the two behind her. Their back seat had snapped forward on impact and pushed them to the floor.

151

Very fortunately for us, the driver behind had left enough space and stopped without hitting us – though his car and the one behind had been crashed into from the rear.

"Malcolm and Lorna are alright; we're alive!" Ena's face was a mass of cuts. "My teeth have been smashed," she said. "I think my arms are broken."

I tried to get out of the car to help. I became aware that our luggage was out of the cases and all over the roadway.

I looked ahead to check on the other driver, now about six feet in front of me. He seemed alright, but frozen in horror. I became aware of his wife loosening her seatbelt.

I was now out of our car and suddenly felt I was going to faint. I told Ena I'd have to lie down on the tarmac. The middle-aged woman from the other car strode towards me angrily, and yelled: "Look what you've done to our car!" The man put his head out his door and screamed over the car bonnets to his wife: "Shut up and get back in the car!"

I was lying on the roadway by this time, a "Good Samaritan" trying to mop the blood from my face. My faintness left me as I became aware of son Malcolm (aged seven), clambering out of our (two door) car, tears all down his face, running up to the other driver, thumping him on his chest: "LOOK WHAT YOU'VE DONE TO MY MUMMY!"

Ena and I felt no anger, just relief and concern for the children and each other's pain. The doctor who tended our wounds in Bridge of Earn Hospital – picking the bits of broken glass out of Ena's face so very gently – was called Darling.

The nurse who stitched my forehead and brought tea for us and turkey sandwiches for the children was a "darling" too.

Brother-in-law Norrie and my sister Jean (no mobiles then but I used the hospital phone) came to pick us up and take us to Edinburgh and then drive back to Dundee.

Some weeks later, I inquired from the police and learned

the other driver's name and address. He and his wife had been on their way to Aberdeen for a grandchild's christening. He was never charged. We saw a Presbytery elder lawyer and arranged trustees for our children just in case of a future accident – also without charge.

A KIRK MINISTER IN
GENERAL PRACTICE

ON BEING "CALLED TO THE HOLY MINISTRY"

"Nobody Should Become A Minister If They Can Be Something Else"
(Bill Martin in the British Weekly)

It was a really big surprise when I realised in 1955 that God was calling me to the Holy Ministry. Just how Ena took this in her stride – two years into marriage with a potential actuary still astonishes me.

Of course, such a notion might actually have been a temptation to my vanity from – to avoid here a longer definition – "the devil". After all, it was commonly said that the real test for the authenticity of a call from God was whether you could survive the training!

This didn't just mean the six years at a university (including compulsory Greek and Hebrew). God eventually got through to one probationer who came to me after he had satisfied the requirements for becoming a qualified engineer, then later a psychiatric nurse, and thereafter three years' divinity in Glasgow, only to find that when he got into the South Leith pulpit there was no "fight or flight" in this crisis for him and he just "froze." (Poor man: I think he'd mistaken the call to be a Christian for a call to the ministry).

For myself, the real test was spelt out in the 1950s *British Weekly* by congregational minister Rev Bill Martin: "Nobody should become a minister if they can be something else. "

Previous work experience

The jobs I'd had in life beforehand could not be seen as stepping stones. They all taught me valuable things about human nature and the need to apply myself, but delivering pitchers of milk in Abbeyhill, working as a butcher's boy in Easter Road, making brooches out of stag antler in the Dean Village and selling shoes for the South Side Parker's Boot Stores were all just for getting some money, while exercising the duties of a sergeant in the Army at Port Said was simply a result of unwanted National Service.

On being discharged home from Egypt, I found myself absolutely clueless about any career. The careers' master at Heriot's in 1947 had said he could see me as a lawyer but the legal firms in Edinburgh were all family controlled, with no scope for promotion. My parents, knowing the limits of their experience, invited a neighbour who worked for Kalamazoo to advise us. He stood me beside him and told us I was not tall enough to go into sales. He looked at my Highers' certificate and then provided the address for me to write to the Standard Life Assurance Company. By return of post, I had an appointment with the deputy manager, Actuary JB Dow. He gave me some sums to do and dictated from The Scotsman editorial. The written offer of a job as a clerk in the pensions department at a starting salary of £190.00 a year settled things for the immediate future – though the army had paid me four guineas a week along with my keep, uniform, accommodation and longer holidays.

The work of re-costing and administering pension schemes was certainly interesting, demanding even, and serving a good purpose. The office pay rates were low throughout, with older men back from war service – including a Spitfire pilot – wearing their pre-war tweed jackets on

Saturday mornings. Three years later, aged twenty-three, when Ena and I decided it was time to plan marriage, I asked for an interview with the group manager but he told me the company did not pay a salary to support married life until aged thirty.

An extra mural evening class in vocational guidance that I attended at Edinburgh University had given me no pointers as to my personal future. Generous grants encouraged "mature" people to train as teachers, but the prospect of 4 years at university was unthinkable. Meanwhile, the Standard had appointed me deputy and then acting head of the pensions H–P department (staff of 20) – and also pressed me to take insurance exams because I was being promoted over people who had already done so, with expectations.

Finding my future through the Iona Community

My real life, however was with the Christian Workers League. The inspired worship of George MacLeod, leader of the Iona Community, and the obviously absorbing and satisfying vocations of Community Members like George Wilkie, John Summers, Penry Jones, James Maitland, Duncan Finlayson, Ian Reid, Uist Macdonald, Tom Colvin and others applying biblical teaching to tackle the needs of people in industry and new housing schemes, got through to me.

On the jetty as Ena and I were leaving Iona after a fortnight's summer holiday in 1955 my wife encouraged me to raise my realisation with Rev James Maitland. He responded, "I am sure this is of God" and sent me names and addresses of people I should contact.

Handing in my notice when the maintenance bursary had been refused

That there was no other job I could do became undeniable when I hadn't heard about my (late) application for the government maintenance grant ("bursary") by the time my month's notice to Standard Life was due and I learned confidentially from an understanding clerk in the education offices that my application had been refused, but nevertheless decided – with Ena's approval – to hand in my notice anyway. (Jim Maitland wrote immediately from Iona telling me to object and ask for an interview with name, address, telephone number.)

Reactions that surprised

The group manager by that time was an ordained elder in the Kirk and, indeed, a Sunday School Superintendent. (Unknown to me then, his brother was a parish minister and a Calvin scholar.) The phone call for me to come and see him arrived within a few minutes of my letter being handed in. Despite his own life and commitment in the church, he found it hard to understand.

"If we had given you further promotion in the summer would that have changed your mind?"

(I was already the youngest employee to be at such a level in the company but obviously now they had been discussing my future unknown to me.) And then, "Do you think that the ministry is the coming profession?"

(Words I particularly found difficult to receive from such a man.)

My immediate line manager, an Assistant Actuary of the Company, whose personality I knew a little better because

I took the department's problems of the day to him every morning, called me down to his office. He divulged that he had been mystified at the lack of any reaction from me on Thursday past when he had told me of the rise in my salary for the coming year, but now he understood. (As a matter of interest to church officials just along the road in George Street, and to the church at large, the minimum stipend after six years at university would be less than the Standard's rate for me when I resigned. Mammon has no part to play in a Call.)

Four weeks later, I matriculated at Edinburgh University, knowing less about the life there than Chamberlain knew about Czechoslovakia in 1938, and I started to search for the one student I did know a wee bit, hoping he would show me the ropes. (John Watt, a son of the Manse and a candidate for the ministry, took me straight to the library and showed me the Professor of Political Economy's "History of Socialism from Moses to Lenin"!)

NAME DROPPING WITH A PURPOSE: ADVICE FROM CLEMENT ATTLEE

It all started with Charles Martin. The "Charles" is significant: no other Scots baptised with that name ever used it. Even the still romantic, regularly talked about Young Pretender of 1745, the Prince Charles Edward Stewart of academic historians, had always been referred to as Bonnie Prince Charlie. But when working-class Charles Martin decided in the early 1950s to take advantage of the then generous teacher training grants and stepup in the world to become a student at Edinburgh University, he became "Charles". He also put a "bool in his mooth". And became a "character" around the Old Quad.

Surprisingly, perhaps, he and I got on famously. Then I discovered that he lived in a Corporation tenement in the Pleasance, and I had visited his wheezing father there on a door-to-door campaign when I was chairman of Holyrood Ward Labour party.

Charles and I met first in the University Labour Club, and quickly saw ourselves as Christians together in the cause.

Charles, I should say, was a practising Roman Catholic. He once brought me a copy of "Rerum Novarum" to prove that the Prince of his church, and Pretender to mine, was actually a socialist, and in this country would be a Bevanite like me. Later, just before his Honours Finals, Charles was to reveal a side of his church's piety less attractive to a Presbyterian when he asked me to pray that he would get a first.

Friendly Christians together though we were, we were never "in cahoots" against the others in the club, and it came as something of a surprise to me—as much for Charles' genuine ecumenism long before the days of Pope John 23rd – that during my first year he put forward my name to succeed him as President of Edinburgh University Labour Club.

Hardly was I elected, than the said Charles, man-about-town and gown, came to me with the news that Earl Attlee was coming to give an evening lecture at the university. "We could maybe get him for lunchtime!"

Well, I called a meeting of the executive committee, who all thought this a marvellous idea, Charles said he could make contact through the university authorities and I said we should invite Attlee for lunch. The trouble was that none of us ever ate out in those days – we couldn't afford to – so where could we take him? I remembered that a girl in the Standard Life, where I'd been back to work for the summer, had mentioned having been taken out for lunch by an uncle to The Epicure restaurant near the Caledonian Station. At our meeting the next day, Charles (The man-about-town and gown) said he'd now made enquiries and "The Epicure is definitely the only place to take him."

The restaurant was very suspicious indeed when I phoned to book a table for Earl Attlee and nine members of the Labour club. I was asked again and again: "Clement Attlee?" "The former Prime Minister? And you say you're a student?"

The great day came and the hall we'd booked, the new Adam Hall in Chambers Street, was packed to the door, with people standing. (A far bigger attendance than for the formal lecture that evening.) I was in the chair, of course, but the able and confident Charles introduced Attlee with a story of one occasion when our speaker had been visiting Edinburgh during the time he was Prime Minister and Charles, a policeman then, had been on point duty at the foot of the Mound. He it was who had held up the traffic so that our National Leader's car would have free passage.

The "wee" man then took over from the "big" man and, speaking easily and without notes, held the whole hall spellbound.

But it is our lunch for him that I'd like you to picture. We had no sooner climbed the unexpectedly shabby stair, sat down, and had an obviously much-used menu put into our hands, than our guest asked me about the wine list. None of us on the committee had any experience of wines at all, of course, but I spoke to the waitress, a second piece of paper was produced, Attlee studied it for a moment and then asked, "What year is the claret?" We were all dumbfounded. I beckoned to the waitress, the poor woman dashed off to ask the boss, and back came the humiliating but inevitable truth. "They're all non-vintage!"

Thereafter the former Harrow boy, army Major, Deputy Prime Minister in the Second World War and controller of Cabinet and Commons from 1945–51, who had taken over a country in such terrible debt and legislated for a totally free National Health Service, a comprehensive National Insurance scheme and nationalisation of the 19th century mines and run-down railways all in less than four years, read our situation accurately, and became the most modest, relaxing and interesting of conversationalists.

On being asked, I answered that I was hoping to become a parish minister. Real interest being indicated, I went on to enquire if Attlee could offer me any tips for moderating Kirk Session meetings out of his experiences when Chairing the Cabinet! "Well," Attlee replied. "You'll probably have at least one Emmanuel Shinwell. When I first formed the Labour Cabinet, Shinwell used to speak on every item on the agenda, and at length. He knew what we should do about everything and had no respect for the others. So on one occasion I interrupted his flow sharply: Mr Shinwell, 'surely' is not an argument."

"Very soon I decided that the best way to manage him was to make sure that at every meeting there was one specific piece of business shown prominently on the agenda under his name but well down. As soon as he began to speak early in the meeting, I would say: 'Excuse me Mr Shinwell, I see there is an important matter from your department that we want to hear about from you and I do hope to complete the agenda today. I had no trouble after that.'"We students all found this hilarious and our admiration for the man overflowed with this new side to his character.

Chairing church meetings

Actually, I never did follow in the church what was such splendid advice for managing a Cabinet of careerist politicians. I always thought that in Presbyterianism it was essential to draw elders out, rather than inhibit discussion. Meetings would last longer but the gifted shy would be able to give their insights, and moderating elders would emerge to stump the bletherer. Ministers of the Church of Scotland should not seek to control their elders. The Holy Spirit should be allowed free rein for His Guidance to emerge. And some very hard working pillars of the Kirk do earn the right to be respected, even when they are boring.

Attlee story with its own surprise

Another wee story Earl Attlee told us at the lunch was a lesson about speaking at meetings and arranging speakers.

A Junior Minister in the first Labour government had been invited to undertake a speaking tour in an America suddenly bewitched by the advent of a Labour government in Britain.

At the welcoming press conference, the visitor announced that he was delighted to have come to a country that believed in freedom – from a country that practised it!

Unsurprisingly perhaps, the speaker realised quickly that his lectures were not going well and began to weigh up the possibility and consequences of abandoning the tour. When the programme took him to cowboy country, the (paying) audience became particularly unsettled, some of them so restless that they were fondling their holsters. Considerably alarmed, his eyes scanned round the walls and realised there was no way out except through the audience.

When one man actually drew his pistol and began examining the magazine and barrel, the speaker panicked and turned to the chairman. The chairman responded, "No need for you to worry. It's the person who got you that they're after!"

SURPRISED BY AMERICANS

At New College

It was a big surprise in 1958 when I arrived in the Faculty of Divinity and found that eighty of the one hundred and twenty students were over here from the USA. I quickly learned that this had been the case for quite a number of years; it was even joked that every Sunday you could hear the sermons of J.S. Stewart from the Atlantic to the Pacific!

The staff at New College, of course, were all among the finest scholars and teachers in the world. Its reputation was such that one morning Faculty Secretary Professor Norman Porteous was teaching our first year Old Testament class and told us that we were going to be particularly lucky in our second year because he had persuaded Professor James Barr to come back from Canada; "the most important thing I've done" because the Old Testament Department is now guaranteed to be in excellent hands until (far-off) 1993. The possibility that a professor might choose to leave prestigious Edinburgh before his retirement date was beyond his imagination!

"Ministry as a career"

But these clever American Ministers did not come to New College solely because of its world–merited academic distinction. This was a career move. With no near-equalising stipend system as in the Church of Scotland, salaries in the US churches were fixed by individual congregations according to their wealth. Salaries therefore varied enormously and there was no possibility of being considered for a "top" job unless you could display the title "Doctor" for the status-conscious churches.

"Socialist medicine"

During US Presidential elections for many decades now, we in this country always hear strident objections to "socialist medicine" and I have often wondered how those American Ministers and wives I got to know from 1958–61 might be reacting. The normal practice in those years was for American Ministers to graduate BD, marry, and then come here to secure their PhD – and also to have their first baby free on the NHS.

(When Aneurin Bevan introduced the NHS in 1948, he was challenged about the cost of his "idealistic" proposal to make the free treatment available for foreigners as well as British Citizens. His reply was that the cost of administering a closed system would be greater than the cost of treating visitors: and, besides this pioneering example from Britain might encourage other countries to do the same.)

A totally different culture

It was long before we realised that I would become a minister that mutual friends introduced us to the first American couple we had ever met. Ena invited them for supper in our tiny Candlemaker Row flat. What an embarrassing experience it was! The "Divinity Dame" (American minister's wife) spent most of the evening sitting on her husband's knee and painting a green "pussycat" across his forehead! Just married and aged 25/22, we felt not only very Scottish but very, very old!

Racism and "Communism"

More serious evidence of "immaturity" (or worse) came when I took an opportunity – long before we heard of Rose Parks and Martin Luther King – to ask another very pleasant American how he preached and prayed about racism. "Oh, Jack," he responded. "If I preached what I believe about race the deacons would meet immediately and sack me." There was no answer to my troubled "SO-O-O?"

Now, about this time fellow students were telling me (a "mature" student) that I would be the next President of the Divinity Students Council. This was not something I wanted, as I already had too much on my plate, but somehow my name was put forward. And then I was told that a young friend straight from school and the Arts degree had been persuaded to stand at the last minute by Americans "who did not want a communist to have the job," and he was elected.

The finest young American minister

"Man is challenged to participate in the suffering of God at the hands of a Godless world" (Dietrich Bonhoeffer)

"I would go out and plant an apple tree" (Martin Luther on being asked what he would do if he discovered he was going to die tomorrow.)

The finest young American minister we got to know was the Rev Ian MacDonald Tweedlie. He had come over from Detroit to study for a PhD at St Andrews: also to research his Skye ancestry and, still single, maybe to find a Scottish wife!

169

Very soon, however, Ian realised God had more urgent things for him to do in His world. He joined CND and became a member of the Iona Community. Calling at the Community's Central Office at Candlemakers' Hall, he learned that Ena had just been whipped into the RIE for surgery. Straight away, he was up to introduce himself and to see if he could help in any way. The next week he was back to see Ena in Candlemaker Row, still in bed at the time. A couple of weeks later he arrived by invitation, he remarked that this was the first time he'd seen Ena with her clothes on, was delighted that an apple pie had been baked for him, and introduced us to a lovely surprise from America – "Apple pie without the cheese is like a kiss without the squeeze."

A Scottish parish, a Scottish jail and a Scottish marriage

Ian's commitment to justice took him to accept a call from the struggling miners' parish of Lugar in Ayrshire. (Significantly, in the area where Keir Hardie, founder of the Labour Party had his home.) His commitment to peace took him to see a new Protestant case for civil disobedience, so he joined the committee of 100 and went to jail.

Ian's commitment to love convinced a Cumnock girl that he was the husband for her. The surprise for me was to be Ian's best man and to have him tell him just before the service to clean his clerical collar before his bride saw it!

first service in Menzieshill, conducted in the temporary manse.

3

Midwifery In Dundee
1962–1969

The first few residents give thanks for their new house and are inspired not only to build a church but to make Menzieshill a new Jerusalem.

SOUTH LEITH PARISH CHURCH

500 YEARS 1483 - 1983

"Erected when Luther was born, when Leonardo da Vinci was painting the Last Supper, 13 years before John Calvin saw the light of day, 100 years before the University of Edinburgh was founded, God has kept in the midst of His people this token of His presence and of His blessing."
JOHN WHITE, 1909.

Intensive care in Leith
1969-1994

The congregation of an ever-reforming church erected 500 years ago skails in 1983 to persevere in serving Leith and the world beyond.

A KIRK MINISTER IN GENERAL PRACTICE

MIDWIFERY IN DUNDEE
1962–1969

'The key to the future of the world is finding the optimistic stories and letting them be known.' – Pete Seeger

WARM AND WELCOMING
DUNDONIANS

Midwifery For A New Jerusalem

Especially when I look back to the thoughtless and chaotic circumstances of my 1969 arrival to be minister of one of the largest churches in Scotland, the memories of so many people from all over who put themselves about to settle us into Dundee in Christmas/New Year week 1961 is a matter for astonishment more than surprise.

I had been licensed in April and accepted for church extension even though I had resisted pressure to fill an urgent need right away because I was committed to joining the Iona Community's new members' programme for the summer. A totally unexpected invitation (given on the recommendation of Professor James Stewart from an established church offering a stipend of a generosity that shook the members of the Iona Family Group) had no effect on the call I felt to serve in a new housing scheme. The challenging outskirts of the Dear Green Place seemed my family's certain destination. But the Holy Spirit was alerting the Presbytery of Dundee to a unique opportunity.

Dundee City Fathers had determined that their next housing scheme would be planned to try and avoid many of the problems of past experiences. Dundee Presbytery had become convinced that a minister in at the beginning would help the development of both community and church. So Uist and Pat Macdonald invited Ena and me to lunch with their family and – not then having a car – asked their session clerk at

Wallacetown church, Jimmy Towns, to take the afternoon off work and drive us up to Menzieshill.

Thus it came about that on a glorious May day we saw concrete foundations for the first of 3,500 houses being laid and also the herd of Jersey cows then munching the green grass that produced the creamiest of milk on the site where the parish church would be erected and where long-term families from overcrowded tenements overdue demolition would come with hope for a life more abundant (John 10 vs 10) and be enabled to relish the pure spiritual milk of the gospel (1Peter2 vs. 2). The notion of a New Jerusalem was irresistible. Of course we would wait.

Home Economics

The Standard Life had supplemented the state grant and enabled us to keep the wolf from the door (just!) for my six years at Edinburgh University, even after Ena's wages stopped with the arrival of two children. But the £10 a week for the Christmas, Easter and summer holidays was continued after the 1961 summer on Iona.(This was actually a good deal for the Standard as well as a necessity for us!) Throughout the years and thanks largely to my wife, we managed to keep a hospitable home and to stay out of debt by doing without much more than was normal for our neighbours.

Forced into the dreaded debt

Just before Christmas, I got a phone call to say that Dundee Corporation had handed over the keys for one of Menzieshill's first houses and could we please move up right away because there would be public anger if the church was leaving empty a key worker's priority house while so very many were kept on the waiting list. Unfortunately, the Presbytery could not meet to ordain and induct me until 11th January, so I could not be paid for the time before that – and on 31st January my stipend would be for 21 days only. The possibility of seeking help from the department of Social Security never occurred to us. This was not something we could share with others anyway. But our very close friends Tom and Jean McAlpine of Hamilton, with whom we had shared so much of life, instantly pressed a loan of £30 on us. And when we arrived, Ena crossed a red line by getting a "Store Book" – food by credit from the local Dundee East Co-operative Society.

Arrival in a blizzard

On 28th December, we left our prefab in Pennywell and took the train to Dundee. Expecting the furniture van just after noon, Jimmy Towns met us again, this time leaving his wife with us and the flask and sandwiches she'd brought "just in case". As we arrived at 363 Charleston Drive, the totally empty temporary Manse, snow began to blow across the hill and quickly we were in a blizzard. The furniture van could not help but be delayed. Ena Towns – not known to us beforehand – took turns with Ena carrying and sitting on the stair with 23 month old Lorna the whole afternoon. Our next door neighbours were out at work.

It was after 4 o'clock and completely dark when the furniture van eventually arrived. There was further delay and stress when snow was blowing heavily into the back and the driver got stuck in an unmade road when he drove off to turn it. Somehow the stuff was eventually brought in but the men, very understandably, were in a hurry to head for home. Furniture and tea-boxes heavy with books had gone down on crumpled carpets not carefully laid out flat. I am glad we were not old enough to be grumpy!

"Robin Hood, Robin Hood"

Suddenly car headlights (a taxi) shone into our windows while turning, voices shouted out, our next door neighbours arrived home from work with their three children and their television blared out, "Robin Hood, Robin Hood with his mighty men". There was a knock at our door and Ellen Butler came in to welcome us: "We're your neighbours but we're no braw!"

(Our Malcolm and Lorna who'd had such a terrible day inflicted on them were instantly agog with the excitement from the television. Thereafter, every night one of our neighbours' children would knock on our door and invite them in to see the box. That's when we abandoned our carefully considered agreement never to expose our family to the coming television culture that, in those early days, many educated people dreaded was on the way!)

The wellies

Next day, with Ena continuing the clearing up, I plodded in the deep snow through the building site and across open country to find the shop in Charleston/Camperdown parish and buy food and wellies.

Hogmanay and New Year's Day
OUR FIRST FOOT

Listening to the wireless at midnight, it was a surprise and a delight to hear a banging on our back door and find we had our first foot. David Marshall, an elder in Meadowside church newly moved into the row behind us, had plodded across the snow to welcome us to Dundee and wish us a happy new year. David told us that Barbara his wife had belonged to Invergowrie and they used to walk across Menzieshill – between Dundee and Invergowrie – every Sunday during their courting days. This was the Promised Land for them.

David had brought a bottle of sherry but kept it in his pocket until he found out what kind of minister had come! What never occurred to him was that God had provided Menzieshill Parish Church's first session clerk of its own.

The first parish visitation

The sun came up on New Year's Day and I went round all the houses so far occupied – thirteen other families. Seventeen houses in all had their curtains up. The deep snow making proper neighbour contact problematical, I told each family something about their neighbours. I was to learn that, unlike Edinburgh, one third of Dundonians were Catholic – descendants from the Irish who had fled from famine a hundred years before to find work in the jute mills – but I was welcomed very warmly by everyone.

The formal establishment of the Church

There being no church building or congregation in the parish, Logie church in the West End provided their premises for my ordination and induction by the Presbytery. A coach brought people through atrocious weather, including my parents – though my father was loath to be at a church service, members from St Bride's and Drylaw where I'd been student assistant.

Such was the interest and concern of Dundee people – alerted by the D C Thomson press characteristically thriving on local news stories – that the pews were full. Logie women supplied tea and food for all present. We met recently married Betty Northam who decided to transfer from Logie to Menzieshill after our church building was erected, giving a great deal of time as an unpaid secretary and, joined by her husband Mike, setting up a youth fellowship.

In the (Presbyterian) Church of Scotland you can't have a minister alone, even seeming to be in charge, and a team ministry of elders forming a Kirk Session enables decisions to be agreed and the work of care and mission done. Nine congregations released a proven elder to serve Menzieshill for its first 18 months. I was introduced to them after my ordination service and called our first session meeting for the next evening (Friday 12th January 1962).

In our Corporation house living room the next evening – with Ena ironing and preparing supper in a narrow very cold kitchen – they took some persuading that we could have our first service on Sunday 1st. One even suggested that, knowing Mr Fitchet the milkman, he could get unused forms from his church hall brought up. ("But what would we do with our furniture?").

Next day Jim Henry, the city's cleansing director, having agreed to be our session clerk for the time being, had a white board with red lettering hammered in at the edge of the pavement in front of the house: MENZIESHILL PARISH CHURCH HEADQUARTERS CALL ANYTIME. I duplicated the briefest of notes and put them through the letterboxes of our few residents. Our immediate neighbour Ella Butler came in to say she couldn't come as she didn't have a hat: "Those were the days!" Ena said that she wasn't going up to our bedroom to put on a hat to come down and sit in our living room. She also told Malcolm and Lorna that they could attend if they were good: no alternative anyway!

Forty six people, young and old, squeezed into our living room, hall and stairway. I opened with Jesus' Promise, "Wherever two or three are gathered in my name there I am in the midst" (Matthew 18 vs. 20). I talked to them (or helped them to realise fully) that the church does not need a special building: not in the first century, not on the battlefields of war, and not here. Our only material necessities were the Bible, water for baptism, bread and wine for communion. I ended by welcoming them and inviting them to stay for tea. Isabel Binnie – one day to become William's godmother – saw the look on Ena's face and went straight out the backdoor across the mud to get another tea pot and more cups.

Very soon, my Saturday invitation intimated alternative services at one o'clock and three o'clock. Duncan Murray, a young family man – later to become a parish minister himself – brought me ends of jute carpeting to put in a message bag so that I wouldn't be taking mud onto the black vinyl tiles we all had covering our underfloor heating. (He called me –until I heard of it! – the "Paki man.")

In no time the growing Menzieshill Parish Church was not just about integrating new residents and taking part in public worship. We were agitating for telephones, a pillar box, a bus service, and for spaces to be left for boys to kick a ball.

The help that others gave

Back in the 1960s, in the different spirit of that age, I just took the then norms for granted. Looking back, it is a matter of wonder that people from all over the country gave of their money to help others they did not know, trusting committees of ministers and elders to implement the second part of the church's traditional policy: "From each according to ability and to each according to need." Thus hundreds of thousands of pounds were passed on to pay for ministers, buildings and community needs in far flung new housing areas.

For Menzieshill moreover, a Dundee Jute Baron paid anonymously the cost of a new Manse. Jimmy Shand, visiting from 'Muchty the family he had digs with as a young unknown, was brought by Isabel Binnie to meet us, looked at my broken motorbike en passant and told me what had to be done, then sent his world famous band to play for an opening dance when our new wee hall, finished first, was ready.

"Nappy Wet"

An amusing and absolutely undisturbing incident occurred after the church itself was complete, but not yet the Manse. George Paterson, a former church extension minister, and now the Secretary at 121 George Street paid for out of the Kirk's common purse to advise and support new housing charges not yet in full status, asked if he could preach at a morning service and get the feel of the place. Ena and I made up a settee in our living room and gave him the use of our bedroom.

Early next morning, George – married but without children of his own – came down the stairs with little Lorna in one hand and her nappy in the other. During the night she had come into "our bedroom" announced "nappy wet", dropped it on the carpet and climbed in beside him!

OUR SESSION CLERK
'EXTRAORDINAIRE'

Presbyterian incense

There came a day when the Clerk of Works for Menzieshill's
First Development visited to say that the pavements had now
been built as far as the Direct Labour's hut and we could use it
for our Sunday service. So that Saturday afternoon, David and
I went along with the key, hoisted the men's still wet jackets
up across the rafters, swept the place out and positioned the
forms and table to give us a traditional Presbyterian church
setting. Our little house-groups were delighted to be together
and to begin anticipating the joys of having a proper Kirk
building. But there was one complaint – the stink from the
wet working men's jackets hanging up to dry.

So David's wife Barbara joined us on the following
Saturday, sprayed the whole place with aerosol and also laid
lengths of material along the seats. (I had learned from Old
Testament studies of incense being introduced 'to send a sweet
odour up to the Lord,' but this was more Presbyterian!)

Democracy at work

Sometime after we did move into a real church building, some
members began to ask for a carpet to go down the central aisle.
I myself had always felt the sound of the elders' feet on the
wooden floor as they brought in the elements for our monthly

Holy Communion very reassuring, helpful. But others definitely felt the sound of "marching" feet distracting. Extra money for a carpet started coming in. The monthly meeting of the Committee of Management decided that a carpet should be bought. I put it to them that I was worried about the colour we might get; half of you might want blue to match the walls, the other half prefer a red that would inspire a different association, and voting might result in a compromise grey which none of us wants. "Has anyone here had experience of choosing carpet for such a large building?" David's hand was the only one to go up. Unanimously we voted to entrust him with the choice.

Politics

One of our openly socialist elders once told me of a discussion some of them were having prior to an election during which David said, "I know I'm the only Tory in Menzieshill!" Notwithstanding, David was trusted by the local Labour and SNP office bearers; definitely 'proven', as the Church of Scotland service for the ordination of elders stipulates.

FULL STATUS, 1968 When the General Assembly recognised that Menzieshill parish church, with more than 900 adult communicant members now, had achieved the Full Status of a parish church – in a record 6 years, as it happens, and despite having started off with such tiny numbers – David came to tell the Manse family that a ten-day holiday at Crieff Hydro had been arranged for all five of us. Only the thoughtful and long-experienced-elsewhere David could have enquired about such a thing.

'A church grows up – and so does the community' was a main theme of the brochure we produced to celebrate a move forward with full status in 1968.

THE BEGINNING OF 'TEAM MINISTRY'

In the 20th century the term 'team ministry' came to be applied to the professional staff of a congregation where not just the traditional parish minister was employed, but also for example an assistant or a deaconess. But I have always insisted that the Kirk Session – that is, the parish minister and ordained elders – was established following the Reformation in order that the responsibility for the congregation and parish might be undertaken by a team.

The beginnings of "Staff" Team Ministry in Menzieshill My first assistant minister and inspirer

The young Reverend John Cook of Blairhall mining village had completed his academic training with an MA and BD at Edinburgh University and came to Menzieshill in the 1960s to satisfy the Iona Community's requirement of two years' experience with a Community member in a new housing area. He first arrived in Dundee just to see the scheme and so that we could weigh each other up. Now, John was hard of hearing; he spoke with a strong Fife accent; he was wearing a donkey-jacket with a torn pocket. I took to him –and so did Ena –right away. John had the background and zeal for mission (in all its aspects) in a working-class community. He knew – as Charles Peguy had put it – that "fishers of men" must be able not only to fish with a rod and a net but also to change the water in the pool. He was phenomenally effective and actually chose to stay with us for three years.

John was very independent, his own man – "No. Thanks for the offer; I'll find digs without troubling you." So when he came to start work, John had already got digs in Lochee and then he quickly became quite well known by finding Saturday night relaxation in a pub: only men used pubs in those days and a lot of customers were Roman Catholic because so many Roman Catholic families had escaped from the 19th century famine in Ireland to work in the local jute mill and indeed a part of Lochee was still known as Tipperary.

When Ena wanted to repair his jacket, John smiled and wouldn't let her. On the afternoon John began to share the door-to-door visitation of newcomers to Menzieshill, Ena had a phone call from "his" multi-storey to say someone claiming he was the assistant minister had called to invite the family to Harvest Thanksgiving. He didn't look like a minister and had a terrible accent: Ena realised that what she meant was it was not Dundonian and not RP, so confirmed that this must have been our assistant minister alright.

Now, this being my first experience with an Iona Community assistant, I assumed that we might meet daily or at least weekly to undertake together our half-hour spiritual discipline of prayer and planning. But this was not for John either; he started to come up to the Manse from Lochee after lunch and he dried the dishes for me as we talked.

I remember an early sermon where John – quickly loved and respected by the congregation – spelt it out that if everyone got off their backsides we would have a better church and a better world. When the church needed more storage than the architect had provided, some of us wondered about digging through the hillside at the back of the Hall of Fellowship. Having worked on the roads for a year after university, John led the pick and shovel team.

The American war in Vietnam was horrifying us. John somehow got hold of an anti-war order of service prepared by a non-conformist minister in the south of England which we adapted and used for our service one Sunday and this was warmly appreciated by the congregation. (Much later the country was able to learn that President Lyndon Johnston had been leaning heavily on our Prime Minister, Harold Wilson, to ally Britain to America "even if you send in just one company of the Black Watch.")

When the new documentary film "The War Game" was publicised and then immediately banned from public distribution, we managed to hire it for a private showing: absolutely no publicity permitted. We set up a special evening service with Moderator-to-be Professor James Whyte of St Andrews preaching and the pacifist Reverend Norman Orr leading discussion afterwards. The church and the new hall were full.

To extend and broaden our youth work beyond the Boys' Brigade (100 members) and Girls Brigade (approaching 200 members), John enlisted one of our young adults (Dave Clark) and together they got a group of 20–25 young folk meeting on Sunday evenings to follow up the Regnal Circle pattern for mental, spiritual and physical development.

Through fellow community member Duncan Finlayson we had good relationships with Monifieth St Rule's church. At a joint open disco for young people of both parishes, a hooligan started a fight. Non-violent John took a battering and eventually restrained the culprit by sitting on him until he accepted he must now go away in peace. A story went around that John was taken to the Dundee Royal Infirmary, Accident and Emergency Department, joined the queue of drunks and gave the doctor a wee surprise when his turn came and he identified himself. But John says now that he didn't go to the DRI, " I just had a black eye."

To Easterhouse

It was no surprise when John chose to accept appointment to an extremely challenging charge in Glasgow's Easterhouse. My first surprise there was when I attended the Presbytery induction service and couldn't help but see a very prominent notice up on the wall above the minister's chair in the vestry, something no couple turning up to see the minister for marriage could fail to see:

WEDDING FEES
Mon – Fri £5
Sat morning £7.50
Saturday afternoon – £15

John explained that the previous minister had been an ardent Kilmarnock fan!

Family man

As I and my own future had been blessed by Ena, so John found his life-long love in Isobel from Kinlochleven.

I don't imagine that all the local gangs could have been Roman Catholic, but in Easterhouse the Church of Scotland minister came almost universally to be called "Faither" – or else "wee John."

Becoming a good neighbour Parish minister in Leith

Some years later I was surprised to receive a phone call from the Interim Moderator for the vacancy in North Leith. In interview, the Vacancy Committee had learned that John started off as my assistant: "What did you think of him?" I replied with hard evidence of John's faith, industry and effectiveness – an unqualified recommendation. The Interim Moderator said they were probably looking for someone "more up market". My disappointment, and then anger, must have been obvious when I finished the conversation with, "Then they will no doubt get the minister you and they deserve!" They eventually wrote to John to say they couldn't take him away from his valuable work in Easterhouse.

Not long afterwards an elder I knew and respected on the Vacancy Committee for our neighbouring parish Leith St Andrews asked me about John and then responded instantly, *"I knew he was the man for us."*

A prophet I learned from

From a televised sermon/ lecture John was selected to deliver in the historic newly restored St Magdalene Chapel in Edinburgh's Cowgate, I still remember and rely on his theme:

A man or a woman with a vision and no task
Is a dreamer
A man or a woman with a task and no vision
Is a drudge.
A man or a woman with a vision and a task
Is a prophet.

VESTRY HOUR

When "Life and Work" published an article by me in 2003 about being a parish minister, one of the letters I received was a thank you from a senior person in the Church Offices at 121 George Street because – to my astonishment – she had never realised what a minister did all week after Sunday services. Some details from a couple of my experiences of the traditional Vestry Hour may therefore provide for a little more understanding.

Now, with every house having a phone these days, personal mobiles and emails being in constant use, and far more people having to work in the evenings, Vestry Hours are probably no longer necessary for parish ministers to make themselves known to be available to the public. But in my 33 years, it was normal for a parish minister to be in his vestry on a fixed night every week, and people would come enquiring about marriage or baptism, needing a signature for passport applications and family legal entitlements, to discuss family or work problems, hoping for money or for help from a local benevolent fund, and latterly for food.

The pregnant 15-year-old

One winter Friday evening in Menzieshill, a 15-year-old girl arrived, telling me she was pregnant. Her parents had recently arrived in the scheme and handed in their "lines" (transference certificate) from the Original Secession church in the centre of Dundee, as it was closing. So, knowing them to be strict and authoritarian, I was particularly concerned right away if she'd managed to tell her parents.

"I kept my coat on and my bag in my hand, because they had warned me that if I allowed this to happen I'd be put out of the door… but my mother burst into tears and they both put their arms around me."

(This is the way of church parents, isn't it?)

I nevertheless did mention that I could help arrange an absolutely confidential admission to the Kirk's Mother and Baby Home in Glasgow, with the possibility of adoption, if Cathy (as I'll call her) came to feel that was best. But the girl continued throughout her term in the family home until one day I was advised that she had been admitted to a maternity ward in – why, I don't know –Foresthill Hospital, Aberdeen.

Up I drove, found that the birth was being induced and sat beside her bed for the afternoon, not saying much, but holding her hand and praying.

About six weeks later, the wee boy was baptised in church and presented to the congregation for their prayer and care. No father was present, but the strictly Calvinist Grandparents were – of course.

A lady in a splendid lemon suit

One lovely spring evening, there waiting for me was a lady I did not recognise, wearing a splendidly stylish lemon suit. Coming into my vestry, and before sitting down, she proffered what turned out to be her lines. "I've been in church one or two Sundays and I hope I can become a member here."

Now, I should explain that by this time, with new houses being occupied steadily, the church was almost full on Sundays, chairs sometimes having to be put behind pews and down the centre aisle, so there were always "strangers" present and I was not embarrassed for not having recognised this lady instantly.

It turned out that this newcomer had chosen to venture into our Corporation scheme from private housing in the well–churched Perth Road area. She was the first Consultant Child Psychiatrist I ever met, responsible for Tayside from Perth to Stonehaven. (Dundee is definitely not Edinburgh! When a private developer came to build houses on a green site in the Edinburgh Parish of Muirhouse, application was made for this area to be transferred to Davidson's Mains and a high metal fence was built to keep it separate from the Muirhouse Corporation houses.)

Needless to say, I asked "Marion" if she could please be ready to put me right with any misunderstanding I might reveal in my preaching and praying.

A couple of weeks later, our church (diligent civil servant) covenants convenor came to see me because the financial commitment given on the form Marion had passed to him was so high she must have misunderstood what was what and he'd have to go and see her!

NEVER MIND THE VOW OF CELIBACY: WHAT ABOUT THE POVERTY AND OBEDIENCE?

One of the great joys of my ministry has been the warm relationships I and my congregations have built up with Roman Catholic priests and neighbours. On our first visit to St Mary's Star of the Sea – to join their Good Friday Stations of the Cross service – wide-eyed South Leithers raised more questions about their having a pub in their halls, than about the totally unknown and sometimes biblically dubious liturgy. I recalled that after our first experience of shared worship in St James' Scottish Episcopal Church some years earlier, our people's main talking-point was not the "English" prayers but the Arctic temperature. Christian Leithers did not want to argue and just seemed to "accept one another, as Christ has accepted us" (Roman 15 v7).

When I arrived in South Leith in 1969, I was sorry to find the Roman Catholic congregation did not belong to the Leith Council of Churches. Father Sean Hynes OMI – originally from Cork – assured me that he would like to belong, so I wrote with a proposed amendment to the constitution. One of the two small Baptist churches in the Ecumenical Council promptly dropped out. One of my elders resigned from our Kirk Session – but partly because he imagined I must somehow have arranged the next Leith Council of Churches meeting for the date when he would be at our Kirk Session meeting, and so be unable to object!

Before long, Leith Council of Churches was organising a United Day of Prayer for Peace in Northern Ireland, and when Father Hynes brought his hesitant Roman Catholic contingent at 6pm he said publicly that he would be using the "excellent" prayers made available by the Church of Scotland Minister. No one could have imagined such a thing beforehand.

Now for that vow of obedience

One day I heard that Father Hynes was seriously ill after emergency surgery in Leith Hospital. I went in to see him in the quiet of the evening. From our conversation it seemed clear to me that his church was under-staffed and he was keeping himself on a treadmill of overlong hours. I put it to him that this illness might be seen as a Providential warning and that he'd become even more seriously ill if he did not get a move.

"I was due away last year," he responded, "but they've been unable to get a replacement."

"Why doesn't the superior of your Order just tell someone to come?" I asked.

"It doesn't work that way," was the reply.

"But don't all of you in the Order make their traditional vow of obedience?" I persisted.

"Oh, yes!" said Sean. "But nowadays we never give an order to someone unless we know he's ready to obey it!"

And now for the vow of poverty

My first and only other charge was the new housing area of Menzieshill in Dundee – in with the first houses on the 28th December 1961 – and away only when both scheme and church were fully established, St Patrick's Day 1969. By 1963/64 Pope John 23rd's exhortations to his clergy that they should begin to recognise the existence of other Christian ministers and congregations had begun to reveal that local priests had thought of this for a long time, although privately of course. The Anglican chaplain at Dundee University phoned me to say he was hoping to form an ecumenical group and would I like to join. Of course I jumped at the chance.

There were three Roman Catholic priests in the group: John Knowles, a Servite Prior, Basil O'Sullivan from the Cathedral, and a young Franciscan. We who were Protestants were astonished at their friendliness, and very soon, meeting every three weeks, we were all discovering where our denominational learning had got us side-tracked.

Now I couldn't help noticing that the Franciscan was a chain-smoker. This was quite a normal thing for ordinary people in those days before the link with cancer had been proven and publicised.

"How can you afford to smoke?" I asked him, over coffee and cake one morning in Menzieshill Manse. There was such an inability to understand the question that I began to wonder if this guy was cocooned from the world the rest of us had to live in. Eventually, after confirmation that the vow of poverty was definitely still in operation among Franciscans, I was told, "Well, you see, we really do work without pay and have no money. If I need anything I have to ask for it from my superior. Because I smoke, he gives me an allowance for cigarettes."

The golfing holiday in Troon he'd mentioned, and the new coat he was wearing, had come only on the same basis, of course.

I put it to him that if I felt I wanted to start smoking again, or to go on a golfing holiday (even for the one annual break) I wouldn't dream of putting it to my "superior" as it would be unfair and she would get terribly upset. In the Church of Scotland we did not take a vow of poverty, but the stipend at the time required scrupulous monthly budgeting between husband and wife, with a lot of even basic priorities not being afforded.

Perhaps a Protestant/Ecumenical postscript is in order!

My wife and I met each other and came into the church through the missionary work of the Iona Community in Edinburgh's Canongate, Dumbiedykes and Candlemaker Row. As the Christian Workers' League, we learned from the Iona Community's publicised discipline of a shared economic witness. By the early 1950s our members were disclosing their wages every Friday night, pooling 10% of the disposable income and deciding together on its use. (The one problem I remember is that a particularly good chap who had been exceptionally generous in helping a fellow member through a period of unemployment – when we all increased our 10% to make sure £3.10/- a week was handed over – just couldn't bring himself to accept money when he lost his own job totally unexpectedly.)

When I had felt called and trained as a minister, I became a full member of the Iona Community. I was really shaken to find that the Economic Discipline in the community's "rule" was left entirely to the conscience of the individual member: in effect, almost voluntary. On the recommendation of the then overworked (and saintly) Deputy Leader, Ralph Morton, who knew all about CWL, I was appointed to be the Treasurer / Secretary.

For four or five years I produced forms and reminders so that every member would account. I "leant" on the non-participants and introduced a development that passed over all responsibility to local family groups, who knew each person's circumstances, and might produce better self-discipline through appropriate understanding and shared friendship.

But I do think that the "commitment" (the vow) still amounted to much less than an outsider reading "The Rule" would expect at the time. (I notice that in recent years – very understandably – the wording of the Economic Discipline rule has been amended considerably for today's members.)

I remember one member wanting to stay in membership, but writing to me that he was not going to commit a share of his tight family budget when another member who had not even replied to blunt reminders or delicate enquiries about his "health and soul" could spend his summer driving a Maserati about the Continent.

Looking back, I think the Community's Economic Discipline of that time was too idealistic for the lowly paid middle-class people living among better-off families, and most of them already very abstemious because of their lower income as well as their vocation. The most we sought and achieved eventually was probably the best any could manage: that every member did account. And the giving away of the common pool was decided democratically at a plenary meeting.

Postscript

Was I still too legalistic about the Rule? Bruce Kenrick was absolutely one of the most committed and self-sacrificing Iona Members. After war service as a Paratrooper, he trained for the ministry and then wrote the best-selling record of his experience with the East Harlem Protestant Mission "Come out the Wilderness." Back home he was a leading founder member of Shelter, the campaign for the homeless. This established, he turned his campaigning to the struggle of black immigrants invited to London from the West Indies and now suffering racial and economic persecution, pioneering the formation of the Notting Hill community and the cause for public celebration.

Well, Bruce wrote to me once at economic witness settling-up time with no specific mention of it but with a story of his landing in Morocco during the war. The Allies wanted to be sure the local people would be prepared and see them as arriving to free them from the German Occupation, not as invaders to be resisted. So they drew up a statement, had it translated into Arabic, and sent planes beforehand to drop the message all over the country. When the army arrived, they found the people totally taken by surprise, asked about the leaflets, and learned that the message the "translator" had actually sent was that his family tea business was coming back!

Was I being told to lighten up?

THE STUFF OF THE KIRK'S ELDERSHIP

A single example from a Dundee new housing scheme: strong and gentle

I first met Tom Penney on New Year's Day 1962 when I sloshed my way through the deep snow to wish a happy new year to the thirteen other families who were the earliest arrivals up in Menzieshill. Dundee Town Council had learned a lesson from the development of previous housing schemes, and so, to help encourage the development of a strong community sense from the start this time, began building in what would be the centre, meaning that we first residents were all isolated not just by the snow drifts but by the absence of a bus service and convenient telephone connections, not to mention shops, schools, a church building.

Tom was a big man in heart, I quickly realised, as well as in physique. He was proud of being a "County of Angus man" and a policeman. I later learned that he was actually the inspector in charge of traffic, and also the anchor for the police tug-of-war team. As soon as we were permitted to ordain our own elders, Tom – already working in his spare time on the church grounds – agreed to join the Kirk Session.

With the death of his old aunt, Tom lost the vegetable garden he'd looked after for years and asked if he might have one end of the long, over large garden that had been provided for the new Manse. Before long, I was to find him one day starting to dig the other end of the grass field. "This is your one."

Two really big stories about this giant of a man.

One sunny Sunday afternoon, our 5-year-old daughter Lorna came running and screaming in to the kitchen, bees swarming round her head and sticking in her curly hair. Some boys passing by had seen the couple of hives we'd naively agreed our organist's husband could keep in the large garden and had begun to throw stones, disturbing the bees. Just then, Tom arrived – surely no "coincidence". Tom took over from us city parents right away. "Hush, lass, just keep your back against the door." He cupped his unprotected hands, picked out the bees one by one and released them out of the Manse. A big, strong, and also very, very gentle man.

Another big event came when I had joined him in the garden digging my end and he said to me that he'd never been baptised and had always been too embarrassed to tell anyone. Getting over my surprise at this unexpected news from a communicant member of the Kirk, confirmed long before moving to Menzieshill, and then ordained with us, I hastened to assure Tom that even if the traditional church sacrament had not been administered the Holy Spirit had very evidently baptised him into full membership years ago. But Tom needed to right the formal omission and feel the experience of baptism in church. The next date for the sacrament – first Sunday of each month – we agreed on and we alerted the Kirk Session.

Tom's open example brought similar relief for a second elder! Duncan Murray, one of our BB officers, told me that he had not been baptised either. His birth certificate showed that he'd been blessed in the Unitarian church his mother had belonged to, but this was not baptism in the three-fold name. So both elders were baptised together during the normal (infant) baptism service. (And, incidentally, a few years later, Duncan resigned from his highly skilled engineering job and trained to become a parish minister.)

Another example from South Leith:
Loving friends and enemies

The best story of sharing I have ever heard came from one of the elders of South Leith. I had first noticed the tall figure of Andrew McIntosh when we lived in the Iona Community's Candlemakers' Hall, and J & R. Allan's food hall opened nearby to herald the end of food rationing. Andrew was deputy manager there. His arresting presence next came into view when his daughter brought him to a communicants class years later in South Leith church.

Talking to him in his home, I discovered that Andrew had spent most of the war in a prison camp in Austria. "Were you ever hungry?" I asked this seller of high-class imported delicatessen. "Had it not been for the Red Cross parcels, we would have starved to death." "What about the Germans?" I asked him. "They were hungry too."

"It got so bad that we actually became more and more desperate. Eventually we realised we could not last one more day, and that if the Red Cross parcels did not arrive, we had no alternative but to get out of the camp somehow and go on the hunt for food.

"I was regarded as the leader– after all I took the Sunday night Bible study group. My close companion, Jack Fermandez, who had been born in Yugoslavia, had emigrated to Australia and joined the army there, was captured in Greece like me. That night, after lights out, he and I, dead scared, climbed over the perimeter fence, crossed the road in the pitch blackness, and then got over a railway line, expecting to be challenged at any moment. Suddenly we heard a moo from a field. Picking our way through the dark we discovered a new-born calf. We could hardly restrain ourselves. We got it on my shoulders. Back over the railway and over the road we went. We managed to make it to the fence without being detected. Somehow we got ourselves over that too and returned to our hut."

"No one could restrain themselves at our good fortune. Inevitably, the noise of excitement was heard by the guards, and all the camp lights were switched on. Quickly we thrust the calf into our hidey-hole beside the fireplace, and got under our blankets, feigning sleep. Guards burst into the hut! What's going on? We were all, of course, affecting innocent incomprehension, when, suddenly, the calf moo-ed. "What's that?" a guard demanded. My friend Jack – whom people did not regard as a leader but just as one who went along – let out another moo, as a kind of groan from his bed and said he had suddenly developed terrible toothache. The guards were not convinced, but who could have imagined that a calf was in the hut?"

"The next morning we got an old oil drum and boiled the calf up – skin and hooves and all. It was delicious. The lifesaver. Our stomachs were not able to cope with a big meal, and, looking at what was left, Jack said "What about our guards?" So we got them in and they finished it off."

"Two hours later we were all on parade before the camp Commandant. A local farmer was complaining bitterly that a new-born calf had disappeared. We were all scratching our heads in apparent amazement that such a thing could happen, guards included. We knew nothing."

TRANSFORMING LIVES

Oh, How We Learned And Laughed Together!

I will conclude this chapter with an extract from a letter sent from Menzieshill to the session clerk at South Leith as my retiral was being prepared for. For obvious reasons, I have omitted things that it says about me personally. What is more important is that it tells about the effect of church life on the writer and gives evidence of the transformation that many find comes through active involvement. And the surprise I add at the end is a sad revelation about the way things can work in our politics and the consequent loss of benefit to the general public when even outstanding talent can be made available and passed over.

Sunday School: Christmas not a birthday

When our church premises became available, Sandy Binnie, our first Sunday School superintendent – previously a lapsed Congregationalist – presented proposals for the children's first Sunday School Christmas Party to the Committee of Management. Our second ordained elder, who had transferred after long experience in Glasgow's Barony church, asked about the cost and the proposed price for tickets. Sandy said the party would be free. John, who must have been conditioned for years by a policy of austerity and cut-backs, expostulated vehemently and at some length that in our financial situation we had to charge for parties like everyone else: "Birthday parties are certainly free, but this is not a birthday party." Sandy remained silent, just looking at his senior brother. And suddenly we all burst out laughing, and, very slowly, John got the point, was helped to overcome his embarrassment, and joined in the laughter.

The Boys' Brigade

It was our Assessor elder from Martyrs church who started our BB Company and transferred his membership to Menzieshill. His gifts extended to the fathers of the boys (and of some girls in the Girls' Brigade too), because before long at least four of them – never having imagined such a thing – found themselves training to join him as BB officers. The discipline Bill engendered was not the stern strictness of the ex-Scots guardsman I had experienced as a boy. The Menzieshill lads looked as if they were free to be themselves but were never out of control. Management was clearly there and respected.

It was always obvious that the company was part of the life of the church. And somehow Bill got the boys to put our one page 'Kirk and Folk' news and invitation through every letterbox in the growing parish every month, (3500 houses when completed.) But when the BB Company took on responsibility for a major fundraising Christmas card campaign, Bill told the fathers to stay away from the big sorting out and distribution arrangements, as the lads got on better without their 'help'! By the time we left in 1969, there were 100 boys in the Boys' Brigade

Girls galore!

And now to the 1994 letter from the Founder-Captain of the Girls' Brigade:

On Thursday 14th March, 1963, having decided to adopt the Boys' Brigade as the organisation for boys in Menzieshill, the Kirk Session decided to introduce the Girls' Guildry for girls. Soon afterwards on a Friday at 4.05pm, possibly following a further session meeting, an almost illegible postcard popped through a young school teacher's letterbox. That card changed the lives of that teacher, her husband and many women and girls in Menzieshill. Over the next six years many 'epistles' passed between the Minister and the Captain of the Girls' Brigade. All took the form of meticulously numbered 'lists'. We have similar outlooks on communication! Nowhere could a young leader ever have found such support and 'know how'.

The 20th Menzieshill grew from an initial 50 girls and three officers to 200 girls and 20 officers. Now, 31 years on, girls from the 20th have maintained GB links in many parts of the UK as well as abroad. Officers have come through the ranks to serve at local, national and international levels.

No sermon is required to stress the major requirement in every sphere of life and living, that of building on a strong foundation. Menzieshill was indeed blessed to have as its first minister a young man who laid that strong foundation. Supported by Ena, he led by example and his efforts were not in vain as he inspired the members of the Menzieshill team. His move in 1969 marked the 'end of the beginning' and what a beginning it was.

Elizabeth J Nicoll OBE
Honorary Captain 20th

And now to 'the sad revelation' that may come as a surprise.

When a time came that I had got to know Betty Nicoll well enough for an expression of my admiration to register properly, Betty – a teacher at Rockwell Secondary School – told me that she had applied for a Head of Department vacancy but had been told that Dundee only appointed teachers with an Honours Degree, and one councillor on the committee asked her if she had passed her 'O' Grades! As a Girls' Brigade Officer, Betty was soon to become the International President and to be awarded an OBE by the Queen.

'The minister's wife'!

Together we were trying to build not just a church but the base for a community. And I cannot end this list of especially talented and time-giving leaders without giving at least a minimal account of my wife's whole-hearted participation. Aware of the public expression in recent years of so much concern about the expectations and 'duties' placed on unwilling ministers' wives (and husbands), it seems essential to register that Ena never conveyed that she felt she *had* to do things she didn't want to do.

The women's group

What Ena did came not as a result of pressure from me or from church members but because she knew herself to be a resident of a new housing scheme far from the city centre with no bus service or shops or school and therefore little chance for women to meet and get to know each other. So – confirmed Woman's Guild member though she had been – Ena formed a Women's Group open to non-church and Roman Catholic women, sitting on the floor of our

Corporation house. (One early sign of the effectiveness of this community initiative was that as soon as a priest was appointed he was told to make the Manse one of his first visits. The evening he called, I was out visiting newcomers as normal, and Father John Ross found himself helping to bath our two children.) Making a point, the first fundraising Coffee Morning of the Women's Group was not for their own needs but for Christian Aid.

The first pre-school playgroup in Dundee – and in Scotland?"

One Sunday, now with a new two-year-old in our family, Ena noticed an item in the Sunday Observer about the formation of pre-school playgroups down in Cambridge. A correspondence course about parental participation in the development of individual play, complementary play, co-operative play and so on was being prepared, so Ena wrote off and registered.

The benefits for Menzieshill's circumstances were obvious. In no time quite a number of mothers were bringing their children and extra money was being raised for a see-saw, a chute, pottery clay and other items. And then, would we be eligible for (free) school milk? Up came Dundee's Medical Officer to investigate our situation, approve the application, and leave with congratulations for a good arrangement to allow mothers to get out to the shops!

INTENSIVE CARE IN LEITH
1969–1994

'Experiences are not what happens to the mind and heart, but what the mind and heart does with experience' – George Vialant, paraphrasing John Milton.

THE KEELIE'S KARNIVAL

'Keelie' (Scot), a town rough: a boorish vulgarian (Chambers)

A leaving "do" and a life lived out

One of the big surprises for my retiral from South Leith Parish Church was an invitation to 'The Keelie's Karnival'. Now, in the Edinburgh of my youth I often heard talk and read reports of Leith Keelies – as if the capital did not have any! But gradually many of the young lads from Leith's congested streets developed as leaders of all sorts of highly respected organisations: in politics, of course, as I've illustrated elsewhere, but also the Springboard Diving Commonwealth Champion Peter Heatley, the Professor of Scottish History at Edinburgh University, Gordon Donaldson, the Professor of Sculpture at Munich, the Chairman of Debenhams, were all among other established leaders.

And some of them had adopted 'Leith Keelie' almost as a title, certainly as a matter of pride, as if they belonged to an exclusive club. Retired police Chief Constable Willie Merrilees, a member of South Leith Parish Church, was the greatest propagator of this privileged status, and not just in Leith, but across America: not only did he provide his dog for Walt Disney's Greyfriars Bobby film, but he made the introductions that facilitated the adoption of a baby by Roy Rogers and his wife, while to this day you can order coffee from a Californian restaurant with 'Wee Willie Merrilees Broon Sugar.'

It is absolutely astonishing that Willie ever became a

policeman. He was far too wee to meet the inflexible height qualification. His formal school education was elementary. Working as a boy in the Leith roperie, he'd lost two fingers. His accent was and remained unmistakably the way born Leithers spoke. But after he'd dived into the docks to save a number of young lads from drowning, the Lord Provost asked him if there was anything he might do to reward him and the Secretary of State duly approved Willie's plea to join the police.

Among Willie's successful ventures was pretending to be a baby in a pram so that he could follow and eventually arrest a German spy in the Waverley Station! His most important contribution to the life of Edinburgh was to invite people he met at the formal dinners where he was a guest of honour to come up to police headquarters, see around, and have a coffee.

What it would do for good police/public support today if his successors were so bold! But when state papers were opened to the public after the 30 year ban, we learned how the civil service establishment of the time despised this unpolished Leith Keelie and prevented the honour due from being awarded.

So, to be recognised as a Leith Keelie in 1994 was a genuine tribute.

During the Karnival while Ena and I watched ONE HUNDRED AND SIX young Leith lads and lassies queued up to dip their hand in paint, press down on parchment the right hand of fellowship, and write their names as a permanent testament which they rolled up and placed in my hands. This was a moving experience.

And when I reflected on the thirty-two years of my life as a parish minister, I warmed to the word Karnival too.

OUT OF THE BLUE AND INTO THE RED – AND THEN THE PURPLE SURPRISE AFTER SURPRISE ON THE WAY TO SOUTH LEITH

What a way to get a new minister! A phone call at teatime in Dundee 'out of the blue' congratulated me for getting on a short-leet of three for a vacancy I hadn't even heard about. And then I was told – within seconds – that the Vacancy Committee had made arrangements for the 'candidates' to take services for them in Edinburgh on three Sundays running and unfortunately there was only one date for me because they'd had the wrong phone number and the other two dates where taken up.

Things got worse. I had called my trusted friend George Wilkie to ask about South Leith. He said right away that the Leith situation was a terrible mess and – no doubt out of concern for me – advised that I should not proceed. But then George did not know that I had felt very recently that I could not accept a call from a charge which another member of the Iona Community had retired from because they kept telling me that they had no problems at all and everything was going swimmingly. So I decided, with my eyes open, to fall in with South Leith's convenience. And on that day, more surprises came one after another.

Crushed into a small vestry after conducting the normal 11 o'clock parish service in a church in Joppa, I was seated where I could not see all the members of the large Vacancy Committee and they couldn't all see me. Then the convenor – a solicitor – said he hoped I wouldn't mind but they had drawn up a list of questions to ask all the candidates and the first one was: "Why do you want to be minister of South Leith?"

The faces I could see were instantly taken aback by my reply at first. "I'm not a candidate. I didn't apply. What has happened is that you've approached me. With my church extension charge having achieved full status, I now have to consider what God wants me to do next. I am considering whether South Leith might be right for me and you're considering whether I'm the right minister for you." The expression on the faces of the people around suddenly changed to show intense interest. I asked why they had approached me. They said they knew they needed change.

More disappointments

But more disappointing misunderstandings showed themselves when the convenor and the session clerk/treasurer drove me round to see the church, the halls and the Manse. Taken up to the back gallery to view the church, I asked why the lighting all went downwards and left the magnificent hammer-beam roof in near darkness. The session clerk responded that the lighting was new and they had accepted the advice of a consultant.

Embarrassment and disapproval

As the car turned into Craighall Road to visit the Manse (No. 70), the convenor said that Mrs Brown, the widow of the last minister, was still living there and knew we were coming. I was most embarrassed by realising the strain this must be for her and asked him to stop the car and turn back. I didn't need to see the Manse anyway.

"But there's Mrs Brown out in the doorway already."

I was in and out of that large Manse – complete with snooker table on the top floor, with tattered leather seats along one wall and an open gents' urinal along the other – in the fewest minutes possible.

Back in the car, I confronted the convenor and session clerk, asking what kind of Kirk Session was it that had allowed their minister and family to stay 26 years in an over large Manse without any redecoration or modern heating, and so far from the parish too. (My father later told me that the boiler system must have been introduced when coal was a shilling a bag and maids ten shillings a week).

Sole nominee

The Vacancy Committee were due to meet on the Monday evening and – to my surprise again – the message telephoned was to ask me to be Sole Nominee. To the added offer that they were ready to change the Manse if I required this, I said that the Manse was not really a material consideration as I sought God's will.

Two days later, Ena and I felt it right to accept. Within a week or two, we were invited to come down to see if the house at 7 East Hermitage Place was acceptable to us.

The 'call'

The details the session clerk had sent me before we met declared that the number of members on the communion roll was '2850 (active membership considerably smaller)'. The number who went to the trouble of signing the formal Call after I'd preached as Sole Nominee was 1209, while 42 adherents signed a Paper of Concurrence.

The arrival surprise

Ena had to leave Dundee by train very early on 17th March to collect the keys for the new Manse from the Solicitors in Leith Walk. (With such a large roll, why could not someone have been asked to do this? I was later to read and understand very well what Dr Swan, minister in the 1920s, meant when he said that people did not join South Leith to get saved but to get lost!)

When Ena arrived, the solicitor could not hand over the keys because the purchase price had not yet been paid! All unknowing, I was driving down with the three children after our beds had been packed into the furniture van(loaded the previous day). But there would be no cup of tea waiting. Despite the special circumstances, there was no welcoming party either! I discovered that Ena had had to stand for a very long time outside the Manse door in the cold and the snow that had begun until someone arrived with the keys. St Patrick's Day, AD 1969.

The organist

A message was waiting that the organist and choirmaster needed to see me urgently – before the next evening's weekly choir practice. The new Manse now being in an awful state, I nevertheless left Ena and the children to meet with the organist in the church vestry. I had posted a (changed) order of service a few days earlier and Mr Dempster was telling me he could not accept it and was resigning there and then if I insisted!

I explained that one important reason for the changes was that the Vacancy Committee had invited me because the church needed change and this would let the worshipping congregation know that things were now going to be different.

I would accept his resignation, of course, but it might be wiser if he accepted the new order for six weeks during which time I would preach about the significance of the changes in liturgy (and elsewhere).

The 'establishment' in South Leith

A few months later, by which time the session clerk and I had become such good friends that he found himself able to call me Jack, Norman Hendry beamed at me and asked, "Do you remember when *you* interviewed the Vacancy Committee? What an eye-opener that was for us... And then when you suggested those big changes to the front of the church? When Andrew Mowat replied, 'Well, we'll think about it, Mr Kellet' that meant, not on your life!

"You were changing the longstanding power structure when you responded with, 'Good. That's what I asked at the last session meeting and we'll vote at our meeting on Wednesday.' "

I learned that in the session room certain experienced and status-conscious businessmen elders, who took the slightly elevated seating on both sides of the Moderator's chair, had controlled the decision-making for many years. Back in the time of Leith's independence, the work of the church's administration had been undertaken by the Town Clerk (and his office staff). When Leith no longer had a Town Clerk, the elders got a young and extremely able and committed man to do the work for them, providing a small, never-discussed honorarium.

Norman, by now the MD of a small warehouse business, divulged that he sometimes felt they treated him like the office boy. No longer!

PURPLE PATCH FROM THE PAST
"Oure Kirk"

"Erected when Luther was born, when Leonardo da Vinci was painting the Last Supper, 13 years before John Calvin saw the light of day, 100 years before the University of Edinburgh was founded, God has kept in the midst of His people this token of His presence and of His blessing." – John White, minister, 1909.

POVERTY AND RESPONSIBILTY

Bacon rinds and police boots

Seeing, as I have, a mother in Leith obviously under strain as she hauls three kids through wind and hail while wearing the cheapest of light plastic coats and shoes, she herself dragging hasty puffs from a fag, inevitably raises questions about the reality of poverty and responsibility.

How can she buy cigarettes for herself when she cannot afford winter clothing for her children? Or else, is it only the soothing effect of the nicotine that enables the poor soul to cope?

Well, there was absolutely no doubt about the reality of both poverty and responsibility in one of the first stories I heard in Leith.

Bacon rinds

Starting to visit very old housebound South Leith church members, I was surprised to find that I myself was being pastored: where was I brought up and what about my family and the old people in my life?

It turned out that one old lady had a story to tell from the primary school my father had attended.

Michael was a wee boy whose clothes were absolutely mingin' and the stink was upsetting the whole class. Eventually, the teacher got Michael to take off his jersey and then his shirt, to find that old newspapers had been wrapped round his body.

Inside the paper had been folded rinds and rinds of bacon, all presumably to try and protect the wee lad's chest from the cold winter weather.

The teacher gave Michael a note to his mother. When the lad came back from school next morning the teacher got the note back with a message on it. "Michael disnae come to school to get smelt. He comes to get telt."

Police boots

This witness to the poverty prevalent in the area reminded me that my mother had once spoken about my father's shame at having to wear "police boots" in school. All parents could not afford to buy footwear for their children so they were left to go to school and play in the street bare foot. Such was the level of public concern that the police came to be responsible for making sure needy children were properly shod. But so dominant was the concern of the powers-that-be to prevent the valuable gift being sold or pawned that the boots had to be stamped with a clearly obvious number. The required spirit of understanding and support did not come from the more fortunate fellow-pupils either!

The South Leith Postie and the Edinburgh Hospital in Nazareth

When I led my first pilgrimage to the Holy Land in 1973, we visited the Edinburgh Medical Missionary Society's hospital in Nazareth. Now, previously, in the early 1950s, I had joined a visit by local Labour Party member to witness the work of a free and very busy out-patient clinic run by church (and also socialist) medics of the E.M.M.S. in the Cowgate, then and still one of Edinburgh's most densely populated and poorest communities. Here now in the Nazareth of 1973 was a hospital the E.M.M.S. had set up and raised funds for in Scotland for the town where Jesus had been brought up and which was the poorest in all Palestine. Before we left, Runa McKay, the doctor in charge, showed us the memorial stone for Doctor Malcolm Kerr of Leith, a pioneer on whom the hospital had for long depended.

Back home, I learned that long-dead "Postie Kerr" was still remembered as an elder of South Leith and that his son Malcolm had had to be one of our barefoot laddies.

PETER THE COALMAN

When I came to be minister of South Leith in 1969 I joined Amnesty and within a few months the Edinburgh Amnesty decided to erect a "cage" at the east end of Princes Street, beside the Duke of Wellington's statue. We put ourselves in the cage, as if we ourselves were Prisoners of Conscience. We tried to attract the attention of passersby and solicit their concern and support. Well, all sorts of people passed by, some even offered us bananas! Most people ignored us, some did give encouragement, but others looked on us as objects of fun.

Suddenly, I heard a voice saying, "Hello, Jake." Now, Jake is the name by which I had been recognised in the Canongate many years before and I hadn't heard it for a decade. I looked and there was this tall man with a long black coat and a Homburg hat. He said "Hello, Jake, it's Peter." I could hardly believe that this distinguished figure was Peter the Coalman, whom I had known when he was a member of the Old Kirk Christian Workers' League in West Pilton. He went on, "You will be surprised at the way I'm dressed. Well, I'm an elder now at St Andrew's and St George's church in George Street. All these lawyers and judges, and me a former borstal boy!"

The voice was extremely coarse, unchanged from the time I had known him to be a coalman. In those days he went around with a hundredweight of coal in a jute sack on his shoulders, jaggy bits sticking into his back, and the coal dust enveloped his nose and throat when he tipped it up into the coal cellar in people's houses. His damaged voice told me that here he was, Peter the Coalman.

I asked Peter what had brought about the change. He replied that his whole life had changed. "I'm now even enlisted for a Children's Panel. Nowadays, children and teenagers when they get in trouble with the law, they come before a panel who recommend what's best for them. I'm now undergoing the course. Just last week I was out visiting the borstal at Leadburn (Wellington School) and when our little group went in the door the prison officer on duty looked at me, said "Hallo." And I said, "Hallo," back. We were given a guided tour. Then when we were about to leave, word came that the Governor wanted to see me. So back I went to see him, and he greeted me with, "I'm told you're an old boy of this place: what made you change your way of life?"

"Yes," said Peter, "well, it happened this way. As a borstal boy I was taken to the Iona Community outdoor youth centre at Camus on the Isle of Mull. While I was there George MacLeod, leader of the Iona Community, came over to make his weekly visit, looked at all of us and said 'One of our Abbey guides has left Iona, and I'm needing a replacement.' So I said, I'll do it."

"George MacLeod took me aside and said, 'Peter, it will be marvellous if you do this. Now, you have to understand that there will be some money and watches lying about on the floor where you sleep with a group of young lads. If anything goes missing, you are the first person I will come to. But if you tell me you are not guilty, I will believe you, and that will be the end of it'."

"I thought to myself, someone believes in me at last. And that was the beginning of my change."

223

A PREACHING PRIZE-WINNER AS MY 'ASSISTANT'

MORE ABOUT THE EFFECTIVENESS OF TEAM MINISTRIES

How fortunate I was in South Leith that – as at Menzieshill – my first assistant minister, again nominated by the Iona Community, was another genius of exceptional commitment, sensitivity and courage, David Graham.

Now, a standard joke among divinity students was that when you started work as a young probationer, the parish minister would give you a bundle of assistant minister's visiting cards to leave with people when you saw them – and then a second bundle with the minister's own name on them to put through the door when the person was out!

But I had such a horror of having a personal servant that I wouldn't even allow the Beadle to help me put on my robes. Moreover, from my departmental boss in the Standard Life Assurance Company (Irvine Mitchell) I had learned to abandon the normal practice when on National Service in the army of commanding unquestionable obedience from anyone of lower rank in favour of drawing the best out of people by recognising the differences between individuals and selecting which person to approach, and in what way, for different tasks. I also recalled the superior effectiveness of Adam Smith's 'specialisation of function' from my Introduction to Economics classes from Eddie Hare at Heriot's.

The near-total absence of non-churchy young adults in

the life of South Leith church had been startlingly obvious right away, so I decided to change the pattern of employing a retired man as assistant minister by a probationer with gifts and concern for reaching out to young Leithers. David Graham was completing his summer training on Iona that autumn. In no time at all, David (and Mary, his wife) were opening their new town flat to youngsters of all kinds every Sunday, and leading them to share not in a class for formal school-type teaching, nor in any of the now-developing model comfortable cafe-style set-ups designed for individual pastoral support, but in adventurous and often boisterous games' activities all over the place, so that the kids really got to know and accept each other. Bert and Ina Dalgleish helped with transport by making their new (and very expensive) Campervan available. David called the group – could you have guessed? – 'the living-and-thinking-about-it-on-a-dull-Sunday-afternoon–group' (later, the L+T). The Sunday programme ended wirh Mary's pancakes in the flat, and then the church evening service suitably adapted to incorporate young people's participation in leadership.

David had engaged with the older Sunday School pupils as a kind of seed-bed and got them voting as their favourite hymn 'Oh, when the saints go marching in'. Now, he introduced the L+T and me to Sydney Carter's songs, and we produced a supplement to the church hymnary, 'South Leith's Let's Live'.

Two or three of the growing group were learning to play a musical instrument. Bill Chalmers, retired BB Captain, contrived arrangements to suit a guitar and a saxophone!

"A soft answer turneth away wrath" (Prov.15.v1)

The kids did not look disciplined and annoyed the session clerk's wife so much that during one 'informal' evening service, she spoke out from her pew about bags dumped on the dais and anoraks even across the Communion Table. One of the girls responded gently, stunning the older adults present by informing us that this was a big thing for them to be in church. Did the lady realise that they had to defend having been in church when they attended school on Monday morning?

The embryonic music group was soon to appeal to the wider congregation and community by appearing on STV's 'One o'clock Gang'.

Easter holiday on Iona

For the first Easter school holidays, David got a group off to Iona. None of them had heard of the place, nor even been on the west coast. Some had never been away anywhere on holiday. On the sea crossing, they were all disturbed by the new experience of the heavy swell.

Next morning, just as dawn was arriving, David and his Community-friend, Erik Cramb, burst into the dormitory rooms announcing that the storm had got much worse during the night. For safety reasons, they all had to grab their things, run down to the jetty and get over to Mull before the storm struck the island in all its force in just half an hour.

Right down to the edge of the water they were urged, watching for the special ferry from Ffionphort. David and Erik slipped unseen to the top of the jetty and then yelled down to them, 'Huntigowk!' before racing for their lives back to the Abbey. It was April Fool's Day.

The planned emergence of a senior group

Before the end of the first year, older kids had 'joined the management.' This led them to form a Sunday evening group – for which a brain-storming session produced the name

Sextant (an instrument mariners traditionally used to aid navigation at sea).

When, at the end of his two years, David handed over his keys for his successor, he said to me that he'd done what I'd employed him to do, and the groups should continue for at least two years. Among them, Ian Galloway and Gordon Oliver found themselves changing their life to become ministers.

Practical training

One of the responsibilities of parish ministers is to help train probationers newly out of academic studies in university for good practice in the ministry. After morning service, I would therefore feel obliged to offer my 'tuppence-worth' of encouragement and advice if not correction.

When I attended the Induction Service in East Kilbride for another very good probationer/become friend, a few years after David Graham, he volunteered that he was now going to have to do the job on Sundays without 'instant retribution'!! I thought it was a nice joke at the time, but years afterwards I was given cause to check up on myself.

David's pulpit work was always more to be admired and wondered at than criticised – tho' Ena would sometimes tease him at lunch in the Manse! But when David came down from Aberdeen to Leith for my retiral 'Keelie's Karnival' and spoke to all so admiringly of me, he murmured privately in his warm Irish brogue that he always remembered the time I'd said to him that he knew the X,Y,Z of leading worship but had forgotten A,B,C!

And then, years later still, when I was invited to play a small part in David's retiral service and celebration, his brother – by then a priest in the Episcopal Church – made mention in his tribute that David had won a prize for preaching at Trinity College, which had enabled him to buy the flat in Edinburgh's New Town. So, from my great height, sometimes I really had been ticking off a modest genius!

RACISM AND BULLYING

In the musical "South Pacific", the anti-racist song "You've got to be carefully taught" – always sung so heart-wrenchingly – is a deliberate and sharp lesson that Oscar Hammerstein felt had to be given to the general public across the world. It has not just been those war time American sailors, or even the heirs of the Ku Klux Klan and modern Islamists who have "taken care" to practise a cultural racism that hurts people they see as different and inferior. Black people in our country today can give countless instances from their personal experiences of how respectable, "liberal", even consciously Christian white people who have no doubt heard the New Testament teaching that, "There is neither Jew nor Greek, there is neither bond nor free, there is neither male nor female: for we are all one in Christ Jesus" (Galatians 3v28) but have never actually absorbed the gospel sufficiently to stop communicating racist sinfulness in daily life. Unwittingly perhaps, we can all reinforce racist attitudes which ought to have been eliminated from our culture centuries ago.

Racial prejudice from teachers

I think Ena and I always supposed that modern primary school teachers, so well trained in Scotland and now with their love of children tested before appointment, would be totally free from age-old uneducated prejudices. But one day our 5-year-old daughter Lorna came in from the new Gowriehill School in Menziehill with a message that the Infant Mistress would like to see her mother at the school immediately after dinner-time. Naturally, we were both upset that some bad behaviour must have taken place.

Ena went down right away, and the Infant Mistress said that Lorna had been found swinging from the beam above the toilet door. Ena was wondering what could possibly be in the teacher's mind, and surely some serious development must be coming when the teacher asked how Malcolm was coping with an adopted sister like Lorna.

The time had come for Ena to explode, "Malcolm and Lorna get on better together than my brother and sister did. And swinging from the beam? Bully for Lorna!!"

(Lorna's reported behaviour was in fact a relief to us, because we had sometimes asked ourselves if she was not *too* quiet! But worse was to come for Lorna at secondary school, which I will record later.)

Godsend number 2

There was a bully in son number one's class at Gowriehill and also Malcolm seemed to spend too much time under a teacher whose sole enthusiasm was showing his pupils how to polish stones (Lapiderary). We don't think he began to learn how to spell and write sentences until he came to Leith. But in the new Menziehill Parish Church (37th Dundee company) Boys' Brigade he seemed to fit in with the boys and had satisfied all the Life Boy (Junior Section) achievements when we left for South Leith Parish Church.

Prejudices in Leith Links Primary School

Just before our arrival in Leith was due, we went to the local primary school to register admission for our three children.

The headmaster at Leith Links Primary School welcomed us warmly, told us he had been minister of Kirkgate Church until his war service in Burma changed his beliefs and invited us to go round the classrooms with him. We were surprised when he lit a cigarette, carrying it with him and then was greeted in each classroom by the children standing up and saying together (loudly): "Good Afternoon, Mr Cassels."

Back in the headmaster's room, Mr Cassels asked if we were registering our children just until places became available in a fee-paying school. We replied in the negative, because we believed all children should be educated together to provide them with a clearer understanding of life in the world. The headmaster then told us that the Links children all came from broken families and he didn't always know who the parents were. I replied that this meant the children were all the more dependent on inspiring teachers and we trusted that he would ensure a good education for ours. He replied that all the teachers with children sent them to fee-paying schools.

Considerably let down by the realisation that the teachers in general had pre-set low expectations for their charges, we hoped that the most important factor for their good really was the family.

But one afternoon soon afterwards, Lorna burst into the Manse to tell her mother that Malcolm was being attacked on the Links. Ena rushed across the road to find Malcolm was now sitting on top of the boy, holding him down, shaking like a leaf, and shouting at him that he must never try that with him again.

Malcolm was never very athletic or football-minded, which didn't suit the normal priorities of our Boys' Brigade company then, but he persevered with the staff, and was determined to earn the two highest awards – The President's Gold Badge and then The Queen's Gold Badge – although one of these required him to get up at five o'clock and go to the baths in order to get his speed for the long distance option up to the required standard. He was promoted to sergeant, as his grandfather Kellet had been (whereas his father had left as a corporal) and Malcolm also became the senior NCO.

Malcolm's way of celebrating his eighteenth birthday was to give his first pint of blood and drink his first pint in the pub! (This was January 1976.)

I don't think that anything would have delighted Malcolm more at the time he got a job than to become a Boys' Brigade Officer somewhere. But those were Maggie Thatcher days and he had to go to London to get his first career job.

Teachers' strike

Malcolm had become very *bolshie* in his Highers year during the teachers' strike of the 1970s. The Leith Academy Secondary Teachers minimised their loss of pay by organising that only 10% of them would be absent each day. The strain fell on the pupils because the staff would not declare what teachers' would be in at 'work' so all teaching was suspended, while 90% of teachers' cars still filled the playground, At home during the day Malcolm used to swing back in our rocking chair, "If they're not working, I'm not working."

Not easy for properly concerned parents! But it was no surprise when Malcolm completed a useful university degree course, added extra qualifications in England, became a senior Lecturer in one university where he added a Masters and then moved to a better university. Malcolm later caught (unexplained) encephalitis and he has since had to retire early.

Back to the 10th Leith Boys' Brigade

There were other easy targets for school bullies, of course. My sister Margaret told me that a boy in our BB Company whom she was helping to look after was being made miserable at school because of peer group opinion that he was homosexual. I spoke to the then captain of the 10th, he spoke to the older boys in the company and the boy was released from his sore predicament at school.

Godsend no.3

We don't remember Lorna ever complaining about any bullying among the girls at Leith Academy, though round the dinner table one day, she made us laugh hilariously by telling us all that the Religious Education teacher – of all people! – made girls seen not to be paying attention to stand up on their table!

The great thing for Lorna at school was the hockey. She made sure she got a Saturday job that did not interfere with the match times. Sadly, poor father that I was – for my priorities made Saturday an unavoidable working day – and, indeed, I remember a funeral in the morning, three weddings in the afternoon and Sunday preparations at my desk until two or three am. But of course I should have done all I could to reorganise as many Saturdays as possible so that I might be with my wife and children when they would have liked that.

Anyway one Saturday morning I did go up to watch Lorna play hockey. Only then did I learn that she was the goal-scorer. "Lorna, Lorna, Lorna," rang out from players and spectators. An eye-opener and much more!

How delighted we were when Lorna was awarded her colours and Ena sewed them on to her blazer.

It was only after she left school that Lorna explained that these were only half colours. "I ought to have got full colours, and much earlier, because I took a job that allowed me to be an ever-present but the PE teacher in charge is a racist. If it had been up to her I would never have become school sports champion. But for that it was a straight-forward adding up of the points for each event."

I've sometimes wondered if Lorna's knowledge of this racial prejudice affected her confidence in the exam room. Lorna was incredibly self-disciplined in the time she gave to study at home. But the results hoped for were slow to come.

And then when Lorna started work the professional qualifications came rapidly: Two nursing registrations, two university degrees and two Masters from two different Universities (one of them Harvard); the rank of lieutenant colonel in the Territorial Army involving Matronships in Iraq and Afghanistan.

Racism and Godsend no.4

When William was just six years old he came home at dinner time from Leith Links Primary School with two huge weals along his hands and up his wrists. He told us they had all been talking in the playground line before going into school and he had been called out and belted.

Ena and I were furious both at the fierceness of the punishment that left such a wee boy's hands and wrist still so inflamed and sore, and also because the only prominent black one in a line of boys had been picked on. The recently appointed Head Teacher told me that the teacher responsible was a lay preacher in the Episcopal Church. He came into the room smiling broadly on seeing a minister but I refused to accept the hand held out, before telling him my complaint, asking him for an explanation, and weighing up the sincerity of repeated apologies.

Not "a time to keep silent"

William did provide one sign that things were not right at school. The love of music and rhythm he exhibited on the day he first came to us as a toddler led us to buy him a violin when music lessons at school became available. One day shortly afterwards, I went out the Manse door and there was the violin bow rammed down into the garden ground. We wondered whether being the only black boy and also a minister's son, might be more than enough to cope with without carrying a violin too. But questions to William and to the school brought no clue of anything serious.

"A time to speak"

William eventually accepted that the ever-ready grin and quick joke would never be enough to protect him from the bullies and permit a peaceful life. He began to use weights and build up his body strength. And a day came when he crashed out of his room yelling that he had just seen from the window "the bullies" running over the top of our new little white Datsun car parked at the back door. He gave me the name and address of the gang leader and I went along to engage the boy's parents in the facts of the situation and the consequences.

When William started secondary school, he came home furious because his class had just been introduced to the gym and the PE teacher – later to be promoted to assistant head – told William to show the boys how to climb the ropes because his ancestors were not long out of the trees.

But it was only when he was in his thirties that William was able to tell us the extent of the racist bullying at primary school. The boys used to tie him to a post in Leith Links, spit into his mouth, push dirt in, and threaten that they would kill him and his parents if he told anyone.

No wonder there was a lot of bad behaviour at home that we could not understand.

Blood in the bathroom

Mind you, on two mornings I got further signs of what William had to put up with. When I went into the bathroom I found blood splattered across the wash hand basin and bath. William had come home after we were in bed, without disturbing us. It turned out that on the first occasion he'd been asked at a disco in Leith to help the management push some hooligans out the door: when he left for home he had found the gang waiting for him.

The second occasion I can't forget and that pains Ena and myself still is that coming home another night someone in the street shouted a term of racist abuse at him and attacked with what William thought was a long stick. After fighting his assailant off, William felt blood from the blow on his back, made for the Royal Infirmary and was told it must have been a sword: all this before letting himself quietly into the Manse.

What led William eventually into his present state of serious mental illness was an attack from behind while he was discussing a little private business in the up–market Rutland Hotel at Edinburgh's West End. He himself refuses to accept that this was a racist attack, even though he was the only black man in the room, because there was no racist abuse shouted at him. But William never saw the faces of the four men who laid him low and left him not only with nightmares but the constant dread in the daytime that they might be coming to get him from behind again.

Just how William can have become a good man, always concerned and doing what he can about badly treated people here and all over the world, despite his own stresses and isolation, is due to his own decisions and determination. But the Grace of God plays its part with us all.

New ways to stop bullying urgently needed still – a new hymn for family life

"The Peebleshire News" of 3 January 2014 reported that almost 400 schoolchildren in the Scottish Borders had requested to move schools following complaints over bullying in just over a year.

The following hymn appears in the most recent Church of Scotland hymn book CH4 (No. 692) and might not be known to too many people:

1.   Jesus puts this song into our hearts,
Jesus puts this song into our hearts;
It's a song of joy no one can take away.
Jesus puts this song
Into our hearts.

2.   Jesus teaches how to live in harmony,
Jesus teaches how to live in harmony;
Different faces, different races, he makes us one.
Jesus teaches how to live
In harmony.

3.   Jesus teaches how to be a family,
Jesus teaches how to be a family,
Loving one another with the love that he gives.
Jesus teaches how to be
a family.

(Graham Kendrick© @Make Way Music, reproduced by permission)

"I'VE BROKEN MY BACK"

Bob Barker was the Sir Anthony Eden of South Leith Kirk Session. Tall, slim, with the same moustache, long black coat, the Homburg – and the Public School hairstyle when he removed it to smile and greet you. I had already visited him and Margaret in their grand, first floor flat at 2 Gladstone Place, and admired the large trophy above their fireplace which Kalamazoo had presented to their top salesman. The day I heard he'd had an accident on holiday and been admitted to Leith Hospital, I was in to see him.

"I've broken my back," he said. "We were down on the south coast of England and I took a spin in a speed boat. Suddenly we must have hit an unexpected big wave or something. There was a huge lurch, I was thrown forward, and heard a big crack. The pain was excruciating but I was determined to drive home and somehow we made it. They've done x-rays and given me pain killers."

The concern and empathy Bob realised any friend would have must have been very obvious on my face, and he changed tack almost right away, slipping into commercial traveller mode with a "confidence" – two, in fact.

"I've just had a visit from two Irish penguins from St Mary's (The worthy Sister Margaret and Sister Anne from the Convent in St John's Place is what he meant to say!) I watched them come into the ward with their little list in their hand. They visited one or two beds, went back to the door, consulted their list again, and came back in to talk to me."

"I'm not one of your flock," I told them, "I'm an elder at South Leith Kirk."

"We're sorry to have troubled you," came the response. "We saw your name and thought you might be a Catholic. But you look very uncomfortable the way you are lying. We'll help you."

"Before I could work out how to react they then took one arm and shoulder each and hauled me up the bed."

"Oh-oh-oh!"

"What brought you in here, anyway?"

"I've broken my back."

"You've never seen two people scurry from a ward as fast as they did!"

The boy David and the good Goliath

And then came the second confidence. "How's your wee lad getting on?"

"He's a bright boy," I replied.

"Shortly after you arrived in Leith," Bob went on, "I was driving along Leith Links past the Manse when suddenly something hit the windscreen and I had to stop right away. The road was almost deserted so I got out of the car, looked around, and just caught sight of William peeking out from behind your hedge. He turned round and ran in behind the door when he saw what had happened, his face white as a sheet and a sling still in his hand."

"That was terrible!" I responded, properly embarrassed. "You never told me or I would have apologised and done something about it."

"Och," said Bob, "William was probably aiming at a tree. I just went home to the telephone, postponed my appointment, and ordered a new windscreen."

Bob was a typical Elder, eh? Definitely not the Sir Anthony Eden who invaded Suez!

VISITING PRISONERS IN JAIL

According to chapter 4 of St Luke's gospel, Jesus read Isaiah's word that "The spirit of the Lord is upon me because he has anointed me to preach good news to the poor. He has sent me to proclaim release to the captives." So I visited Leithers in jail.

Corntonvale

"Wee, sleekit, cow'rin', tim'rous beastie. O what a 'panic's in thy breastie!"

Ellen was about thirty when she died, "of Aids," the death certificate would say. This happened a few months after I retired, so I personally was not able to tease out in the public funeral service the church's love for her, while also trying to communicate the love of God to distressed and disturbed mourners.

Ellen, warm and friendly as she was when we did see her over the years, never responded to telephone calls and notes through her door from our team. Maybe she didn't want to deceive us about some things in her life that weren't really all the police's or someone else's fault, and so she was cow'rin' away. The last time I saw Ellen, thanks to a kindly phone call from Bob Mathers, the chaplain, she was in the City Hospital, sores had begun to break out on her face, legs and body. But the visit I most vividly recall was during her second spell in Corntonvale Prison; this time, I'd drawn Ellen's whereabouts from the confidence I'd built up with her embarrassed but loving Dad. I found myself in a bright dayroom with Ellen in a particularly bouncy mood, possibly playing up a bit for the benefit of some other young girls who were about and started joining in the conversation from time to time, as they saw that I warmed to them too.

Suddenly, Ellen said; "See what's still up on the wall." I followed her across the room to view two sheets of black paper. The writing on them, in carefully stylised script, was in white. We read out together Burns's *"Tae a moose."*

Now, I'd heard of Ellen many years before when she was about 12 and her father had phoned to say that his wife had died. Ellen's own mother had died some years previously and now her poor father was trying to cope with the early death of his second wife. Young Ellen, for whom this was a second bereavement, too, of course, was out of the house. "I don't know where," said Dad. Ellen, I guess, was trying to escape the ordeal in the company of her pals.

Over the years, a wall of silence was to grow up between father and daughter. It had been difficult enough when father found himself a sole parent and thought daughter would do as she was told. The second death so stunned both that neither could help the other to understand and to cherish.

Ellen got into trouble not just at home. She was expelled from school (and I do wish the Rector or Guidance staff had told me at the time). Much later, Ellen was to tell me she had been gang-raped.

As we approached the Burns' poem, Ellen told me that this was what she had produced with the materials I'd sent her during her first spell in jail. (South Leith church always kept me in money – in food too, indeed – so that I could express in practical action as well as words our concern to people in need.)

I remember being aware of Ellen looking at my face, as I stood beside her, and then she climbed up to reach her art-work, took out the drawing pins, rolled the sheets up, and put the poem into my hands:

"Wee, sleekit, cow'rin', tim'rous beastie, O what a panic's in thy breastie!"

I'd often wondered about Burns' concern for a mouse. Mice eat the farmer's crops and are universally seen as pests to be killed as quickly as possible. Do you think it possible that just maybe on this occasion, from the plough, Burns was put in mind of some wee lassie of his acquaintance knowing what it was to be sleekit, cow'rin', timorous and in a panic?

The things we do to wee lassies! There must be a better way than the jail.

Stepps prison

I first went to see Kenneth when his salt-of-the-earth Grandparents told me he was in trouble with the police and hoped I might be able to help. I found him tall, slim, very well dressed indeed in a light grey suit, utterly charming, confident and delighted to talk with the minister he did not know. "I'm getting a lot of hassle from the police," he volunteered and answering the obvious question he said he was a Hibs Casual.

"Are these new Football Casuals not violent?"

"It's violence that turns me on…"

Some weeks later, Kenneth's name was in the Evening News as being responsible for an act of violence and receiving a jail sentence. I duly got the help of the prison chaplain to arrange that I might get in to talk with him. This was not in the usual type of reception room or cell with a table and chair that I was used to when visiting jails, but standing in a long, empty, newly built cement possible workspace. And there was a prison officer standing five yards away. Kenneth presented himself apparently unchanged, apart from an increased sense of injustice that the police had stitched him up. I ventured that although innocent in this case he must have done this kind of thing before and got away with it. "Oh, yes, but I was not involved in this one: I'm innocent."

Maybe I could become more useful to Kenneth and his family now that an engagement with him had been entered into…

(When the time came for me to retire and notice appeared in the press, Kenneth's mother called at the Manse and gave Ena a bottle of malt whisky for me, with her thanks for having visited her son.)

NOT ALWAYS GETTING IT RIGHT

"Paint me warts and all" (Oliver Cromwell, Puritan Reformer and "Lord Protector") – when a portrait was insisted on.

Newly inducted as minister of South Leith in 1969, word reached me that a young Gold Award girl in the Guides, unmarried, had become pregnant and moved out of the family home. I managed to find out where she was living – far from Leith – and went to support her. A teenage boy answered the door in the tenement and was obviously uncomfortable – and almost hostile – at the appearance of a minister, but eventually he couldn't refuse my request to see Susan and he let me in.

Susan and her family had known my predecessor so, of course, sad though the girl evidently was, there was no resentment from her at my presence.

Immediately I asked how she was, however, the boy, who had positioned himself behind me, standing against the shutter of the window, registered his objection. I turned my head to face the boy and said that I had come only to help.

Sitting beside Susan, I was soon telling her that the church had two benevolent funds from which I could help buy whatever she needed, without anyone at all knowing who received the money. Understandably, this was a message I had to repeat and explain to the young woman who seemed totally at a loss.

The young man, obviously not paying any attention to what might be being said, persisted in his antagonism and kept interrupting.

I got so angry that eventually I swivelled round and declared, "One more word from you and I'll throw you through that bloody window!"

Mea culpa.

Understandable violence

When Jesus visited the temple in Jerusalem on what became the first Palm Sunday, this was already a particularly holy week for the Jews and Jesus was so horrified that the establishment had turned the "house of prayer" into "a den of thieves", making a mint out of overcharging the pious poor for the approved pigeons they were required to sacrifice, that he "whipped out" the money-changers and overturned their tables. (Mathew 21, vv12-13)

Violence – and who would blame her??

"You're the very man! That elder of yours has just hit me on the head with my frying pan!"

This was the greeting by a church member when I rang the bell and she opened the door. I had paid the visit at the request of one of the South Leith elders because she was desperate about the constant drinking of a niece and the dangers to which her two young daughters were exposed. Nan herself was checking up once or twice a day but could not get Elizabeth to change her ways and be careful. Twenty minutes before I arrived, Nan had used her key to get in, found the house full of smoke – the children elsewhere, thank God – and two chops burning away on a high gas. She seized the frying pan to stop the flames, turned off the gas, ran through to find Elizabeth still asleep in a drunken stupor and in her rage and panic struck her niece with what was in her hand.

(Pastoral Care is not always predictable, comforting and properly prepared for in college. And sadly, not many months afterwards Elizabeth was to perish when her house did go up in flames.)

Violence – and who could not understand??

Andrew Smith had been ordained to the Eldership – and indeed had been Sunday School superintendent – long before I arrived in South Leith. Andrew, determined man of action, was proud of the fact that when the 2nd World War was declared and his intention to enlist in the Armed Forces was frustrated because he was in a Reserved Occupation – that is required for the Home Front – he and a pal had gone up to Stirling on a bus and made sure he was accepted there.

A time came after the war when Andrew and his wife Mary decided to use their longish summer holidays to visit the various beaches where Andrew had landed as a commando. So, immediately after the service one Sunday, Andrew made the long drive to the south coast of England in their campervan. They got on the Channel Ferry, but then discovered that a French strike was preventing all traffic from leaving to the place where Andrew and his comrades had put their lives at risk in order to free the very people who were now determined to stop him and his wife in a time of peace.

Andrew was not a man to frustrate! After weighing up the situation, he determined to move out and somehow managed to drive though the pickets, though all the while the strikers were not only shouting and gesticulating but actually pushing the van on its sides to try and make it topple. All the while also, Mary was extremely frightened and screaming for Andrew to stop. But Andrew had been brought up on the Leith motto (Persevere) and somehow he got through.

A short distance along the main road, Andrew saw what must have been the pickets' cars parked along a side road. Out he got and before driving on to their destination he let all the tyres down.

SURPRISED BY A NON-BELIEVER

My uncle Jimmy Simpson was not just a run-of-the-mill, couldn't care less, non-believer: he had become President of the National Society of Rationalists. So it was a real surprise – and a challenge – when I was asked by his daughters to join the close family for his golden wedding celebration dinner in his Leith Corporation house, and be ready to say a prayer or a blessing if this would seem right at the time.

Now, Uncle Jimmy and his wife Auntie Pinkie – as they were always known to us in our family life – were not really related to us. Agnes Pinkerton and Millie McKay had been harum-scarum pupils at school: they once escaped together from the classroom by "dreeping" from a window down into the King's Park.

Millie married William, Pinkie married Jimmy, and each couple had a son and three daughters. Uncle Jimmy became Chief Engineer on a Granton trawler. "Cousin" James told me of his 14-year-old start as a boy-cook; of the necessity to get all the fish gutted, as soon as they were lucky enough to get a catch, however long it took, with the knife cutting his hands and the salt water healing them; also of the rush to break the bond and get at the whisky immediately they left harbour, and then the panic when the engine failed before they got to the three-mile customs limit on one occasion!

During the war, Uncle Jimmy arrived on a visit in the uniform of an Officer in the Royal Navy. Such an appointment was astonishing, perhaps unique. The senior ("snobby") service only commissioned middle-class men who'd been educated in "Public" schools. But a man of

Jimmy's calibre and expertise was needed for a training college in West Africa.

When Uncle Jimmy was an old man, cancer struck him down and confined him to his bed just when the date of the Golden Wedding approached. The two daughters who had emigrated to Canada got back to Leith in good time. James, however, who had emigrated to Auckland – where he became President of the Rational Association of New Zealand – would not be able to get away and had sent his congratulations.

On the big night, Uncle Jimmy had somehow got himself up and dressed and seated at the table for dinner. Then to our amazement he managed to push himself up to make a speech. At this point, one of his daughters explained that above the din she had heard the phone ring, lifted the instrument and, lo and behold, there was James's voice ringing out a greeting. And then the door suddenly opened and James himself walked in from the spare bedroom where he had been hiding. Uncle Jimmy and Auntie Pinkie collapsed to their seats, totally overcome. I saw the sisters' nod to me that now was when words from a minister-friend would help the family.

Ministering to people outwith the church

Hans Kung interpreted the Incarnation as God showing he was on man's side; that is not just for believers.

It was cancer that took my mother-in-law's life too. Annie Barker, who had suffered a great deal from the behaviour of other people throughout her life and yet remained a resilient woman, had never in my company shown any interest in the Christian Church or voiced any opinion at all on the will of any God, suddenly found herself seriously ill and admitted to the Eastern General Hospital. Ena and I went in to be with Annie that evening and found her little room crowded with family. Some attempts were being made to tell Annie that she would get better now, but she interrupted the talk: "Will you all go out for a minute and leave me with Jackie?"

And then to me, "Jackie, will you say a wee prayer for me and then ask the others back?"

"PROD ME WITH THE ODD": SURPRISED BY RUDOLF

One Sunday when I went up into the pulpit to start morning service, sat down to pray privately as usual and then stood up to begin to speak, I was absolutely astonished to find a tall African man right in front of me. His black face and his white teeth beamed up to me from ear to ear. That huge smile never left his face the whole service long.

Now, no black African people lived in Leith at that time and this was the first time one had appeared in the Sunday congregation. Afterwards I learned that his name was Rudolf, he had arrived in Leith the previous night, and his B&B landlady had told him how to get to South Leith Parish Church.

I asked about the smile and he replied that he was a Lutheran minister from Namibia and this was the first time in his life that he'd been able to worship with white people.

Ena came over and invited our visitor to lunch. In the Manse, we discovered that Rudolf's knowledge of English was not very good but realised that the words of the church service had not been what was important to him.

For Rudolf, this was just an overnight stay in Leith. The World Council of Churches, preparing for the day when Namibia would be free, had somehow succeeded in arranging for Rudolf to go to Sweden for further study – nothing political of course!

For pudding, Ena had baked an apple pie and she supplemented the custard sauce with a big blob of ice cream. Sitting opposite Rudolf, she suddenly saw shock on his face and sprang to her feet in horror!

"What's wrong??" Rudolf looked down at the steam rising from the ice cream on top of the pie just out of the oven and said "I thought it would be hot!" He had never seen or tasted ice cream.

A year or so later, tragedy was to befall Rudolf and his family. Back in Namibia he disappeared. Evidence such as there was led to the conclusion that this man of the gospel of peace had been kidnapped by the South West African Police. His case was taken up by Amnesty and he was prayed and campaigned for, but to no avail.

"The Word of God"

The writer of the Epistle to the Hebrews tells us (chp13v2), "Be not forgetful to entertain strangers: for thereby some have entertained angels unawares."

Scholars of church history have long told us that the Epistle to the Hebrews only got into the canon of the Bible because it was attributed to St Paul: and scholars of New Testament language in recent years have asserted that the writer of St Paul's epistles could not have written this one.

Our family's experience with Rudolf – and like Christian action by others too, of course – is convincing evidence that whoever wrote the Epistle to the Hebrews, whether apostle or not, whether man or woman, gave us "Word of God".

TELEVISION

"New ways to touch the hearts of men"
(From an Iona Community prayer)

"Television is for appearing on, not watching"
(Malcolm Muggeridge)

To the new and young parish minister of Menzieshill housing scheme, Hugh Douglas, the long established minister of Dundee's main parish church (St Mary's), had always appeared lofty and unapproachable, but then he made time to write that he'd had to come in to Menzieshill on a bereavement visit and had been surprised and delighted to see how attractive and well cared for our church grounds had been developed. And then Ralph Morton, Deputy Leader of the Iona Community, told me that Hugh, though 'only' an Iona Associate, was a better member than many officially on the membership roll. So, when I saw him speaking on a television programme very easily – convincingly indeed – I ventured to let him know how his work for the gospel on the screen was greatly admired.

And then, to my "not something I could do," Dr Douglas spelt out a lesson: "It's easy when you are actually in the situation because you realise that the television people are relying on you. Their livelihood depends on a good programme."

"Late Call" before I M Jolly

I think it's quite forgotten nowadays that Late Call appeared seven nights a week and was a very popular TV programme.

It used to be commonly said that the household demand for electricity and gas in Scotland almost disappeared when people went to bed after watching this programme. But this was before the incorrigible micky-taker Rikki Fulton (himself an every Sunday attender at his parish Kirk) and the BBC (seizing on an ideal opportunity to steal a march in the ratings war they seemed to become obsessed by) put a stop to the programme's good work for the nation.

It was in May 1979 that the Rev Dr Nelson Gray, STV's Religious Programmes Editor, telephoned and then wrote inviting me to work on television for the first time. My dates were 28th Sept to 4th Oct and the seven scripts of four and three-quarter minutes "direct speech" were required three weeks beforehand. I should avoid wearing dark clothing or a white shirt. One change of jacket would help confirm the notion that each Late Call was live on the night. If I remembered to blink occasionally that would stop viewers realising that I was reading from an auto-cue. I "should put something of myself into it."

What were the most valuable things to say to the general public and how best to get through? Well, it happened that I had recently been struck with what was called a Hippy Prayer, with the line "Dear God, prod me with the odd," and I used this insight as the cutting-edge.

I asked the Rev. Dr John ("Ian") Gray, the rigorously honest Head of Practical Theology at New College, to try to view "Late Call" for the week and then give me his detailed assessment of its truth and helpfulness.

A surprise at the recording

There turned out to be no strain or stress at all with the business of recording. A lady spent a couple of seconds putting powder on my nose and forehead. I was sat in the chair for a voice check and to make sure I could follow the way the words were on the auto-cue. There was no run-through, just a voice check of a couple of sentences, and then, "That's fine. Are you ready to go?"

And now for the surprise. There I was concentrating my sincerity to communicate effectively what I thought were among the most important things that anyone could hear when I realised that the technician who had helped set up the camera and lighting had sat down in another chair just one arms-length away to my left and was paying absolutely no attention to me, just reading his morning paper! Needless to say, immediately I finished I turned round to see which red-top and which page!

A Leith woman volunteered to me that most people she knew made a point of watching Late Call every night, though some decided after Sunday or Monday whether to make a point of it for the rest of the week.

Nelson Gray wrote that he and his family thought the talks were "great" and enclosed a payment of £30, which helped keep my car on the road. Sometime later he asked me to conduct a morning service for the network, live.

Leith Motto

The fact that Leith's traditional motto was "Persevere" seemed widely known elsewhere, but it turned out that many contemporary Leithers had not heard the old spelling lesson of the Port's schools in: "Let Every Individual Try Hard."

LEITH DEFINITELY NOT EDINBURGH!

Leith was always choc-a-bloc on Saturday mornings in the 1980s and early 1990s. Grandchildren from the schemes in Edinburgh were brought in to see Granny and Granddad, and the weekly messages could be collected by former Leithers before leaving the beloved old port.

Nowhere was the traffic busier than in Henderson Street, near Great Junction Street, where South Leith Church's new halls were built and opened by the Duke of Edinburgh in 1982 – starting a year of celebrations and spring-boarding for the historic church's 500th anniversary. Lothian Region buses stopped and started and jammed against inconsiderately parked cars. Quite normally, as many as three double-deckers would get caught up in the junction, as they tried to go different ways, while all the time pedestrians would step off the thronged pavements with nothing but their own intentions in mind, and even grimly held Zimmers with net baskets swinging from the front would add to the chaos. The noise was colossal, the people were cheerful and accepting of the crowd and chaos – except when more than one engine was revved up suddenly and a mouthful would come from a frustrated driver.

Saturday mornings

South Leith Parish Church ran a shoppers' coffee morning every Saturday. A nearly new stall allowed young families and poorer pensioners to supplement their clothing for almost nothing. A "One World Stall" sold fairly traded goods to help really poor people abroad – and also pricked our consciences. The church magazine on every table meant that non-church folk could see what the church was doing and possibly become involved. I would look in to support the workers and deal with any pastoral messages – "propping up a wall for the Kingdom's sake" as Ernest Marvin of Bristol described this ministerial practice to me in Iona in 1961 when I was preparing to become a parish minister.

"Hingin oot the windae"

One Saturday when, approaching noon, I left the busy halls and dodged my way towards my car, a sudden yell "Hi Tam" came right out over the top of the traffic from across the road. I looked up, first to see a woman in her 50s hanging out of her window in no.13, hair-curlers in and totally unabashed; and then down back to my pavement, to notice the man being addressed coming towards me, cloth-capped, maybe in his 60s, a plastic shopping bag at the bottom of each arm.

"Hi Aggie!" was his response.

"Still gaun the messages?" quizzed Aggie.

"Still dyeing yer hair?" re-joined Tam.

Leith is definitely not Edinburgh!

Leith so different

Of course, the reality of Leith's historic and characteristic separation from Edinburgh has gradually been disappearing. My former colleague, the Rev James Scott Marshall, one time Dux of Leith Academy and Minister of Kirkgate Church from 1947, used to say that the polite Edinburgh silence of the tram journey from Princes Street would reign until the trams left

Pilrig Street, when the passengers would all begin to talk as they now knew they were all Leithers. In 1969, when I first went into Leith Academy as chaplain, many of the staff were former pupils and some still stayed in Leith: by 1994, the staff had grown considerably in number, but not one was a former pupil and only one to my knowledge had chosen to come and stay in Leith. By that time also houses in middle-class Wardie and Trinity were not spoken of as being in Leith by their owners or their lawyers or estate agents!

Now, it is probably true of at least Scottish human nature that we can love our neighbour in Africa easier than people in the next town. When middle-aged Hugh Davidson, minister of Inverleith Church, heard I'd be retiring to Walkerburn, he told me that he had been brought up there where his father was parish minister, and he still couldn't hear the word, "Innerleithen" without going "Acchh!" This matches the long-term animosity between next door Edinburgh and Leith, which might have been worsened by the fact that Edinburgh is sited above Leith and Edinburgh people have been felt to look down on Leith and its people socially as well as geographically.

Looking down on Leith and Leithers

What had commonly become a sense of innate superiority in Edinburgh was not confined to the status-conscious bourgeoisie. My mother-in-law used to live in a room and kitchen, with common lavatory in the stair, four flights up in Edinburgh's High Street. When she was left on her own in her 70s the family began sustained efforts to get her to flit. About 1978, after our usual Sunday lunch in South Leith Manse, my wife and I decided to drive her home via sheltered flats newly opened in Gordon and Manderson Street. I told her how convenient they were inside and how happy the tenants were to be settled there. My wife offered to make enquiries and see if we could arrange a visit to one of the flats. Her mother was very quick indeed: "Ena, I'm not living in Leith!"

Historic Injustice

The root cause of centuries of mutual animosity – running into hostility by Leithers – may have sprung up in the Middle Ages, when Edinburgh, being a Royal Burgh, had all the rights to international trade. Thus, the Leith Carters, for instance, the poorest of the trade incorporations, were kept out of all the lucrative contracts. The cargoes left to them were the dirtiest and least profitable ones.

After the 1st World War, Leithers did not want amalgamation with Edinburgh: the town was very proud indeed that it had electric trams and a Woolworths when Edinburgh did not! But Edinburgh owned the land around Leith that was needed for housing to replace the densest slums in Western Europe, and a marriage had to be arranged. Leith councillors now joined Edinburgh councillors on the amalgamated town council and ensured that the new housing in areas at Lochend and Loganlea, made possible by the first Labour government's housing and rates act, was made available to Leithers as well as to the unfortunate slum –dwellers of Edinburgh's Cowgate.

But Leith still suffered badly from a City Chambers too concerned about Princes Street, the Royal Mile, and the International Festival to pay attention to Leith's needs.

The most scathing critic of Edinburgh's treatment of Leith was Gordon Donaldson, a Leither who became Professor of Scottish History in Edinburgh University, and later Historiographer Royal for Scotland.

The media to the rescue

And then, about 1970, Shelter, the new British Campaign for the Homeless, produced statistics to show that Edinburgh contained more houses without baths, without hot water and without their own inside toilets than any other city in the country. This Report was seized on by TVs Nationwide, Panorama and indeed media across the world. Shocking publicity for the Festival Capital City! Horror in the City Chambers! Leith began to get some serious attention at last.

The national statistical picture was transformed for Edinburgh almost immediately by the demolition of the offending tenements in Leith. But Leith was left for years with vast derelict areas, and Leithers were transported far from home to Edinburgh's unappealing schemes. Almost as bad, much unworn ready-cut Craigleith stone from the Old Leith tenements was just dumped in the Forth.

The sense of "belonging" in Leith

Mind you, as late as 1980, a Leith couple who had both developed cancer realised they had to get a more suitable house than their small flat in a post-war multi-storey in Lindsay Road. Now, the man had been a water polo Scottish Internationalist and as such had travelled the world. But when he told me he had been up to the city's housing department in Edinburgh's High Street, he said (in all seriousness – something that was "natural" for an old Leither) that he had made it clear that he would take a house *"anywhere – even as far away as the foot of Lochend Road."*

Leith councillor Cornie Waugh did eventually get the council's agreement to change the longstanding letting policy and allow Leithers to have priority for Leith houses that became vacant.

Some things you just cannot get done if you stay out of politics!

Leithers in political power

Better days for Leith only began – so suddenly, it seemed – when it was Leithers who held the key posts of Lord Provost (Kenneth Borthwick) and Chairman of Housing (Cornelius Waugh) while the Labour Convenor of Lothian Region (John Crichton) and the Leader of the Tory Group (Brian Meek) were also Leithers, and Leith MP Ronald King Murray was Lord Advocate. As a matter of interest, the Roman Catholic Church's (only Scottish) Cardinal Gray was also a Leither.

It was a great pity when the parliamentary boundaries commission failed to find a way to keep Leith a single seat, which would have helped retain, nourish and possibly extend the web of care that does exist and flourish where people know they belong in a particular distinct community.

Of course, new developments which would not have come into being without benign influence from Edinburgh will produce unimagined benefits. The building of the new Scottish Office; the Forth Ports Authority; the former Royal Yacht now anchored and welcoming international visitors. All such, and the studied priorities of the Leith-inspired Port of Leith Housing Association – with South Leith Kirk Elders always having been on the committee – help Leith to prosper in a general sense as never before.

Egalitarianism and Affection

But we must hope that the Old Leith bonds of common egalitarianism – sometimes, it should be said a bloody-minded egalitarianism, for the Leith motto "Persevere" can become "Be Perverse!" – that the rare sense of all being Jock Thamson's bairns will somehow persist.

Just before I retired, I was determined to see some of the frailest Leithers whom I hadn't seen personally for a considerable time. People on our routine visiting list were visited by our team regularly every 6–12 weeks at least, and a report was always given at the Friday team meeting. For Mary from Newhaven, who was 90, there was always a reassuring report as her son visited every day and the new Sister in charge of the geriatric ward in the Eastern General Hospital had brought a great deal of life into the place.

Well, this day I duly went to see Mary in the Eastern General Hospital and she was sitting on her own in the day room. Other patients with visitors happened to be seated round the walls, but Mary was in the middle of the room in her chair with the bar across, and a tray in front, keeping her safe. So I duly collected a little chair and sat in front of her, my knees against her knees, took her hands into mine and said, "Mary, it's Jack Kellet, the minister." "What, wha is it?". So I raised myself up, leaned over and spoke loudly into her right ear, "Mary, it's Jack Kellet, the minister." "What, wha is it?"

I moved my head round to her other ear, "Mary, it's Jack Kellet, the minister." "Wha is it?"

By this time, all the other patients and their families were obviously paying a great deal of attention. It was becoming like the two Ronnies' programme, or Billy Connolly without the swearing, and someone shouted to me, "She's deaf" (as if I didn't know) and another joined in "She's blind," as a poor minister wouldn't know such a thing! Then suddenly I had a little brain-wave. I was wearing my clerical collar, so I took her hands, lifted them to my collar and ran them along it. She instantly exclaimed "Oh! It's yersel, ya bugger!"

Later, I learned from my Deaconess Kay McIntosh and assistant minister Fiona Winn, who had been visiting Mary more regularly, that the trick was to take chocolate and slip it between her lips.

PROSTITUTES AND PRESBYTERIANS, PUBS AND POPE

One Saturday night around Christmas, I arrived at our church halls to find that I could not get in because a key had been put in the lock from the inside to ensure that no one, even key holders, could gain access. It happened that an undertaker had just phoned to tell me of a sudden, unexpected death and I needed to get into the office immediately to check out family details before visiting. Moreover, the noise told me that a big party was going on and I was a wee bit surprised that I hadn't known about this because in the Church of Scotland the Minister had to be consulted about the use of church premises.

When Sheena Clark – one of the elders – eventually responded to my ringing of the doorbell she told me that this party had been kept a secret because it was for the local prostitutes and their families. A real surprise to me – and a delight!

The port and the pubs

Now, Leith had been founded as a port, of course. In the Middle Ages, Berwick had become too vulnerable to attack by the English, so Leith, close to the capital, had been built up to become the busiest port in Scotland. In my time, older people told me that the traditional Sunday afternoon activities for families used to be walking round to stare at so many boats from all over the world.

With the boats came sailors, of course, many of them stuck for days, weeks and even months while cargo was being unloaded and reloaded, and necessary repairs were being organised. (A common sight was a crew of Lascars walking through the streets up to Edinburgh in single file following the leader.)

With the sailors – not just foreigners! – came pubs to the highest density in the country. (In those pre-wireless and pre-containership years, church people of the popular and idealist Temperance Movement – which the Labour Party and Co-operative Societies belonged to – raised the funds to build the Leith Sailors' Home, providing cheap accommodation and a social life without the demon drink.)

With the boats, the sailors and the pubs came the scandal of prostitution too. When the area of Iona Street, in the grey borderland between Edinburgh and Leith, and actually in South Leith Parish at the time, came to be rebuilt with high quality tenement housing, it was given this new name as its original name had become notorious for the brothels. "Nice" old Leithers in my time would say that the women came down from Edinburgh because Leith girls would not do such a thing – and even that the clients were Edinburgh men with less fear of recognition in the busier streets of Leith.

The 20th century meant fewer travelling seamen about the place, but the advent of a plentiful supply of drugs put more young women on the streets "to feed their habit." One early evening Ena and I decided to look for something at Kinloch Anderson's shop, realised we'd missed the entrance, slowed down and then stopped to ask directions when a young woman came in to sight. She came right up to my window as I lowered it and then looked startled when she saw Ena with me, noticed my clerical collar too, and covered her face – so young and beautiful – in embarrassment. "I'm sorry, I'm sorry, I've made a mistake!"

The pioneering laity of the Kirk

One of the most dedicated and inspiring groups within the Church of Scotland has always been the Woman's Guild (now just the Guild). Every year, the National Guild selects projects for its branches to prioritise with their support and fundraising: the six projects as I write include Rwanda, Mary's Meals and the Julius Project for the homeless. (The sad fact that more young church members can't break free from contemporary age-prejudice and share in such good work is a tragic commentary on our society.)

Last century, one of the most radical Guild causes was to provide whatever pragmatic support might be acceptable for "sex-workers" on the streets of Leith. Two case-workers were engaged and an old shop was taken over in Henderson Street. Obviously, discretion all round was necessary, but with no implication that we might like to interfere in any way, we volunteered that we might respond to any request that might come to us. This particular Christmas party was one such result.

The Pope and Presbyterianism

Now in the 21st Century, Pope Francis has delighted Presbyterians with his totally unexpected proposal to invite the laity of the Roman Catholic Church to get involved in the decision-making of their church. An absolutely committed Roman Catholic layman friend has voiced his fears that bishops entrenched in their authority and status–consciousness will seek to muddy the clear water-for-life coming down from the Pontiff, but my friend's enthusiasm did get to work with no delays!

May the Pope and his bishops quickly find to their surprise and delight that their laity will lead them to new and more effective ways to implement the gospel of Jesus Christ! Just as the Guild and a lot of Church of Scotland ordained elders have.

BEFORE FOOD BANKS

'*TEA*!!" A plastic mug was being thrust almost in my face the moment I opened the Manse door. It was three o'clock in the morning and as my half-open eyes were trying to focus through the darkness, the street lights behind him across the road gradually revealed the tall figure of a man in front of me, his loose clothing all black, his curly beard both broad and long, the unwashed odour filling my nostrils. The repeated need for tea sounded out as loud and urgent as the ringing of the doorbell had been.

Now, just a week or two before, the deservedly respected Interim Moderator in the South Leith vacancy had warned me that even though the house bought for us in the heart of Leith to replace the distant grand residence in Trinity was new as a Manse, the beggars would find us quickly. And there was no need to give any money: an elder of his congregation was manager of the local Social Security Office and they had staff on call even at the weekends to provide any help and guidance that was needed.

But then, what about a poor soul who could hardly speak and was unconscious of the time in the middle of a very cold night?

"*Inasmuch as ye have done it unto the least of one of these my brethren, ye have done it unto me*" (Matthew 25)

I did not hesitate: Jesus' watchword for us, 'Inasmuch,' is instantly compelling – and not just for ministers, of course. I beckoned the caller in and led him through the porch, through our hall, through our living room and the little breakfast room, where I picked up a chair to seat him in the kitchen at the back of the Manse. Boiling a kettle and making up a cheese sandwich, I sought conversation by risking a few obvious questions, but the confused man just mumbled to himself.

My wife Ena appeared on the stairs, just after the man had risen to leave and we were making our way back through the house. Alert, no doubt, to the risk of infection to the children and the disinfecting she would have to do, Ena told me that next time the tramp should be seen to in the porch. She also told the (growing) Malcolm and Lorna what they should do to help the man if we were out. On future visits, the man – with no name to tell – managed to voice another need we could help with, as soon as he had finished his tea and sandwich: "Have you any money for cigarettes the day?" On one occasion, he said, "You werenae in last time, and your Bahamian lad gave me the tea and the piece." That would be Lorna before she got out of jeans and into dresses.

Freddy freezing on Leith Links

Another poor soul regularly in urgent need who could not have satisfied the arrangements of the Social Security Department of the time or the policy of the Food Banks today – which requires a referral as a worthy recipient from a GP or Social Worker – was a Leither called Freddy. His first call at the Manse wakened me up at 6 o'clock. He was 'freezing', having spent the night trying to sleep out on the white-with-frost Links. His wife had refused to let him in the night before because he was drunk. It was money, and only money that would help him.

Over the years I got to know Freddy well. He was in and out of jail for non-payment of fines. When I consulted him about how life would be for a young lad I was concerned about who was awaiting trial for murder, meantime in a Young Offenders' Unit, and certain to go to jail when he reached the age, Freddy told me he would be 'easy meat.' I said that this was a really tough guy but Freddy responded, "Easy meat, he'll not be able to stop it," and gave me a look. It turned out that Freddy himself had been convicted of murder as a young lad and served his time, so he *knew.*

After many conversations with Freddy about possible changes he could make, I told him that there would definitely be no more cash from me. I spoke with Elio the Fish and Chip man in Duke Street and he agreed to await payment from me if anyone gave him a note I'd signed requesting a fish supper. Freddy accepted the note very easily. But in his next emergency, he told me, "No more chitties. Last time I just held the supper up in the pub next door and asked who'd buy me a pint for it."

A slightly more perturbing failure of policy came when two men I did not recognise called at the Manse, obviously the worse for drink, insisting that only cash could buy the ticket home or wherever. Eventually, they saw they had no hope and accepted my offer of something to eat. From an upstairs window, I watched them crossing the Links and throwing the sandwiches up in the air for the seagulls. (Mind you, when feeding the multitude who'd come looking for help and hope, Jesus did not ask his disciple distributors to sort out the 'unworthy' from the 'deserving'!)

The demon drink and the best-loved schemes

On one occasion, two drunks were particularly aggressive with Ena after she'd insisted they'd have to come back when the minister was in, and after she locked the inner door they urinated all over our porch. The church Fabric Convenor immediately advised that Ena should keep the main door shut and ordered one of the new clever peep-holes which looked from the outside as just a nameplate.

Unfortunately, it was fitted in our absence too high for Ena's eyes to reach!

THE GIVING OF THE POOR FOR THE WORSE OFF

For my first years in South Leith the town was classified formally as an 'area of multi-deprivation'. But when I dedicated the collecting tins after my first Christian Aid week in Leith, by far the heaviest – this was 1969 and a time for coins – came from the worst slum street in our parish.

When the Trades Fortnight arrived, an elderly woman member from another of the most squalid tenement buildings, also scheduled as 'condemned' and awaiting demolition, passed me an envelope to send to some poor country. Her annual rent was collected only 50 weeks of the year and this was her rent for the two weeks' 'holiday'.

Understanding my word of concern for her, she smiled, "Well, my mother always said that a "gi'ein' haund's a gettin' haund.""

Planned charity from the better-off

There had always been many, many poor people in Leith and the minister of South Leith was an *ex-officio* Trustee – in some cases the only Trustee – for quite a number of funds that wealthy people had bequeathed – for communicant members of South Leith Parish Church, for people in the parish with no church connection, pensions for Leith women in need over 55, even the closing balance of the long-demolished King James VI Hospital Trust and educational grants for the children of deceased ministers of the Scottish Episcopal Church!

Just before Christmas, a cheque signed by a Building Society manager started to arrive, accompanied by an unsigned explanatory letter. This was an Income Tax rebate the donor had received but she felt that her accountant had been administering her affairs to avoid tax she herself thought was due. So would I please pass the money on to Leithers in need?

(I learned that the donor was the wife of a Leith solicitor, when she phoned one year to apologise that the donation would not be available until after Christmas. This lady happened to be a member of St John's Episcopal Church at Edinburgh's West End – "Busy just now, incidentally, scrubbing out houses for the expected refugees from Vietnam.")

Other surprises

Sometimes there were surprises of a different order. One old, aged Leither, stuck in the tenement flat that had very obviously known no improvement or badly needed decoration since his father had got it decades before, constantly poking away at his smokey fire when he was not spitting into it, had repeatedly refused the absolutely guaranteed private gift of an electric fire, or the wage for a painter or a cleaner, told me on his death bed in hospital that he hoped I didn't mind, but he'd willed money to the Epileptic Society, membership of which I had long before arranged for him. After he died, I was dumbfounded to learn that the bulk of his (unknown) wealth was coming to South Leith Parish Church (£42,000)!

One Christmas Eve I took a telephone call from a man I didn't know to say that he would deliver six unsold turkeys, now roasting in his oven, if I could get them to six families who wouldn't be having one. Now we ourselves had not been able to afford a turkey for some years, but the donor, not imagining such a thing, meant me to give them away! (A similar thing had happened in Dundee. Have I been too puritanical for my common sense, as well as my family's good?)

Gi'ein' and gettin'

The sharing of our wealth – however great, however little – has always been as much the essence of the life of the people of God as the praying, praising and preaching. The Old Testament made it a condition for life after slavery in Egypt that the Promised Land would provide for the poor, the widowed, the fatherless and the stranger. Over the centuries God kept raising up prophets who risked their lives by denouncing the corrupt and the greedy (sinners all, whatever their 'religious' practices).

In the New Testament, we learn that as soon as the first Christians sensed the power of the Holy Spirit, were baptised and 'broke bread' together, they sold their possessions and 'distributed them to all, as any had need' (Acts 2). A medieval church in East Lothian has "Remember ye poor" carved into the stone-work wall beside the pulpit where no worshipper can miss it. An early tower in South Leith Parish Church had an office where deacons paid out what money had been given to help folk in need. Wealthy elders would take money for coal in the winter to people in their district: I remember being told by an old man that he still recalled his mother's distress when her elder was ill and didn't come.

But in living memory the great John White, minister of South Leith early in the 20th century, upset a lot of the working-class faithful by emphasising that the church was a place for giving as well as getting – and he specified amounts for the offering!

Bill Swan, his successor as minister, spelt out the consequences of the motor-car having enabled the well-off to move to a home and a church in more salubrious areas around

Edinburgh. When I was inducted in 1969, South Leith was still commonly referred to as 'wealthy', with the largest congregation in Scotland. The sad fact, however, is that the ordinary members, made more comfortable by full employment, felt no need to change their habits and give generously week by week.

At my first Kirk Session in March 1969, the Finance Convenor published the accounts for 1968 and said that something drastic had to be done because there was a deficit of £8000 – a colossal amount then – even though the carefully calculated fair allocation of financial responsibility for the Kirk's work at large had not been met and the full minister's stipend had not been necessary for six months (owing to my predecessor's death).

When the last days of the month arrived, the Treasurer told me he had not enough money to pay my stipend.

The generosity of Leithers when they're in-the-know

Drastic action was taken. I was the first member to have to declare what I would give every week, and how I'd worked it out. Some members I visited told me how hard up they were and only softened after I asked them what holidays they were managing to save up for. A former Boys' Brigade captain inspired fellow elders by insisting that the young Sunday School Superintendent charged with tasking him about his level of giving had told him to hand over the card showing his target, looked at it, and signed with the response that it was not much more than he was giving already.

Two sets of envelopes

Apart from essential normal running costs, our pipe organ needed some thousands of pounds to be spent on it and the lead of the stained-glass windows had begun to bend and bulge the lights dangerously inwards. Then a site close to the Kirk became available for new halls that would better serve the community's young and old. I suggested to the Kirk Session that every member be given a second set of Freewill Offering Weekly Envelopes, the giving in which would be reserved for the new halls. Sometime in 1982 the Solicitor of the Church of Scotland in 121 George Street, an elder at Cramond who had got to know us when we employed him in a dispute with our builders, telephoned to say that the new Year Book had just been published and South Leith showed the highest 'Christian liberality' (income) in the country.

Serving old and young, rich and poor

All the work of the church was faithfully placed before all the elders meeting in Kirk Session every month – questioned, discussed and decided upon. We employed the largest professional team ministry in the country to assist the parish minister and elders in pastoral work and community service. We did not foresee or adopt the un-presbyterian management system of Tony Blair, whereby preferred decisions were actually made in advance by small carefully selected committees, all agreed before the coffee was drunk and so much time was thereby 'saved'. Our normal attendance was 50 or more. Consensus would not have been possible or even desirable. Majority voting was the norm – and I recall one occasion when the result was 22 to 22, so that I had to give the casting vote (a few having abstained).

The communion roll was pruned of 'dead wood' while more and more traditionally South Leith families were moved far away (and to other church rolls). But the Boys' Brigade officers attracted the largest company in the Leith and later the Edinburgh Battalion – bringing in computers and robots long before such were even seen except by specialists at work. (Sadly, the officers also made all the boys Hibs supporters.)

The new halls accommodated a Leith lunch club for pensioners whose premises were being pulled down. A young woman doctor's receptionist asked about providing Sunday breakfast for the growing number of homeless around: we promptly made her an elder and the attendance – without having to attend church which George Orwell objected to as regards the Salvation Army – is currently about 70 (2014). On Saturday mornings, a weekly coffee morning was quickly established, with cheap nearly new clothing and Fair Trade goods available.

The routine priority visiting list of members and non-members numbered nearly 300 in my time. A Christmas Day lunch for people otherwise on their own became a fixture. A church history was published while the building itself was renovated, floodlit and Saltire-topped.

Back to our own 'food banks'

Way back to 1982, we invited the congregation to begin bringing non-perishable food and thereby quickly had food available for anyone who asked in the church, the halls and the Manse.

SCOTLAND'S CARTOON CHARACTERS IN THE KIRK

Two startling images of the Kirk's key office bearers have stayed in my mind since my teenage years when George Wilkie spirited the Canongate Christian Workers' League off to Iona Abbey.

The first cartoon, of a very self-pleased preacher booming, "Blah – blah – blah" while the Cross of Agony and Grace beside him had been hidden over by an All–Things–Bright–and–Beautiful floral arrangement, I had to keep as a permanently necessary reminder to myself when – still astonishingly – I found myself a minister.

The second cartoon, of "The Elder", depicted as domineering, stern, and saying "NO!", I quickly learned to be a calumny –

"Full many a gem of purest ray serene.
The dark unfathomed caves of ocean bear". (Gray's Elegy)

The Elder with his gifts of stinking fish

All elders are not forever youth–alive and care–committed, of course. When I first met a certain George, I wondered how he had become an elder. He did attend church every Sunday, he presented himself unfailingly for the monthly Kirk Session meetings, he (still, then) had a district to look after but there was something obviously wrong and inadequate about him. The elders who knew him from his earlier days told me that George had had a bad war.

It was many years before I got any details. George's condition had deteriorated, he had lost his job, I would see him from my car trudging the streets, obviously a lonely man, with his head bowed and a plastic bag in his hand. Then George started turning up at the Manse. The bag always contained a gift of fish – haddock from an old contact in Newhaven Harbour or else a surplus of trout from an angler. Maybe some people had begun to see George as a nuisance, wanting to come in and talk and smoke. On one occasion, George told me he'd called on four days before getting me in. We could understand why the fish was sometimes stinking.

I asked George about the war. A 16-year-old German boy had thrown a bomb at the truck he was in, "Just as well I was in the back with the lads and not up front as I should have been with the driver, who was killed."

Not long before this, George had actually been dropped behind enemy lines. It was when the daring and ill fated air borne landings to capture the three bridges across the Rhine and to Arnhem were about to take place. "*Somebody*" was needed to check beforehand that a particular bridge had not been mined, ready to be blown up before it could be captured, or the waste of life would have been even worse and in vain.

Thus I learned that George was also one of the gems from the dark unfathomed caves of the Eldership.

(And, *Oh!* we have to note that elders too can sorely need friendly understanding and spiritual care.)

PASTORAL VISITATION – AND COLLEAGUES WITH SURPRISES TO RELISH

When James Marshall, former Minister of Kirkgate Church, retired as our part-time Associate, the Kirk Session agreed that we should maintain our priority for pastoral visitation at its existing level and we were extremely fortunate to secure the services of Iona Community fellow member Richard Fraser Baxter. I had started to get to know Richard when he was Menzieshill's Missionary Partner in Nyasaland and came up to preach about our responsibilities there – characteristically singing away almost incessantly while in the Manse for lunch with our family. Richard was then heading up a Laity Training Centre. These were the days when politics could not be avoided, because the Kirk was one with the African people in their opposition to Central African Federation (and the risk of creeping apartheid).

Richard Baxter

Before leaving the newly established country of Malawi, Richard chaired a National Commission for the government which was of such importance that the Queen awarded him an OBE. The Wardenship of our then ecumenical centre in Dunblane (Scottish Churches House) followed and thereafter a brief experience as a parish minister which led Richard to realise that this was not the kind of job for him. But the invitation to develop a part-time associate ministry to shop and office staff in Edinburgh's George Street did appeal and Richard's rare range of talents produced a remarkably effective ministry in circumstances few ministers could have risked. When the very polished 'chaplain to Jenners' joined up with the Leith Keelies, we relished surprise after surprise.

The regular visiting list and the staff meeting

All of us in the professional team – Parish Minister, Associate Minister, Assistant Minister, Deaconess and students assigned to us – together with some elders who volunteered to do their bit – took part in the systematic visiting of hospitals, care homes, families carrying special burdens and also people bereaved, chronically sick, frail and lonely at home, consigned to prison – members of the church and non-members referred to us by the community at large. Every Sunday morning, I would hand out the lists on a card with space for a report on the visit. Every Friday night after Vestry Hour callers had been served, I would read out the reports to the team, starting normally with my own in order that the students in particular would find it easy to confess their personal inadequacies as well as find confidence in their insights. Together we would decide what actions we might take to help our people, which of us should be the next visitor and how soon. Approaching midnight, I would deliver our directions through the letterbox of our (supposedly) part-time and certainly committed Clerkess, Mrs Dorothy Thomson.

Kay McIntosh

Such was the system I had introduced and persevered with, but Friday nights were exhausting for many years and eventually concern about staff tiredness was raised at a Kirk Session meeting. Richard drew and circulated one of his cartoons right away (see below). Kay McIntosh, our imaginative deaconess, instigated a change of regime for the good of us all.

" The Vestry staff are showing some wear + tear." (JMK)

Richard   Kay   Ewan
           McIntosh   Aitken

At a meeting earlier when I had actually begun to worry about the unrelenting programme and the constantly growing pastoral needs we were detecting, I noticed in 'The Scotsman' that Andrew McLellan – the extremely able parish minister at St Andrew's and St George's, with whom Richard had previously worked – had accepted yet another phenomenally demanding responsibility from the General Assembly, and I remarked to Richard that I couldn't understand how that amount of time could be made available. Richard, with all his varied experience behind him, and what he remembered of his father's parish work in Clydebank too, replied that he had never known a church where so much visiting was done – and needed to be done.

A baby in an incubator

When Kay survived a particularly dangerous pregnancy and the tiny mite – not expected to live – was isolated in an incubator for some weeks, I would pray from the bottom of my heart with my eyes open and fixed on the wee face. Richard sang to her!

A bobby-dazzler bishop

Visiting a very elderly wheelchair-bound South Leither in the Royal Victoria Hospital, I was asked: 'Who was that bobby-dazzler you sent last week?...... with that smart suit and the wooden cross round his neck. I thought he must be a bishop!' (All spoken in a delightful Highland lilt.)

Preaching out of his own pain

From the pulpit, Richard deepened our understanding of him and our openness to one another. People in the pews having to struggle through life learned that the preacher on the love of God had not been a protected species when Richard felt able to share with us the experience of his young son Martin's death during their time in Africa.

War and peace

Richard knew about war too. As a boy he'd been bombed out of the Manse in Clydebank.

When old enough to join up, he had trained as a commando: having specialised in cliff climbing and abseiling, he was sent to Holland! Invited in his old age to tell of his experiences on a video for the new Commando Museum, Richard asked the young marines who were escorting him with some awe, if anyone recognised him, because he had been arrested three times at Faslane! Just a few days before his very sudden death in 2009, Ena and I were enjoying a postretirement dram or two with Richard in Crieff Hydro, when, characteristically, and with his ever-youthful panache, he launched out before leaving with his current party-piece: 'GIN I WAS GOD'.

A DEEP SADNESS OF MY MINISTRY

Mr William Smith Penman BL (OBE forfeited)

Not many preachers can have had a member of their congregation stand up and walk out in the middle of a sermon, but this happened to me three times. The first occasion was the consequence of a simple mistake, when at a watchnight service in South Leith two Roman Catholics, who really should have known where their church was, took a second look at my Genevan Gown and, after some audible murmuring, moved out of their long pew ("Excuse me, excuse me, excuse me, passed about ten people, and all during a prayer, presumably so that I would not notice!)

The third occasion was a really serious and sad one: my friend Bill Penman suddenly got up out of his every–Sunday pew during the sermon and hurried out through the side door. Quizzing a mutual friend immediately after the service, before visiting Bill at home, I learned that he had left once before – unnoticed by me. Both times it was while I chose to refer with horror to the dropping of the atom bombs on Japan.

Ever since 1945 I have remained appalled that what was seen by the rest of the world as "the Christian West", and often then declared itself as such, should have wrought such reckless – literally unimagined – death and destruction on so many helpless men, women and children in Hiroshima and Nagasaki. I have been told that it was all basically an experiment, rendered inevitable by the years of preparation and excited curiosity – two bombs exploded in different circumstances on cities deliberately lulled into normality, so that the effectiveness of the scientists' and politicians' labours could be seen. Certainly the Japanese knew they were beaten before the atom bombs were dropped, for the United States Air Force's massive fire bomb raid on Tokyo had already destroyed their capital, killed more people than either atom bomb would, and so converted the country's leaders that they were prosecuting enquiries about peace terms via Moscow.

But Bill was not able to listen to such evidence, or even argue his opposing view. The one thing that Bill would say to me was that in 1945 he had been posted to Hong Kong, with so many others, to get ready for the invasion of Japan. I was left to ponder that thousands of these men, hundreds of thousands in all, were preparing to die and would have died but for the war's sudden and dramatic end. I realised that for Bill, and no doubt his contemporaries in that situation, there could be no questioning or discussion about the events that brought about such sudden, totally unexpected relief.

Since I first met him in 1972, Bill Penman gave me reason after reason to accord him not only the affection of a friend but the highest respect one churchman – one human being – could have for another.

As a member and later convenor of Presbytery's Readjustments Committee for eight years of unparalleled change, I had to battle, often in vain, for congregations to accept that the world round their doors had changed, and that the neighbour they now had to learn to love was not in Africa but in that rival building just a stone's throw away! But in 1972, out of the blue as it seemed, Bill Penman, then session clerk of the small Kirkgate congregation in Leith, telephoned me, minister of "big brother" South Leith Parish Church, and asked if we might meet to consider a possible union, with the members of Kirkgate coming over to South Leith.

It was a very moving occasion for many many Leithers when Kirkgate congregation walked over to the ancient mother church, led by minister James Marshall carrying their pulpit Bible and session clerk Bill Penman carrying the communion roll.

We had agreed that our first service of public worship together would be Holy Communion. In South Leith Church we left the central front seats free as a sign of our welcome and the importance of our "new" members.

It was extremely distressing to learn at our first Kirk Session meeting that Kirkgate Church used individual cups and were not all ready for our common cups to be circulated among them!

When our newly united congregation planned to build new halls, Bill soon became the unanimous choice as convener. In 1982, Prince Philip, the Duke of Edinburgh, opened the finest set of church hall premises any of us had ever seen, all paid for and within a relatively poor community.

Thereafter, the ancient Kirk building, last rebuilt in the 1840s, was obviously now in need of repairs and refurbishment. Though Bill would insist in ceding major credit to the technical expertise and long working hours of fellow elder Robin Arthur, Bill himself was the convenor who carried the session, dealt with outside authorities, and got the whole job completed in time for my retiral – a springboard for our successors.

Bill's respected wisdom and leadership were not just for church, of course, but were for God's world. At work, he became Keeper of the Registers of Scotland, no less: and I understand that it cost him the normal OBE for this office when he defied the Thatcher government's blanket insistence to reduce the civil service in every department – on the grounds that his staff had become increasingly efficient, and cost the country nothing, as their services were sold to solicitors at a profit.

On retirement, Bill took on the (unpaid) job of chairman of the Port of Leith Housing Association – splendid new houses every year for hard pressed Leithers!

Always a man of principle, Bill was to resign from our Kirk Session in 1992. For years he had been troubled by what he saw as an unfair, left–wing bias in the General Assembly's Church and Nation Committee: was not one good word ever to be said for the government? Then the Parish Education Committee of the General Assembly refused to accept a first "No" for its view that children should be invited to participate in the Lord's Supper, amended its proposals to make such a provision permissive and selective, but persisted in advocating this practice as the new norm for the whole church. I was very close to (private) tears when I failed to persuade Bill that the good work and fellowship of South Leith, along with our own decision–making power, should be paramount for him as for me. (Despite his resignation from session, I made sure before I retired that Bill – to his surprise – got his particularly well deserved long service certificate from the Moderator of the General Assembly, and joined his fellow recipients on the dais to receive the congregation's sung blessing.)

It was no surprise to me that, notwithstanding his resignation from the session, Bill was elected to the Vacancy Committee formed after my retiral, and recognised as the best person to be the convenor.

And now I must approach and confess to what is the most serious failure on my part, in relation to a very good man, whom I counted as a best friend. Bill –like some others on the Vacancy Committee – consulted me privately about possible successors. Eventually, after making clear where responsibilities lay and I definitely did not want to know or intrude or interfere in any way, I did offer one or two names of people who might be approached and should be considered.

I therefore had a heavy heart that the person I regarded as the congregation's leading servant became so upset under the new ministry – however hard working and imaginative and attractive it was to so many – that he stopped participating in public worship in South Leith. Stubborn though he was, Bill Penman earned enduring honour and affection.

When some time into my "retirement", Bill found himself diagnosed with terminal cancer, he asked, asked and then tenderly insisted that I conduct his funeral. Ian Gilmour graciously gave his consent. My immense sense of privilege and thankfulness was deepened further a few days afterwards when a former work–colleague (not known to me) wrote to say that I had "got Bill to the life".

Well done, good and faithful servant now entered into the joy of the Lord!

Advice For Ministers And Elders – Also For Politicians And All Others With Strong Opinions

"You should not attempt to argue against a widely held point of view until you have so understood it as almost to be convinced by it."

John Macmurray, Professor of Moral Philosophy, 1956.

PRAISE FOR UNDERTAKERS

Surprise surprise

One morning I left my Leith Manse at five to nine to conduct an early funeral starting from the bereaved family's house. To my absolute consternation my Morris 1000 Traveller was not at the backdoor where I had parked it just before midnight. It must have been stolen. And the most grieving of the mourners would be expecting me in a few moments.

Now, at New College we had all been told that it was one of the undertaker's normal duties to collect the minister and return him home after the funeral. But I found that this meant a lot of hanging about while the undertaker's responsibilities to the family were being completed. With my own car, I could avoid wasting time and press on with other pastoral priorities immediately.

That morning, my own car not being where it should have been, I was back into the Manse like a shot and telephoning McKenzie and Millar, Leith's main undertakers, with apologies and explanations for the urgency. Bob McGillivray, the manager, understood my predicament right away, said he was sorry all his cars were out but he would shut the shop and collect me in the wee blue van if that was acceptable to me. What a relief! He was at the door in no time at all – and it was only as we were arriving at the house and I could see the waiting funeral cars that I remembered that this was not a McKenzie and Millar funeral but a Co-op one!

A cry for help to another undertaker

One of the earliest funerals I found myself conducting in Leith – before I had access to the communion roll and the parish boundaries map – was for another man whose brother had said South Leith was their church. The same day – normal practice – I went to the house to support the bereaved brother and also to find out something about the man who had died so that I could prepare a personal and appropriate service. This turned out to be a very distressing experience for the living room was dirty and uncared for: and as I pondered what kind of life had led to this state, a mouse ran across the floor between us. Sadder still, the man I was there to help and depend on could not indicate his feelings or provide me with basic information.

The service was to start in the funeral parlour of a long established undertaker in Duke Street and this was my only time there before the business closed. My first surprise was to find that the front door of the shop opened directly into the small parlour, with an open coffin taking up almost all the length of the room, the mourners seated in the single row that there was room for along the three sides, while the position for me was just a foot from the deceased's head. All of us present, indeed, were just a foot away from the exposed dead body.

But no sooner had the undertaker motioned me in than there came a surprise that was really alarming. A burly man in his 50s, just a yard or so to my right, rose to his feet and lunged across to try and punch me, yelling out his anger that I had been asking questions about the family.

More than just taken aback, I moved myself right back and out to the pavement, enabling the undertaker to bring some order into the room so that the service I had been asked to take could be conducted

What kind of life had that angry man experienced?

How many near impossible situations do undertakers have

to cope with? (By the way, does the general public realise in these changed days that parish ministers –Church of Scotland – conduct funerals without fee?)

The undertakers' experiences and training of young probationers

Shortly after one of my early Assistant Ministers arrived complete with a three or four year MA and the traditional demanding three year BD of the time, I learned that he had only been at one funeral in his life and that was his father's, many years ago. To supplement the insight, training and experience I could share I suggested that he sit at the back of the crematorium for the whole day at different services and then talk with me about his surprises. The manager of McKenzie and Millar readily agreed to meet with him and speak of the problems and troubles people arranging funerals have (and may choose not to reveal to the minister).

"Goodness, gracious me,!" A Gold Watch

After I arrived at South Leith I quickly realised I had to reduce the number of funerals. Apart altogether from the fair and sensible considerations of Church of Scotland policy, the history of depression and the glaring weaknesses in South Leith Church's structure and practices demanded leadership that only I could instigate. So I got copies of the Presbytery's parish boundaries map to the various undertakers and spelt it out that though the general public still thought that South Leith covered almost all of Old Leith, the other churches had each been given part of the parish as part of their responsibility way back in 1929. Henceforth South Leith Parish church would only take funerals for members and their immediate families wherever they lived and non-members who lived within our parish boundaries. Neither the (young) assistant minister nor the (older, mainly part-time) associate minister was to be approached first, except when I was on holiday, and nothing at all should be promised for us before agreement was given.

This did bring immediate relief, though overcrowding was still so great that I remember five funerals in one week (plus weddings on the Saturday, of course). Very conscious that I was the "called" minister, I made sure that where I had not conducted a funeral myself, I paid the follow up visit the next week.

When, after nearly twenty-six years, the time for my retiral came I was surprised to receive an invitation to a lunch in my honour in McKenzie and Millar's premises. I found that all the other Leith ministers had been invited. The manager – by then part of the Co-op Funeral Group – presented me with a gold Rotary watch!

A SURPRISED "BISHOP OF LEITH"

My young adult life in Canongate Church, the Christian Workers League and the Iona Community meant that I was long an "ecumaniac" when I was inducted as minister of South Leith Parish Church in 1969. (Jesus had something to do with this, of course.)

When I had been approached by the Vacancy Committee, one of the assurances I needed was that the congregation had no involvement with the Leith anti-RC Protestant Action Party of the 1940's and 1950's. Soon after I'd been inducted, I asked the parish priest – Sean Hynes, OMI – if he would like to belong to the Council of Churches (and his superiors approved). When the Council of Churches notified us that all parties had approved, an elder that I myself had nominated and ordained accused me of manipulating his absence from our last Kirk Session meeting and resigned in high dudgeon!

I also contacted David Maybury, Rector of the Scottish Episcopal Church of St James the Less in Leith, and asked if he would be agreeable for us both to cancel our morning service in turn and worship together.

A day duly came when, with the unanimous approval of South Leith Kirk Session, we all crossed Constitution Street to join the service of the Scottish Episcopal Church. To our surprise and discomfort, it was not the different liturgy that presented difficulty, but the freezing cold that our neighbours worshipped in!

Sometime after the return visit, I was disappointed to learn that on the morning of the united service in South Leith Parish Church, our neighbour church had felt it necessary to arrange an Episcopal service in their building beforehand.

About a dozen years later, it became public that the Scottish Episcopal Church had decided to sell their over large and expensive-to-maintain building in Leith, so I wrote to the then Bishop of Edinburgh, saying that I was prepared to approach our Kirk Session and Edinburgh Presbytery and see if our ancient Kirk – out of which St James had emerged in 1688 – might be made available for their services. The bishop telephoned to say that St James were going to use their own hall for worship, but could he come down, renew his acquaintanceship from Dundee days and see round our newly built suite of halls? Thereafter, he wrote to say thank you and that he'd never seen church premises with such a large safe!!

In 1988, I was honoured to be invited to preach at the 300th Anniversary of St James' Scottish Episcopal Church in Leith.

When we proceeded into the hall-church, I was led to a special seat in the front of the congregation, with Richard Holloway, then the Primus of The Scottish Episcopal Church, being shown to a "Throne" on the long wall to my right, while some twenty or so members of the Scottish Episcopal clergy from all over the country – and all in white surplices – squeezed themselves into crowded seats round the altar, up on a raised platform.

Just a few days before–hand, I'd received three biblical lessons from which I was presumably expected to preach, thereby dishing what I myself had been preparing to say. My Genevan robes made me highly conscious that I looked very different. When the time for preaching arrived, I found myself standing now at the lectern and facing the congregation. I said, "It really was an honour to be invited to preach here on your very significant 300th Anniversary, and I realise that there are historical reasons why Leith's gracious Scottish Episcopal Church might consider inviting the minister of South Leith Parish Church. But with all those white gowns behind me,

I now feel like the black sheep of the family." The douce and disciplined people exploded in laughter.

Thoroughly relaxed now, I fell for a temptation and stepped across to stand facing Richard – whom I had only known of, rather than known, when we were both members of the Iona Community – and declared: " And I abominate bishops. " The congregation roared in what seemed like acclamation. And Bishop Richard declared "So do I!"

Thanking me at the close of the service, Rector Andrew positively beamed at us all, referred to my 'abomination of bishops' and said "But everyone around here calls you the Bishop of Leith."

When the time for my retiral came in 1994, I received a very fine Celtic cross by Fiona Danby, picked out and painted in wood, "From your friends at St James' Episcopal Church, Leith."

AN ORGANISER (?) AND A BOLSHIE

"There is a variety of gifts but always the same Spirit: there are all
sorts of service to be done...working in all sorts of ways in different
people... The particular way in which the Spirit is given to each
person is for a good purpose"
(Ist Corinthians 12, Jerusalem Bible Translation)

It was with some surprise – to a relatively raw parish minister
– that one of the elders in my first charge of Menzieshill
chose to say that I had a real gift as an organiser. Now this
man intimating to the Kirk Session his impending departure
because he had been appointed Head of Maths in a school
in another town, had had considerable experience as an elder
elsewhere, and the conventional thing – as I learned afterwards
– would have been to refer to the minister's characteristically
distinctive duties in the conduct of public worship and pastoral
visitation.

But surely I should not have been surprised that he called
me an organiser, for was I not (when I thought about it later)
the boy who organised the ball for football and the weekends
away in the (always kindly) radio padre and Canongate
minister Ronald Selby Wright's hut at Skaterow? Then there
came the members' democratic leadership of the CWL, the
Edinburgh University Labour Club's demonstration against
the Suez Invasion; the Iona Community's economic witness;
the pattern of church life for a new community without
church buildings, and so on?

But actually, from a sermon preached by Penry Jones at a
CWL conference more than a decade before, I'd learned that

the guiding principle of my life had become the text that the prophet Isaiah left for us (Isaiah 6v8): "Here I am, Lord, send me." The notion of seeing oneself as an organiser was not part of my mind-set then because it seemed to smack of self-importance.

Also, from the days of my youth, I recognised and rejoiced that I was a bit of a bolshie. CWL had taught me to be aye ready to challenge the establishment. The weekly Bible Studies revealed to us that God's prophets had to rebel against the status quo. The Investigations convinced us that the law was often ignored by employers (as is still the case today, of course).

So, I remember challenging the President of the Christian Youth Assembly (which CWL had helped found). Then, at eighteen, hearing our platoon sergeant on my first week in the army on National Service telling us that "the purpose of a soldier is to kill the enemy," I actually heckled him from the ranks – for this was December 1947 – *"What enemy?"*

As a young minister in the General Assembly of Fathers and Brethren, I joined those arguing for equality of stipend. And when the powerful Secretary of the Maintenance of the Ministry Committee sought to close the debate by trailing a series of red herrings across the issue, I reminded him and my fellow–commissioners that "Mr Greenlaw was made for the Assembly not the Assembly for Mr Greenlaw."

Within the Labour movement, I was a supporter of Aneuran Bevan against leader Hugh Gaitskell when the idea of charging everyone for prescriptions, thereby breaching a founding principle of the NHS, first came from the Labour Leadership.

Thus, long before I was 65 and approaching retirement, I had grown to be very content with these two sides to my personality, and how they both helped in my discipleship. (And here I'd like to record for the benefit of any reader who might have experienced painful disappointment during an engagement with one of our understandably fallible ministers or who might have fallen for the all-too-prevailing shallow and dismissive "jokes" by media pundits who have never actually known a Scottish parish minister, that the prophetic characteristics of bolshie and organiser are typical of us, and rightly so.)

Civic Reception

Shortly after I'd given notice to my Kirk Session and congregation that I would definitely be retiring on 31st October 1994, I learned to my absolute astonishment that the Lord Provost and City Council where going to honour my work for Leith and South Leith Parish Church with a Civic Reception in the City Chambers for up to 315 guests.

It was very important to me to learn that the motion had originated with a Liberal Leith councillor (who happened to be a minister in another denomination) and two Leith Councillors who were Tories (one of them a practising Roman Catholic), while Norman Irons the SNP Lord Provost gave his support.

Needless to say my wife, family and South Leith congregation were delighted. But I myself was to experience considerable feelings of embarrassment when requested to provide a list of people to be invited as guests to share in honouring me! My main concern was that the elders and other fellow–labourers working for a better Leith and South Leith Kirk should receive a personal invitation, so I did get down to supplying some names.

Ronald Selby Wright of the Canongate, retired Moderator, now living in a Grace and Favour House of the Queen, telephoned immediately to offer congratulations and said he'd never heard of a Civic Reception for a minister before. An old Leither phoned Ena to ask where the City Chambers were – "Is it in Chambers Street?" Ron Brown, the Leith MP, wrote to the Edinburgh Evening News to express thanks to me and also to complain that he'd not received an invitation. In his diary, Alex Cheyne, Professor of Ecclesiastical History, recorded that 350 people attended!

In my speech, I voiced my surprise, for what had been achieved over my 25 and half years was a team effort of Leithers – not least my wife. All I had done had only been my duty as a parish minister, and "duty" is mentioned only once in the gospel, as being not praiseworthy at all: "We are unworthy servants: we have only done what was our duty." (Luke 17v10)

Organising in my genes

"Organising things" does seem to be in the Kellet genes. My father had run his RAF Unit football team during the war – in Holland, a gang of entrepreneurs raided the team's truck, so he was dreading his demob might be delayed by a court martial! After the war he eventually stepped into the shoes of the works foreman at James Gray and Son – a firm owned by the Treasurer of the City Council – and cleared up the clutter of 100 years.

His brother, my Uncle Ian, had been honoured by King Edward VIII for his work pre-war, and then organised wireless communications for the Admiralty in the Western Isles, Hamburg and Cyprus. My uncle Charlie was mentioned in Dispatches as a sergeant major in the Royal Scots. My Uncle Graham ran his works' Hearts supporters' bus. (He also ran the weekly sweep – so "successfully" that he became known as "Lucky Kell!")

"PHYSICIAN, HEAL THYSELF" –
MINISTER KNOW THYSELF!

When our daughter came home from her summer volunteering job in Iona Abbey, aged 17 years, she announced to us with evident relief, that she'd now decided what she wanted to do with her life – become a psychiatric nurse. Now, this came as an absolute surprise to us, so my wife and I exchanged a quick glance before beaming at Lorna and saying how glad we were that she had come to such an important choice for the future. "Let's talk about it tomorrow, at teatime."

The truth was that I had been in and out of all sorts of psychiatric wards and visiting mentally ill people of all ages at home too, around Dundee and Edinburgh, for 15 years by then. But it would have been very unwise to respond negatively right away!

The next evening arrived, and I opened the conversation, saying for her mother and myself how pleased we were…but would it not be better to do a general nursing course first, and then choose any specialist field in the light of the three years' experience. There followed a very short pause, and then a gentle but firm, "No."

"Tell us Lorna why do you want to be a psychiatric nurse?"

"Because I'd like to understand my parents."

Laughter all round, and then, a good bit later, "I knew exactly what you would say and worked out the right response."

Well, Lorna is now Chief Nurse at the Royal Edinburgh Hospital and Associated Services, with experiences behind her as Matron in both Iraq and Afghanistan. But what about understanding her Father?

It so happens that some years ago I found myself attending a two-day conference for ministers working in team ministries. Part of the programme was for a much respected deaconess with a special interest and experience in personality studies and group relations, to take us through a series of questionnaires especially designed to assess and better inform us about our natures.

Later in the afternoon we were told the conclusions resulting from the study – each given a paper purporting to show the personality group we belonged to. Then we were asked to come forward one by one, and duly lined up along the wall, in an order governed by the revelations of the research. I found myself placed at the extreme end of the thirty-odd participants; a real odd guy, eh?

My personal print-out ran as follows: *See appendix 2*

Whether this would have made my very young daughter – or anyone else, for that matter – any the wiser, I could not possibly say! But it all does seem to me to be technical and speculative jargon, compiled from so much box-ticking that it provided such a range of "results" that made it not fit for the purpose of helping us get to the core of our unique personalities and the roles we had to play. Not much use. Gobbledegook!

So I offer now – in many fewer words – how I might have replied if asked to explain myself; "a natural organiser and a bit of a bolshie, blessed with uninherited and unearned faith, hope, and love." And I am certain that if encouraged to tell the whole truth in love, my very able team-mates would have rid me of any self-delusion!

"Minister, know thyself"– recalling the academic philosophy tradition.

Surely, no longer the egotistic "I think, therefore I am."
Nor yet the macho "I act, therefore I am".
But rather, what rings truer from life-long experience, "I respond, therefore I am".

JOY AND FULFILMENT IN PARISH MINISTRY

I don't understand why more church members have not become ministers. I find it particularly hard to bear that so very, very few children of ministers have been found choosing to accept the priorities of their parents – as once was pretty normal – by opting into what is the best job in the world.

One of my family, when his mother gently mentioned in his maturity that she thought he might have followed his father into the ministry, was very terse "And work his long hours?" But now he works (and drives) very long hours, without – it seems to me – anything like the riches I could relish.

I remember freedom and opportunity, privileges and responsibility, challenges and achievements, affection and respect – abuse only occasionally – and so many happy bursts of laughter. I remember being stretched and absorbed by a job where I had to be ready for anything. It was a life of variety, such as no other vocation could offer, where I could seek to be a gracious neighbour full-time and be of some use in this awful world.

I remember working in a team with some of the finest ministers, deaconesses and elders – some of the finest human beings – who could exist anywhere.

Oh, the fun of it! The first service of parish worship I conducted in 1962 was in the living room of a Corporation house in Dundee and during the second (unaccompanied) hymn, we gradually changed tunes as the session clerk's wife proved her choice was superior to mine!

When our Menzieshill church building was duly erected, I complained to the architect that the bell did not work, demonstrated how hard we pulled and how high up the rope we clambered, only to watch his (Anglican!) assistant produce mellifluous tolling with one thumb and one finger.

If I had not abandoned Standard Life for the Church of Scotland ministry, I would never have scored a goal at Dens Park to the roar of thousands. (I don't tell everyone it was when playing for the ministers and priests against the butchers to provide mobile telephones for Maryfield Hospital and the Dundee Royal Infirmary!)

I remember having the only telephone in a new housing scheme and being called from Dundee Royal Infirmary at 7am one Sunday to go and tell the parents of a young boy who had just died after a road accident.

I remember sheltering with a Leith family in a safe house provided by the police after one of the sons had been murdered and the second time murderer was on the loose, searching for them.

I remember chasing two Daily Express men who had inveigled their way into a house to get a photograph when the mother whose young daughter had just been found dead saw them and became hysterical.

I remember a pregnant 15-year-old girl coming to see me, my asking her how she had told her very strict and churchy parents, being told she had kept her coat on and her bag in her hand as she expected to be put out on the street – and then hearing they had cuddled and wept with her.

I remember, at the height of the Cold War – as a near-pacifist – arranging to get hold of a copy of the banned "War Game" for private showing in our church hall, on the condition that there would be absolutely no publicity and finding the large hall packed to the door.

I remember large congregations listening in church Sunday after Sunday with an intensity I did not always find among fellow students avid for a degree as they listened to their lecturers during six years at Edinburgh University.

I remember instant laughter at the odd joke and smiles of forgiveness when I made mistakes.

I remember learning of and being shamed by the way the love of God was being expressed by church members I hardly knew in devotion to people in trouble day after day.

I remember sensing angels and archangels around the Communion Table.

I remember the first man out after Sunday service, realising no one was immediately at his back, blurting out, "I landed on five beaches as a commando during the war and I'm afraid to go to the doctor."

I remember real discussions, lots of personal teasing, lasting friendships, teamwork that somehow brought about miracles of achievement.

I remember, on retiring, some 150 children and young people holding a Leith Keelie's Karnival and the little ones pressing their hands into paint, so that I could be presented with a scroll of the right hand of friendship.

In what other job do such joys arise?

I do not understand why more church members have not become ministers. I'm sure God still calls.

SURPRISES IN ITALY, ZAMBIA
AND THE BAHAMAS

SINGING OUT TO ITALIANS IN FLORENCE

Ah, beautiful and historic Florence! Cradle of the Renaissance; the opulence of the Medicis; the magnificence of the marble Duomo Cattedrale Di S Maria del Fiore! See the valley of the River Arno in the month of May with its Ponte Vecchio and the flowers at their best. Florence is absolutely a treasure house for guide book writers! A tourist Mecca for the West.

But my Uncle Charlie's experience of Florence was very different. Just back from a post-war visit so that his wife could see where he had soldiered and been wounded, he found his nephew asking if he got any surprises.

"That River Arno," he responded.

"It was just about this broad." (Pushing his hands forward the width of his shoulders).

"But when we waded across through waist–high flood water, with our rifles raised above our heads and the Germans shooting at us, it was at least a mile wide!"

Catholics in Italy opposed to the Pope

My own first experience of Florence, in 1984, was not as a tourist either. Led by Dr Ian Fraser of Scottish Churches' House in Dunblane, we were eleven Christians from different denominations in Scotland and England visiting Basic Christian Communities in Italy to see what we might learn.

Before departing, we learned that there were such

309

communities to see all over Italy (similar to those in South America and the Philippines). The members were devoutly Roman Catholic but had made a decision for maturity. They were not going to have ecclesiastics coming in to tell them what to do. They were working out the faith for themselves.

"Secondly, there is not a political group and an evangelical group. The political is the evangelical."

"Thirdly, they all share in the leadership and the children are among the membership."

Isolotto, a post-war housing area of Florence

It was here that the Basic Community Churches movement started. We met first in their hut with some one dozen plus people and an indistinguishable priest.

The priest had been expelled from the local church because the congregation made no difference between believers and non-believers, Christian Democrats and Communists, and also wanted people to participate fully (the wine as well as the bread) in the sacraments, the administration and the common life.

One reason for alienation from the hierarchy came in 1948, when the Pope excommunicated all the communists. (Today the Communist Party in Italy is the second Roman Catholic party). Many who go to mass vote Communist.

The lesson for British churches too?

This Basic Community now numbered about a hundred. They see their job as not to attract numbers but to communicate their message. They are committed to "do what the state should do for ex-prisoners, people with housing problems, etc." They see their witness as a "prophetic sign," not to make people come into the church but to point the whole community to the values of the Kingdom. The church seeks to divide people. The Isolotto Community wants to prevent the isolation of the Christian congregations.

At 11am we assembled with the Basic Community church in the public square – which turned out to be a bus terminus busy with vehicles – for weekly communion. A table was erected with a cloth cover, one circle of chairs, some seventy people around (plus others pausing in passing), and a microphone to use. The "priest" introduced the service in the three-fold name, articulating that the gospel was for the oppressed poor, reading from Malachi (while the church bells outside were tolling), and we were invited individually to introduce ourselves. Thereafter the microphone was made available to anyone for questions and comment! (The sermon?)

At the distribution, the basket of bread was offered to all, including passersby.

I myself found it strange there had been no singing – our Scottish sign of togetherness and praise. So I started off, "This is the day that the Lord hath made, let us rejoice and be glad in it." The participation from English speakers was instantaneous. Local people joined in when I moved on to "We shall overcome" in English. And then they sang one of their own hymns/ songs:"The street is the only way to discover ourselves. At home you cut yourself off from life. Universal justice does not come by choice. Angels don't make appointments."

Their re-discovery of the Eucharist is experienced as a source of nourishment for life. "When you start to be obedient, your hunger drives you to read the Bible." The integrity of the people who have left the church organisation is that God needs them here.

"No Popery" at nearby Fiesola

At nine o'clock that evening we had a meeting at Abadia Fiesolana with the superior, Padre Ernesto Balducci. This Sunday night EB was dressed in a tweed jacket and an open-necked shirt. He spelt out three ways of seeing churches:

Institutions facing one another – the Pope's kind of church.

Confronting Christ, judging themselves, and ready to die as specific churches.

Churches that face Man's problems and unite themselves solving them.

No confessional difficulties: just churches trying to meet the needs of man. "The hierarchy never listens so there is no point in dealing with them. We need to found a Church without a Pope – Man's Church!"

The power of the Pope in Rome

On Friday 11th May we had a meeting with Giovanni Franzoni the deposed "Life-Abbot" of St Paul's Basilica, the National Church "outside the walls."

Ian Fraser had told us Giovanni Franzoni used to have open meetings on Saturdays at St Paul's for Bible study and sermon preparation by the people. Hundreds came on Sundays and a roving microphone enabled prayers of confession to come from the congregation. Despite his life appointment he was "squeezed out."

Giovanni Franzoni made no opening statement but invited questions right away. Asked about leadership in a community and the problem of avoiding anarchy, he replied that sometimes he was "accused" that "grass roots authoritarianism" could exclude the problems of the individual. But pragmatically it is a lot easier to correct authoritarianism when it does not come "from the top" and there is more chance of criticism being effective. Personally he cannot correct his "censoring" because it came from "the top level – Doctrinal errors". (Unspecified – and told his censure could be lifted if he left Italy!) Giovanni Franzoni was asked if he had any contact at all with the Pope and he replied that sometimes an emissary came down and said the Holy Father weeps for you. The message back was always "and I weep for the Holy Father. Please could I meet with him to discuss theology?"

"Ah the Holy Father is so very busy."

"Yes, I reply, and I noticed on Wednesday he had time for a meeting with a starlet from Hollywood. Why cannot he make time to discuss theology with one of the senior clerics of the church?"

A Protestant reaction to the Pope in Rome

With a very different ecumenical group on a pilgrimage-cum-holiday to Rome in the 1980s the programme took us to St Peter's Square for the Pope's weekly appearance before the general public. At the very front, a small raised platform was obviously reserved for special guests.

I counted no fewer than eleven different cardinals, each one seemingly very conscious of the privileged position as he paraded himself with very little to do, high above the level of hundreds of visitors from all over the world, ushering the relatively few more important guests to their seats in the hour before the Pope appeared.

Surely it was not just Protestant prejudice that caused the sight of such prodigality with the scarce time of key, top level workers to stick in my craw!

With a mixed Scottish group a few years later, the cult of personality in St Peter's Square was even more dominant because hundreds of schoolboys were present that Wednesday, standing on their seats and wearing their football supporter scarves for a long time after the Pope's arrival, while they shouted in unison, "Giovanni Paulo, Giovanni Paulo!"

It troubled me to wonder if the love of star-status is now to be ranked with the love of money as the root of all evil. For the scene was more like the Roman Emperor before his plebs than a Vicar of Christ with his fellow-sinners.

(By the way, the Pope's spokesman welcomed the group I was leading as "from the Archdiocese of Walkerburn" – which is definitely not what my wife called us when the telephone inquiry came!)

Singing together also in Naples and Genoa

The 1984 Basic Christian Communities learning experience took us by train to Naples, where we were welcomed first by two representatives of the Waldensian (Presbyterian) church. When carrying our baggage out of the station, we were confronted by busy, fast–moving road traffic. So it was absolutely astonishing to find that the tall and glamorous young Italian woman–with red-hair "from my Scottish grandfather"– stepped off the pavement with her right hand held high, and the cars all pulled up to a halt to let us (her) across the road!

Our university History Professor – as she turned out to be – and her companion then settled us into accommodation at the new Community Centre in Ponticelli.

Pontecelli had originally been a left–wing peasant community until Mussolini re-drew the boundaries of Naples so that the fascists could control it.

An enthralling lesson followed the history. Pizza originated in Naples and the right way to eat it is to pick the round up in both hands, fold it into a sandwich, and bite into the broad side. Not at all lady-like for us in those days.

It was made clear to us here again that the Basic Christian Community was essentially a "cultural" organisation, acting to take services to people, not to bring people in. Protestants had built a hospital *because of needs* in Ponticelli.

Some 50 or so local members arranged a meal for our late evening in Naples. While the pasta was being prepared, guitars were produced and we began to hear and learn Neapolitan songs.

But the most moving singing during our Italian learning experience came in Genoa. An international arms sale was in progress. Three Italians were fasting in a public protest. A monk from Vietnam was the principal guest. Hundreds of People for Peace were demonstrating (peacefully) in the streets. Then in a packed church hall afterwards a video of the Greenham Common women tying flowers and colourful ribbons to the high fence protecting the British / American Cruise Missiles was shown, all the while we joined in the singing of *"Whose side are you on?"*

SCOTS TOGETHER IN ITALY:
AN ENCOURAGING CATHOLIC/
PROTESTANT SURPRISE FROM
AN ECUMENICAL TOUR OF BASIC
CHRISTIAN COMMUNITIES IN ITALY

Listening to a lecture in Turin from a young man in the Italian Young Christian Workers' Movement, I realised I was becoming more and more uncomfortable on the raised plastic chair. The friendly Glaswegian beside me whispered, "They're Wimpey rejects."

It turned out afterwards that Dr Jim Oates was a Catholic lay member of the Glasgow Archdiocese and he explained how Wimpey commissioned chairs that had a slope on the seat so that diners would not sit too long, thus permitting faster turn-over and bigger profits. Some designs of chairs had been rejected because the slope was a fraction too steep and therefore noticeably uncomfortable on the customers' knees too soon.

Very quickly indeed Jim and I realised that our Scottishness bonded us together and the fact that one of us was decidedly Presbyterian and the other devoutly Roman Catholic was insignificant in this ecumenical group. The real difference for us was with the many other ecumaniacs from south of the border cheerfully talking to each other about their last ecumenical tour abroad and the next one they hoped to get on. 'Milking the system', we agreed.

Jim had to retire early from his professional post because of a physical disability and was now heading up the Archdiocese's project to develop the part that should be played by the laity in church and society.

Sometime afterwards, he invited representatives from South Leith Parish Church to attend a service of blessing for lay leaders in his own parish the church of Our Lady and St George in Glasgow. His was the first parish in the United Kingdom to develop and live this new image of the parish. So we watched Jim hand forty copies of the New English Bible – a translation not bearing the hierarchy's imprimatur, of course – to Archbishop Tom Winning, who placed each one in a member's hands, addressing each recipient solemnly with the message: "This is the Word of God. Read it and obey it."

In 'retirement', Jim worked for his parish, and the Archdiocese. He travelled all over the UK and sometimes abroad, communicating a new way of being church.

His belief was that no one was so poor that they had nothing to offer. In conversations along the way he gave others insight into their true value and worth. In short, how to become what they were always meant to be. Jim would see troubled people in his flat and he said he 'just chatted' with them. There was no fee. Jim understood that payment changed a relationship that otherwise might provide deeper understanding and optimum help.

Two very troubled South Leithers I referred certainly found the chat a transforming experience.

FEAR OF BIRDS CURED BY POOR
PEOPLE IN ZAMBIA

If you're eating your breakfast or tea just now, I hope it's not bacon and eggs. You see, I'm going to tell you about my lifetime fear of birds – and also how I was cured – but it begins with a fried egg.

A year before we were married, my wife Ena went to stay with her big-hearted sister Anne and her family. Now Anne's husband Harry was partially disabled with Multiple Sclerosis as a result of war service, and there were two growing children so – very generously – I was invited for tea, at least once a week.

The very first time we sat down to bacon, egg and chips I discovered it was the family practice – fairly common in those days – to let the pet budgie out of the cage when Harry had come home from work and everyone was in the living room. But I was instantly alarmed by the bird fluttering and flying about, not knowing who it was going to land on next. All of a sudden it chose to land its yellow feet smack on the yolk of Ena's egg.

Some years later, I watched Alfred Hitchcock being interviewed on the BBC about his gift for making films of suspense and dread and inevitable disaster. He referred to that classic picture of Rod Taylor being attacked by birds, and said it was a success because nearly everybody has a terrible fear of birds flying around them, the noise and quick sudden movements, the uncertainty of it all. Very true.

I didn't lose this sense of alarm for many years. Even when the Queen's valet told me as I was leaving after my weekend at Balmoral that her Majesty had put a brace of grouse in the boot of my car, I was filled with dread at the thought of having to handle and pluck them.

And then I went to Africa.

Friends and fellow-members of the Iona Community, Gavin and Rachel Elliott had invited me to spend my sabbatical leave with them so that I could experience and learn from the pastoral skills of church elders in Zambia. I was extremely fortunate to find myself one afternoon in a tiny village in the bush. The life going on around me there seemed unchanged from David Livingstone's time, except, thank God, there was no threat of slavery, and I was told the children could go to school, as places became available and – a government rule – if they had shoes.

What happened to allow me to be there is that one of the elders of Holy Trinity church in Lusaka had been made redundant from his job in TV education. Zambia had been a rich country because of its copper and had been encouraged by the World Bank to borrow money for capital development. With the advent of plastic pipes, the copper market collapsed. The World Bank insisted on the repayment of interest due as a first priority for the country. Government jobs and money for education were slashed! And now there was no alternative for this Western educated man but to return to his village in the bush.

It turned out that he had managed to procure a very large metal drum that could be used to collect and store water in the rainy season. 121 George Street – that is, church people in Scotland – provided Gavin with a wee Japanese pick-up. I was invited to sit up on the back of the truck for the experience.

I remember sharing in the great sense of welcome to the unchanging bush village, feeling accepted myself – though of course I didn't understand the language. The villagers were very busy all the time preparing vegetables and cooking on small open fires along the five or six mud huts I could see.

Later, in Lusaka another elder, the Head of Home Economics in Zambia, was to tell my wife that it took her mother, still living in the bush, all the hours of daylight every day – collecting water, firewood and food, cooking and cleaning – all the hours of daylight just to survive for that one day.

Suddenly, it seemed it was time for Gavin and me to leave. I saw an old woman say something to a boy. He began to run, and there was a lot of squawking and wing flapping. Back the boy came and handed the brown hen he'd caught to his grandmother. The old lady came right up to me, smiled and put the live hen into my arms.

It was interpreted for me that the village had not known a visitor was coming and so apologised for not having prepared food for us. Please would I take this hen home?

I was bowled over by this act of great kindness, from the poor to the rich too. My fear of birds left me. I received and held that hen like a baby given me for baptism. Perfect love does cast out fear.

SIGNS OF HOPE FROM THE DEEP SOUTH

First, the Vietnam veteran in Canada

On the coach tour through Eastern Canada organised by a London Tour company, Ena and I were surprised to find ourselves the only Brits. A little matter of early interest was that the mainly American fellow travellers greeted each other first thing in the morning not with comments on the weather but with the latest news from the stock exchange (affecting their pensions, of course). Cause for real surprise, however, and mind-change came at the end of the week from one of the Americans from the Deep South. He told me he had been preparing a brief act of worship, as he normally did this on Brennan Tours for the last evening – something in a constitutionally secular state that never happens on public coach tours in our Christian country – when it occurred to him that on this occasion he should defer to the Scottish minister on board. I instantly told him how pleased I would be if he continued his practice.

As we began to get to know each other a little better I mentioned that there were no black Americans with us, and realised that racial discrimination was still an important fact of life in his home state. "Not for me personally" he said, "not since my plane crashed in Vietnam. I realised when I came to that I was stuck in a deep hole, I saw two black arms stretching down from above and I heard the shout, "Grab hold of my hands and I'll haul you up."

Secondly, white teenagers from the
Deep South in the Bahamas

Just after I retired –and meaning to be retired – I got a phone call from Richard Mackay, furniture man, and an elder then in Manor Church, asking me if I would help out Lucaya Presbyterian Kirk in the Bahamas as they needed a locum for three months. Ena and I asked for 24 hours to give us time to consult with our children. The three of them answered in the same way: "How many rooms are there in the Manse?"

Now it happened during our stay that a group of teenagers arrived on a week's Bible Mission to (black) Bahamian school children. (We had already discovered that in the local black shanty-town it was a part of family life for the Bible to be studied and enthused over. But Bahamian ministers were anxious to encourage such annual visitations partly because contacts made sometimes led to gifted Bahamian kids being admitted to US Colleges and Universities.)

The American teenagers slept in the Lucaya Presbyterian Kirk hall. Ena, helping to provide their meals one evening, was so impressed by their politeness and keenness to engage with us that I told them that this was not normal for Scottish teenagers with adults and foreigners!

"How come you are all so well-mannered?" I asked.

"If we weren't, our parents would…" And a fist went up.

I had taken an opportunity when they arrived to remark to the young Methodist youth minister in charge of them that none of their party was black. He replied, with a real hint of embarrassment, that relationships had improved but there was still segregation on Sundays.

So, in the little service the American students had asked me to prepare for them, I decided not to speak (literally) down to them but to engage from among them, asking them to join me in focussing up to the huge Caribbean sea-shell

322

dedicated as the Baptismal Font, to the Bible on the lectern, to the magnificent wooden table with chairs around and to the interestingly shaped cross modelled on the huge one erected outside for all passersby to see.

"Why was it decided to put these things there? Think with me about each one in turn."

I reminded them that God so loved the world that he must be happy to see what is the norm for Lucaya Presbyterian Kirk every Sunday – Bahamian black, Bahamian white, visitors from America and other countries in genuine fellowship.

And then, standing by this time in the central aisle of the back row concentrating with them on the closing hymn they had requested, "Amazing Grace", I wondered if I detected a quiet movement beside me. The "Amen" completed I turned to find two girls standing on either side of me, the hair in Port Lucaya extensions, the smiling teeth in American braces: "We came up because we felt you must feel lonely all on your own."

So there is hope for the future alright in Scotland and all over the world if sometimes we do find seeds that have been sown secretly really are growing among us all.

A message sent from the state of Illinois by new American friends, in AD 2013, gives us further inspiration: "I would rather have a mind opened by wonder than one closed by belief."

And it blesses us with, "Go and change the world with grace."

"By the way"

In Grand Bahama, large signs on the main road warned drivers: "UNDERTAKERS LOVE OVERTAKERS."

Would this do any good on the A9?

SURPRISED BY THE PROCLAIMERS, MIKE TYSON AND AT ST PETER'S

TAKING FAMILY FUNERALS – AND THE PROCLAIMERS

One of the surprises that a parish minister might never foresee is that inevitably he finds himself taking funerals for members of his own family, even when he is among the most grief-stricken.

Thus it was when one of my younger sisters died, that her daughters came down to our retirement cottage and asked if I would conduct the funeral service, because I knew and understood their mother so well. And, because Margaret was a fan of the Proclaimers' songs and actually knew them personally since she sat close to them Saturday by Saturday in the Hibs Leith stadium, please could one of her favourite songs be played just as the service began?

Now, an awful mistake it was, but there were always too many church and parish demands and opportunities at Menziehill and then in Leith for Ena and myself ever to have time to enjoy any kind of music, except in relation to work and worship. (Ena still expresses her surprise that we didn't even know about the Beatles until after we retired in 1994.)

But I had heard of the Proclaimers. Iain Macdonald from Skye, roadie for Runrig, a member of our congregation while on a project for the Iona Community, had attended in Leith's Lorne Street the Proclaimers' first press conference after their "Letter to America" astonished the world. He had chortled as he recounted the surprise that the Sun variety correspondent asked how the twin brothers had met! (Iain has now been parish minister in Orkney's Westray for some 20 years.)

So heard of them I had, but I did not appreciate the power of their music and their understanding of human experience until I stood at the door of the Crematorium, ready to lead in my sister in her coffin, when the organ voluntary stopped and the CD came into play: "Sorrow, Sorrow. My heart is broken."

MORE NAME DROPPING WITH A PURPOSE: MEETING MIKE TYSON

Suprises that Appalled

Ena and I got a big surprise on 17th September 2005 when we met and talked with Mike Tyson who, at the age of 21, had become the youngest ever heavyweight boxing champion of the world and perhaps the most world famous man of the time! But the surprise that came just before we parted, and that we had unwittingly facilitated was a very sad experience: appalling.

We happened to be leading a pilgrimage-cum-holiday to Italy and had to change planes at Frankfurt. Entering the departure lounge, we found it very crowded, except for one double table where a black man was reading a newspaper.

"No one's sitting beside him," said Ena.

"Let's go there." (I'll tell you exactly why before I finish.)

Ena asked the man if he'd mind if we occupied the vacant seats beside him and he said that he would not. A few minutes later, the big man's face appeared properly from behind his large open newspaper as he folded it up and laid it down. I took the opportunity to indicate friendly presences beside him by saying that there was no need to ask where he was from when I'd noticed the paper he was reading: "You must be American."

"He certainly is," came a loud voice from a table to our right. "That's Mike Tyson." And suddenly the whole lounge of mainly American travellers who had obviously avoided sitting beside him, seemed agog.

The big man turned to engage back with us, and Ena asked where his home was. "I haven't got a home now," came the reply. "I just seem to be travelling all the time from one place to another." It was a sad man speaking.

I asked where he'd just been, and he answered, "Portugal, but it's not that I have any friends there." Ena's concern was showing on her face as the importance of having a place to call home began to be discussed.

"It's when you're at your lowest you find who your friends are," he said.

And then suddenly, as we talked together, a woman passenger from our left arrived right across the table and took a photograph in an instant, departing as quickly as she came, all without a word.

The excitement all round was now palpable and a man from the same long table to our left piped up: "Would you mind if I was photographed with you?" And hardly had Mike Tyson indicated a sort of acceptance than the man was right up beside him. Mike Tyson began to rise to his feet, and the man went very close snuggling up inside the big man's arm so that he seemed to be being cuddled, and the photograph was taken, again so quickly that we didn't see it coming.

What we did sense immediately was that the human being Mike Tyson was absolutely embarrassed.

Returned to his table, the man who'd taken advantage of an opportunity without a thought for his target's feelings was now announcing with huge glee that he had a sports club in Florida and this picture would be a great asset for him up on the wall.

We ourselves were appalled, not least because we had opened up a situation which led to a poor soul being used unashamedly.

Some five years later (5ᵗʰ December 2010), we were delighted to see a beaming Mike Tyson pictured on the front of the Observer Magazine, his new baby girl now firmly clasped to his left shoulder and a story about how he'd finally defeated his demons.

Our William

The reason Ena suggested we sit beside the isolated black man is because our son, William, had recently returned from a short trip to Iona. On the way there, when he took the bus from Edinburgh to Glasgow, and then the bus from Glasgow to Oban and then the bus across Mull to Fionnphort, no one had sat beside him. There he was, a black man studiously reading his book, and as people approached him up the aisle because the buses were full, they would see the empty space, see him, and then stop where they were.

On the way home, William had the same experience that people were obviously frightened, after what the Americans call 9/11, of a black man with a small holdall. Once again, William was being kept unaccompanied until when one lady was almost upon him, and actually looked at him. William said: "There's a space here, I won't bite you." But she moved away the moment another seat became vacant. On the streets of Glasgow, some people let their friendly city down by shouting "Go home!"

It happened that when William was arriving home he got off the Lothian Region Bus at the top of Easter Road and began walking down towards his flat as usual when he noticed a man coming up the brae towards him who was obviously the worse for drink. William had to be alert and wary, of course, so he moved to try and get out of the man's way but he – the man with too much drink in him – stopped right in front of William, put his hands up to each cheek of William's face, and said to him: "And what kind of day have you had, chocolate boy?"

As William said to us afterwards – "Only in Leith!"

SURPRISED AT ST PETER'S

Can you imagine a passing Presbyterian pastor being invited to use a Pope's Privy in St Peter's?

Well, it happened this way. In August 2013 Ena and I celebrated our Diamond Wedding with a cruise along the Danube. In beautiful Ragensburg, which had first come into our ken a few years before when its cardinal was elected Pope (Benedict), we were almost entranced by St Peter's Cathedral when, quite unexpectedly, my aged bladder came near to bursting point. Seeing a man about as old as myself watering the plants – the Beadle, perhaps? – I approached and asked him where the nearest toilets were. My school knowledge of German had withered away long before, and I was having some difficulty trying to follow his directions (lechts und rechts) as well as in controlling myself, when the kindly gentleman, noticing my walking stick and perhaps having experience himself of my need, summoned me to follow him, turned towards the altar, and then led me along a passage into the vestry. Pointing to a picture of Pope Benedict on the wall, he opened a door and ushered me in.

What a pleasant surprise: celebrity indeed had arrived!

Hardly had I told Ena than an American lady we had got to know on the cruise to be a very devout (and attractively mischievous) Roman Catholic came over to us and I recounted my rare experience. She touched my sleeve and then stepped back in feigned awe, to say:

"And I'm the Catholic woman who touched the arm of the Protestant who peed in the Pope's toilet."

APPENDIX 1

CHRISTIAN WORKERS' LEAGUE

Investigation On Conditions Of Work. Be Sure To Get Facts.

See
- What is your job? How many people in your work?
- What are the arrangements for Sanitation? (No of WC's etc), Ventilation? (No of windows) First Aid (Boxes, First Aid Worker). Who keeps the place clean?
- Are dangerous machines protected? Do the workers use the protecting appliances?
- Does the Factory Inspector ever inspect the work? How are complaints dealt with?
- What notices are up in the work?
- Are there any dangerous or unhealthy works in your district?

Judge
- Are the conditions up to legal requirements? Are they up to Christian requirements?
- What influence do they have on the young worker? His health? His attitude to work? His attitude to God?
- Should there be regular medical examination of the worker?
- Is man to be treated different from a machine? Why?
- Are there any jobs which you think are below a man's dignity?

Act

- What can we do to change conditions? See Employer? Through Shop Steward or Union Official? Write to Factory Inspector?
- Can we influence fellow workers to help?

Legal Requirements

- First Aid Arrangements:
- There must be one first aid box or cupboard for every 150 persons.
- There must be a notice in <u>every </u>workroom stating who is in charge of the box.
- When over 50 persons in factory, person in charge of box must have had first aid training.

Sanitary Arrangements:

- For females – one sanitary convenience for 25.
- For males – one sanitary for every 25 (but not simply urinal) and so on to 100, thereafter, providing also urinals, 1 for each 40.
- These must be ventilated, kept clean and properly screened off, but also always easily reached by anyone, anytime at the factory.
- Those for the different sexes must be in larger factories kept decently apart.

Protection of Machines:

- All dangerous machines must be properly fenced – also flywheels.
- New hands must be properly trained and supervised in every way.
- Cases must be looked at where protection is only arranged or machine stopped when inspector comes.

Ventilation

- This must be adequate – You must have a general feeling of freshness in the air.

Temperature

- This must be at least 60 degrees Fahrenheit by 1 hour after starting work and there must be at least ONE thermometer in each workroom in a suitable position. (special arrangements for exceptional cases)

APPENDIX 2

ESTJ – Extraverted Thinking with Sensing

ESTJ people use their thinking to run as much of the world as may be theirs to run. They like to organise projects and then act to get things done. Reliance on thinking makes them logical, analytical, objectively critical and not likely to be convinced by anything but reasoning. They tend to focus on the job, not the people behind the job.

They like to organise facts, situations and operations related to the project and make a systematic effort to reach their objectives on schedule. They have little patience with confusion or inefficiency and can be tough when situations call for toughness.

They think conduct should be ruled by logic and govern their own behaviour accordingly. They live by a definite set of rules that embody their basic judgements about the world. Any change in their ways requires a deliberate change in their rules.

They are more interested in seeing present realities than future possibilities. This makes them matter-of-fact, practical, realistic and concerned with the here and now. They use past experience to help them solve problems and want to be sure that ideas, plans and decisions are based on solid facts.

They like jobs where the results of their work are immediate, visible and tangible. They have a natural bent for business, industry, production and construction. They enjoy administration, where they can set goals, make decisions and give the necessary orders. Getting things done is their strong suit.

Like the other decisive types, ESTJ's run the risk of deciding too quickly before they have fully examined the situation. They need to stop and listen to the other person's viewpoint, especially with people who are not in the position to talk back. This is seldom easy for them, but if they do not take time to understand, they may judge too quickly, without enough facts or enough regard for what other people think or feel.

ESTJ's may need to work at taking feeling values into account. They may rely so much on their logical approach that they overlook feeling values – what they care about and what other people care about. If feeling values are ignored too much, they may build up pressure and find expression in inappropriate ways. Although ESTJ's are naturally good at seeing what is illogical and inconsistent, they may need to develop the art of appreciation. One positive way to exercise their feeling is to appreciate other peoples' merits and ideas. ESTJ's who make it a rule to mention what they like, not merely what needs correcting, find the results worthwhile both in their work and in their private lives.

NOTES

1. *Foreword p.ix.* I make this point because when, in 1961, after completing 6 years at Edinburgh University, I joined a group of new members of the Iona Community for further training in the understanding of work-in-community, a group of new Episcopalian ministers came up to the Abbey for a few days and every single one of them had been at an English Public school. It happens that all the vicars and bishops I have met over the decades since have come from the same restricted background- with the notable exception of Richard Holloway.

2. *Equerry p.9.* "Official in attendance" says my old Chambers dictionary. A Royals PA we might say.

3. *Security p.17.* When I got back to Dundee, I mentioned to my wise and much more experienced friend Uist Macdonald, minister at Wallacetown, how I'd been surprised that the Queen - then so long serving and at the peak of popularity and respect - had chosen to ask my opinion on a particularly important matter for herself and the country. Uist responded instantly that the Queen would be very glad indeed to weigh up any comments I made because so many giving advice around her had their own private agenda.

4. *After Dinner Mangoes p.18.* President Sadat of Egypt's assassination. Tragically it seemed that hardly was I back in Leith, when another military vehicle raced up towards President Sadat at the airport and assassinated him. I wrote to Prince Charles immediately and received the following hand addressed and signed reply.

BUCKINGHAM PALACE

30th October, 1981

Dear Mr. Kellet,

I was enormously touched by your very kind letter. Thank you so much for writing as you did. We greatly enjoyed meeting you at Balmoral and hearing all about your ministry in Leith. Our warmest gratitude for your prayers.

Yours sincerely

Charles

5. *Shock Horror p.47.* "Only one petition in the Lord's Prayer has any condition attached to it: it is the petition for forgiveness" – William Temple, "Personal Religion and the Life of Fellowship"

6. *Don't Ask Questions, p.105.* But on one occasion Uncle Ian expressed distress that the Americans had sunk Britain's only cable-laying ship because they said they didn't know what it was!

7. *A Working Class Wedding p.108.* Any idea of a Pre-Nuptial Contract would have been dismissed in those days as accepting that a marriage "til death us do part" might possibly be a temporary engagement. But I accepted that Ena would not darn my socks and Ena agreed that we would not be buying the Sunday Post!

8. *On Being Called to the Holy Ministry p.157.* Astonishingly, it was only many years later- and after I'd helped organise an "honest to God' funeral service for him- that I learned from my youngest sister that my Father was a convinced atheist. He never once questioned my call. But Ena remembers that he did raise the subject of my "leaving a good job" with her, privately. (Millie's response to me, incidentally, on hearing of my Call, was "so you're not going to fulfil your boyhood ambition to be a balloon- man, then?")

9. *Disciplinarian Carried… p.108.* Uncle Charlie's bravery led to his "Mentioned in Despatches" award and a commendation in the Royal Scots official history.

10. *A Better Ending p.112.* In my three years' Divinity Studies at Edinburgh University, including "Practical Theology" classes, and also four years of student assistantships with two good Parish Ministers, I didn't receive any advice or training for ministry in such common and important situations. Nor did I think to ask.

11. *Into the Army p.115.* Divorce was particularly expensive for a working class man. The army in those days would keep,

feed, clothe you and leave you with some spending money while using the rest of your pay to cover divorce costs.

12 *The Christian Workers League p.127.* In 1947, the Iona Community published a booklet "The Christian Workers' League – a Movement of Industrial Youth" written by "General Advisor" Rev. George D. Wilkie.

13. *The Christian Workers League p.127.* Ena and I have contributed to a book " about The Christian Workers' League and George Wilkie", by ex - Christian Workers' Leaguer Dr Jim Kelly , "The Iona Community and the Kirk: History of CWL and Industrial Mission," published by Lulu 2014.

14. *The Christian Workers League p.127.* Some of our early experiences of The Christian Workers' League, The Iona Community and Iona itself are recorded in Anne Muir's "Outside the Safe Place" (Wild Goose Publications, 2011)

15. *St George's West p.135.* St George's West: masses of Edinburgh church people, having attended their own church in the morning, used to queue up in Shandwick Place for Murdo's Evening Service.

16. The Investigation that improved scandalous conditions at Ena's work is a splendid example of the General Advisor's service to working –class youth: See Appendix 1

17. *West Pilton p.135.* James Currie was to become one of the best known Ministers in Scotland. Perhaps his funniest story was of the new resident in Pollock who rushed up to him after a packed morning service and said ' Oh, Mr Currie, I've not been in a church for years, and you had us laughing !" (JC) "Next Sunday, will your husband come too?" (Answer) " No, he's a Protestant and never goes to church."

18. *The Christian Workers League p.297.* When Penry Jones – later of ABC Television, ITV and the BBC- became Industrial Secretary of the Iona Community, one of his responsibilities was General Advisor to the CWL which he

described as the seed- bed of the Community's Industrial Mission.

19. The photograph *p.140* appended of the "Regional Rally" held by CWL in the Canongate's Milton House School in October 1947 shows 46 members and advisors, including a very young Ena Barker and "Jake" Kellet.

20. *The Workers Meet... p.137.* Bill Aitken went as a Missionary to Nigeria and, during the Civil War, found himself organising the "illegal" landing of aircraft with emergency food for the Biafrans. Later, he became a Minister in the United Church of Zambia.

21. *Planning a Family p.141.* William McIlvanney - recently described by Allan Massie as Scotland's greatest contemporary novelist - has characterised us now as "a mongrel nation and all the better for it." This is what the Proclaimers' have celebrated with their song.

22. *Planning a Family p.141.* Campaigning crofter Allan MacCrae of Assynt, whose Mother was a genuine Cockney, used to describe himself as "A Hybrid, and hybrids are the strongest plants."

23. *At New College p.167.* I am still tickled pink that when James Barr produced his theological world-shattering "The Semantics of Old Testament Language" he graciously in a footnote gave credit to me for a question I had raised in class.

24. *Vestry Hour. p.190.* Footnote about recent changes in Parish Ministry: Meeting an experienced Edinburgh parish minister in December 2013 he confirmed that he still holds a weekly Vestry Hour. But in today's society, the role of the minister has been greatly diminished and nowadays only church members make use of it. "I think I've still got the best job in the world! And I don't think that most people have lost all faith when they get a non-church 'celebrant' to take their funerals. It's just that they're embarrassed to

ask when they don't officially belong to the church and there are people offering their services whom they can pay for."

25. *Postscript p.196.* "Leant": (Lord) Alf Robens who had led a successful transformation of the Scottish minefields with thousands of Scottish miners leaving peacefully for pits in England, told Industrial Chaplains that one key to the success had been this slogan he kept for himself: "Don't push, they push you back. Just lean.'"

26. *Girls Galore p.205.* Girls Galore! was the headline published in The People's Journal, May 4th 1968 for a photograph of the 180 members.

27. *p.206.* The new wife of one our Assistant Ministers at South Leith - very friendly personally and with wide interests - actually chose to join a neighbouring congregation as she was certain - mistakenly - that there must be a fixed role for the Assistant Minister's wife

28. *Police Boots p.219.* Dr Runa Mackay- who was later to become a member of the Iona Community – told me that in Nazareth they had as their local name "the English Hospital!" "After all, there is a French Hospital where they speak French and we speak English…"

29. *Practical Training p.227.* A Lesson from Thomas Anthony Harris (1967). 'I'm OK, you're OK.'

30. *Permission from the Prince fit… p.31.* Finding the correct leadership to effect necessary change that will prove acceptable is not easy. For some situations royalty is called in to help. Wheeling a South Leith member with MS to the front of a crowd at a Holyrood Palace Garden Party on one occasion, I found myself beside a man who said to Prince Charles that he had seen him that morning at Wester Hailes. The Prince beamed and said that he'd gone because someone had to – and he swung his leg up as if giving a kick!

31. *Prostitutes... p264.* "A new commandment I give to you, that you love one another; even as I have loved you, that you also love one another. By this all men will know that you are my disciples, if you have love for one another" (John 13:34,35)

32. *Civic Reception p.299.* In the Kirk of Jean Calvin and John Knox, "speaking the truth to power" is done to the Church itself as well as the state.

33. *Minister know thyself p.302.* Footnote: Psychosymmetrics. At a time when my second son was thinking of applying for a job in Standard Life, I happened to bump into an old friend, Professor David Simpson, and asked him about the present situation there. "Oh, we are taking on new people just now and the HR Department will put him through psychosymmetric testing. I've told them that the whole technique has been discredited, but they're still using it."

34. *Joy and Fulfilment p.303.* This personal view originally appeared in "Life and Work" the official magazine of the Church of Scotland in August 2003.

35. *Joy and Fulfilment p.305.* When I came to retire in 1994, I was disappointed to realise that six of the students, probationers and ordained ministers I'd helped to train and on whom I had pressed the priority of Parish Ministry were now working in the Central Offices of the Church of Scotland, George Street, Edinburgh.